T0195077

BLACK
BRAINWORKS
2014-2022:

PROTESTS,
POLITICS,
PROGRESS &
A PANDEMIC

PAUL KING

authorHOUSE®

AuthorHouse™
1663 Liberty Drive
Bloomington, IN 47403
www.authorhouse.com
Phone: 833-262-8899

Published by AuthorHouse 07/12/2022

ISBN: 978-1-6655-4921-9 (sc)
ISBN: 978-1-6655-4919-6 (hc)
ISBN: 978-1-6655-4920-2 (e)

Library of Congress Control Number: 2022900525

CONTENTS

*The following 47 BLACK BRAINWORKS by Paul King were published
in N'DIGO MAGAPAPER or on its Online Edition, 2014-2022*

ENRMidwest

Legacy Award

Paul King's Legacy is Opening Up Opportunity

January 25, 2022—*By Jeff Yoders, Engineering News-Record Midwest Editor*

Fifty-three years after leading protests that shut down Chicago worksites, he hasn't given up the battle against racial bias

Paul King meets with President Obama. *White House Photographer. Photo courtesy of Paul King Jr.*

Paul King with the late Parren Mitchell and one of his congressional aides when the businessman and legislator were drafting the federal contract language that would become known as affirmative action. *Photo courtesy of Paul King Jr.*

Fighting for Representation

In 1969, King led a group of 80 Black contractors known as the West Side Builders Association in a peaceful protest that shut down a federally funded construction project on West Douglas Boulevard. It was the first of more than $80 million in closed projects the group opposed, forcing local trade unions and the Associated General Contractors to the negotiating table to discuss how to open the trades and contracting industry to Blacks. At the time, the unions were 97% white. Negotiating for the unions and contractors at the time was Chicago Mayor Richard J. Daley.

"We wanted our fair share of jobs, our piece of the pie," King says. "Blacks would pass construction projects in their neighborhoods and see nothing but white workers. It was a slap in the face and a daily insult."

It would be a career-long fight for King to create opportunities for Black-owned businesses in construction as a leader in both Chicago and Washington, D.C. Whether it was through the Labor Dept., the Small Business Administration or the work of NAMC, King pushed for more access to bonding, loans and the lucrative public projects that can turn small contractors into larger ones. He was named an ENR Newsmaker in 1974 for his efforts.

King was always interested in the business side of construction even before founding UBM in 1975. His father, Paul King Sr., was a successful wholesale produce distributor dating back to the Depression and the first man to bring fresh, Southern produce to Chicago's supermarkets. King's uncle taught him to paint—a skill that became the foundation of his future construction career.

Paul King celebrates five years of business development at Comprehensive Construction Consulting in this illustration. *Photo courtesy of Paul King Jr.*

Actions of Affirmation

In his 2009 memoir, "Reflections on Affirmative Action in Construction," King recalled 40 years of the program meant to set aside percentages of federal contracts for minority-owned firms. As an adviser to U.S. Rep. Parren Mitchell—the first Black congressman from Maryland and a founder of the Congressional Black Caucus—King was instrumental in the legislator's addition of an amendment to a 1976 public-works program that required state and local governments applying for federal contracts to reserve 10% of funds for minority-owned businesses.

"He and Parren Mitchell got together and wrote a lot of the federal affirmative action bills that were actually implemented," says John Bolden, an engineering principal at Comprehensive Construction Consulting and King's business partner. "It more or less provided opportunities, not just only for general contractors in the Chicago area, but it affected general contractors in the construction industry nationwide."

1969: THE PHOTO

ops stand at peaceful parade rest.

In 1969, Paul King and the West Side Builders Association stood up against trade unions and the contractors for which they worked for excluding Black workers and eventually shut down 80 worksites. *Photo courtesy of Paul King Jr.*

That contract language became standard for federally funded projects. "One out of every seven jobs is in some way related to construction. It's a big, big business," King says. "In trying to advance the Black contractor, we're talking about trying to stimulate an agent for the cause of Black economic development. It's not just trying to make an individual rich; it is a process toward Black economic empowerment."

King participated in a Chicago Tribune series of investigative articles that highlighted supposed minority subcontractors hired onto large projects such as the McCormick Place expansion that were only minority on paper, without a Black face on the site.

"Those fronts and those fraudulent people that are doing that kind of thing, every one of them is taking business away from the growth and development of Black firms," King says. "Jesse Jackson Sr.'s brother Noah Robinson was famous for doing that."

Robinson, Jackson's half-brother, operated several Chicago companies that capitalized on programs to aid minority businesses, but often hired white-owned firms to do the work. He was eventually convicted of unrelated racketeering, narcotics and murder-for-hire charges.

King also says that watching policies and contract language deviate from requiring minority representation to requiring minority or women-owned firms has led to more abuse of the process that goes against the spirit of the law's original intent. He notes that contractors that simply list a wife or other female relative in a top leadership role, when the firm is actually controlled by men, suppress Black and minority entrepreneurship.

"Now, it's everybody and their mother and a lot of folks who never even saw a protest march that are benefiting from affirmative action legislation," Bolden says.

Photo courtesy of Paul King Jr.

Educating the Next Generation

A thread that runs throughout King's activism—and is evident in his writings in ENR Viewpoints as well as in the magazines Black Scholar, Black Enterprise and N'DIGO—is that education is what truly creates opportunity.

"You can't have construction productivity or safety without reading, so we find ourselves in a situation where all the Black boys that would be interested in our field are in jail," King says. Programs for teaching incarcerated young men the construction trades so they can be both safe and productive when they get out are as important now as when he started fighting for jobsite inclusion, King says.

His youngest son, Timothy King, has taken his father's teachings to heart by opening Urban Prep Academy, a network of public charter schools in Chicago. Its three schools in the Bronzeville, Englewood and Near West Side communities serve more than 1,500 young men—the first such all-male charter schools in the U.S.

Paul King says more must be done in construction to attract young Black men. "We don't have enough Black young men that are aware of the opportunities in construction," Paul King says. "There has to be a major educational effort as well as a recruitment effort."

He also realizes that the lack of labor that contractors face today is a problem that was created by exclusionary policies decades ago.

Still active in the business, Paul King is today the primary business developer and rainmaker at Comprehensive Construction Consulting Inc., where he gives credit to his partners, Bolden, president Lynn Dixon and principal Doug Conover.

"I love my partners, they allowed me to get out there and showboat," he says.

He has lectured at Roosevelt University in Chicago and is working on a second book, due out later this year. He and his wife, LoAnn, still live in the city.

Writing in the foreword to "Reflections on Affirmative Action in Construction," Gwendolyn Keita Robinson, former executive director of Chicago's DuSable Museum of African-American History, said, "There are not many people who get to see their ideas come to fruition or their lifetime struggles rewarded. Paul King is one of those people, although he would be the first to say 'a luta continua'—the struggle continues."

TNT – THREE COLLEGE CLASSMATES EXPLODE MYTHS ABOUT VIOLENCE…

"Six killed and thirty-one others shot in Chicago's most violent weekend in 2022," screamed the *Chicago Sun-Times*. There were over 622 shootings and 157 murders across the city by mid- April, mainly on the South and West Sides.

There's no escaping the grim truth: Black people are under siege! Calls for more police and better prevention programs ring throughout African American neighborhoods. Yet while there is broad and loud alarm about dodging bullets and avoiding carjackings, one aspect of this crazy mayhem is little discussed – the impact this is having on Chicago's health care system.

Think about it. At the end of these shooting episodes, the victim, whether shot by police or by some rival gang, is typically taken to *Mount Sinai, Christ Medical,* or the *University of Chicago Hospital.* They are merged into a stream of folks seeking care for everyday illness and injuries – a stream swollen to a flood by the stubborn *COVID* epidemic.

Whether a parent taking a child for vaccination, a senior going for a heart exam, or a good samaritan visiting an inpatient friend, we are all affected by Chicago's violence and its effect on our health care system. Now comes

Thomas Fisher, a veteran emergency room physician, with a new book that shines much-needed light into this tunnel of trauma. It's titled ***THE EMERGENCY, A Year of Healing and Heartbreak in a Chicago ER***. And it's nothing short of amazing!

A Little Backstory...

But first, a personal backstory. Back in the day, a *Shell Oil* executive named **Joe Moore** awarded my construction company a contract to build a service station on South State Street. Years later, he introduced me to his journalist daughter, **Natalie Moore**, and we stayed in touch. I recently collaborated with Roosevelt University **Prof. Erik Gellman** to bring author **Ta-Nehisi Coates** to Chicago. Coates had just published a masterpiece on racial reparations in *The Atlantic* magazine.

As with Natalie's keen observations on race (see *The South Side* by Moore), Coates provided me with more precise insights into our political and historical situation. I still feel fortunate to know them both. I was amazed when I learned that Coates, Moore, and Dr. Fisher were already friends and collaborators. It turns out that Thomas (T), Natalie (N), and Ta-Nehisi (T) were all *Howard University* classmates. The talented trio even huddled together at Natalie's 53rd & Kenwood Avenue apartment to discuss Black issues. So I dubbed these wunderkinder "*TNT*."

The Book...

THE EMERGENCY is one of the essential nonfiction books of 2022. It leaves one gobsmacked, and not just because it describes a year in the life of a big city hospital emergency room during Covid. It also demystifies the maddeningly complex U.S. Health Care System and the subtle but devastating inequities that infect it. **Ta-Nehisi Coates** contributed to the book's Forward: "It was not merely that Tom was an ER doctor directly caring for those afflicted by the plague of gun violence that covered the country and leveled a particular toll on Black neighborhoods. It was that these bodies were rushed into the ER from the streets that Tom called home. He was working not just for the Black community in general but for the same South Side of Chicago where his parents had settled and where he had been raised. He was caring for the lives and bodies of his neighbors."

The book describes the impact of a capricious system in visceral, bloody detail. Pain and agony are everywhere visible but looking behind the system's many curtains through a doctor's eyes reveals that Black people do not merely live shorter lives than their peers. Instead, their lives are more physically agonizing. And not just the agony of illness and injury, but racism and its consequences, both subtle and overt. "Your body, like many bodies on the South Side, began accumulating injury and illness before your peers on the North Side," Fisher writes, "And unlike your peers, you had fewer chances to recover and return to your prior health."

The "you" addressed by Dr. Fisher is a journalistic device that enables the author to write about composite "patients" while guarding their privacy ... yet providing plenty of clinical particulars. The author moves from patient to patient doing the best he can, trying to do too much in too little time. He does his best to heal the body – "our most important endowment" – and almost always comes up short. Even as a doctor, he is merely an actor within the system, not the system's author.

The Burden of Blackness...

Dr. Fisher is no foreigner trying to apply medical remedies to unknown people. He is of the South Side, using his craft at the *University of Chicago* mere miles from where he was born and grew up. It is worth remembering the early days of *COVID* when it was said to be "color blind." Maybe we wanted to believe that we would find ourselves together on the same footing as mainstream America in a time of crisis, together in our common frailty. But alas, that was never so. Here we are two years later, with Black people having lost nearly three years of life expectancy – roughly triple the loss for whites. We should have known better and should now understand better. **THE EMERGENCY** helps explain why this is so. Whether it's the plague of gun violence or the plague of *COVID*, the burden is never borne equally.

Fisher sometimes takes us outside of the *Emergency Room* and inside his head. He especially worries about "the worst" happening to him as an ER doctor -- getting *COVID* himself. "How sick would I become?" He laments: "The only certainty (is) that once infected, I would be contagious, and I can't risk passing the disease along to my family, my patients, to the woman I think I love. So, the terrifying months ahead will be spent mostly alone. It feels like I will be without human touch during the most stressful time in my life, but the alternative is to infect the people who mean the most to me."

"Hospital preparations," he explains, "include a schedule for those who fall ill and alternative housing for folks who couldn't go home. I prepared my affairs, set an autopay for my mortgage, stacked my fridge, and withdrew cash as though I'd be gone for six months. So my will is up to date."

Activism and Advocacy...

Beyond personal concerns, however, Fisher grappled mightily with systemic issues, beginning with the *University of Chicago Hospital*. He recalls that the hospital's CEO planned to reorganize the Emergency Department several years ago with ten beds walled off and allocated to *Patients of*

Distinction. (Mainly white patients with insurance.) *Eight Beds* that had been used as a fast track for ankle sprains, coughs, and other minor complaints would be closed. Though *"POD"* made up less than a fifth of Emergency visits, Fisher realized they would take up almost half of the available space and resources.

"I knew separating patients into separate pods to deliver care was used in emergency medicine, but doing so based on the ability to pay was unheard of. Money became concrete, people became abstract," and "I realized how much the plan would segregate the ED racially."

"I decided," he remembers, that "the day they segregated the ED would be the last day I showed up for a shift." He relates how it went: "I offered a counter-proposal to reorganize the ED with a basis in illness severity, not insurance status ... I was admonished to continue.

"Instead, I was partnering with quiet allies in the administration and organizing the hospital's young physicians," he remembered, vowing then that "there could be no compromise that, segregated or otherwise, extracted resources from the poor. Not here, not in the Emergency Room in the heart of the South Side!"

Ultimately, plans to accommodate *Patients of Distinction* were replaced with a design to structure the space by Illness severity. This was a win for Fisher and his group of equity advocates, though some of his allies had had enough. "By the time the smoke cleared a year later," he remembers, "we had lost a department head and four-section heads. All the emergency medicine faculty under thirty-five departed to restart their careers elsewhere. The CEO, COO, & CFO of the Medical Center disappeared as well."

The big lesson learned, writes Fisher, was that "health inequity is not simply the product of benign neglect waiting to be fixed but an active and intentional scheme to take from one community and give to another. I witnessed arguments that tried to elevate the importance of morality and science rendered impotent in the face of a financial imperative. The 'right thing' was irrelevant. Only power mattered."

Diagnosis and RX

Realizations such as Fisher's also occur to those of us who live and operate businesses in Chicago. The intersection of unequal healthcare and sporadic violence doesn't need a traffic cop. It requires intervention, leadership, and critical thinking.

My company employs over 40 technical staff who oversee the construction of schools, medical facilities, roads, and bridges. These employees deserve protection and informed management oversight. If random shooting is occurring on the South and West Sides, it is incumbent upon Black businesses to become informed and involved.

Toward these ends, I provide the following Action Items for consideration. Notice these include references to mental health. **Dr. Gary Slutkin** of *CeaseFire* has long argued that *Violence* and *Mental Health* are inextricably linked. Add to this the social and educational disruption brought on by 2+ years of *COVID*, and new modes of counseling are also needed.

Action Items...

- Chicago is to get $1.9 Billion in Federal COVID Relief. Community Organizations and Health Officials should steer a portion towards reopening city- run mental health clinics in Black areas.

- Research shows too many Black people who have mental illness routinely land in prison. Courts need to order and consider the results of, mental health evaluations prior to sentencing.

- The City should open professionally staffed clinics in minority areas that are free of charge, robustly staffed, and fully accountable for their quality of care.

- Black people don't get information on prevention soon enough. Ways and means must be found to provide info updates via telephone, online, print, and even in- person home visits.

- The city should offer culturally sensitive programs that require staff to understand and consider the experiences of the Black people they treat. Healing must be holistic while considering the historical and societal contexts in which Black families exist.

- A non-police response network should be created that allows social workers, paramedics, and peers to respond to emergencies, especially points of shootings.

- Support Cure Violence – A World Without Violence Virtual Gala on Thursday, June 2, 2022. Contract: http://cvg.org Dr. Gary Slutkin deserves the support.

- Join and Support the Business Leadership Council. This is Chicago's premier organization advocating for Black Business and is fully engaged in these matters. There is room for start up Black Businesses and mentorship opportunities for members and non-business supporters. Info at https://www.blcchicago.com/

After all, it's past time to explode racist myths about urban violence. Try some "TNT."

CENSORSHIP – A TO Z (BEWARE THE EFFORT TO REMOVE TRUTH-TELLING BOOKS ABOUT RACE IN AMERICA)

There is a move afoot to ban books and suppress stories that deal with race.

Education writer **Julie West Johnson** called out this alarming trend in a recent issue of *Chicago Life Magazine*. "The moral panic we're seeing has created an extraordinary environment," she observes. "Many of the books being challenged these days have been sitting on library shelves for years without comment. Some books are now under attack because they tell the truth about American History or explain race and politics in the past or present."

Consider the efforts of **Matt Krause**, a Texas Republican and state legislator who seeks to oust some 850 books from school libraries and curricula that could give white students "discomfort, guilt, anguish or any other form of psychological distress." A school district in San Antonio has already pulled 414 books from its libraries and classrooms, responding to growing pressure from lawmakers and from "a vocal segment of angry parents."

Among books the district removed from circulation was **Isabel Wilkerson**'s *Caste, The Origins of Our Discontents*, which looks closely at the history of slavery and racism in America. Same with **Ta-Nehisi Coates**' *National*

Book Award Winner *Between the World and Me*, in which the writer speaks honestly to his son about his experience as a Black man in America. I have had in- person conversations with these Black authors and treasure signed copies of their books.

This Gets Personal...

The travesty that really got me going, however, was reading about a Wichita, KS school district's decision to include Black poet and playwright **August Wilson**'s Pulitzer Prize-winning ***Fences*** on their list of 29 books to be removed from school libraries. This was a gut punch. This made it personal.

This past winter thousands of Chicagoans got to marvel at the genius of Wilson when his play ***Gem of the Ocean*** returned to the *Goodman Theatre*, where his masterpiece premiered in 2003.

"GEM" is one of ten interconnected plays documenting the culture, history, and lived experiences of African Americans from slave days to the present. It is this writer's opinion that these plays are a must-read-and-study body of literature. Wilson considers each decade of the 20th Century, with ***Gem of the Ocean*** set as the earliest in 1904. My wife Loann and I were privileged to see this play at the invitation of *Goodman Resident Director* **Chuck Smith** during its premiere run in 2003. We saw it again this past January. The earlier performance included dinner with the playwright, giving us a chance to exchange ideas on his motivation and creativity.

"I wanted to place this (Black) culture on stage in all its richness and fullness," he was later quoted as saying, "and to demonstrate its ability to sustain us all in areas of human life and endeavor and thought." There have been, he added, "profound movements of our history in which the larger society has thought less of us than we have thought of ourselves."

The kicker to all the above was being invited recently to stream a live performance of **Gem** on our home big screen TV. This was made possible by the Goodman, and it was terrific! You could pause it, repeat it and see the tension in the faces of the performing artists.

Wilson shows us that, not only is it alright to be different from mainstream White America but these differences must be celebrated rather than repressed. He is troubled by the unspoken desire among too many African Americans to distance themselves from their slave ancestors as if that part of their history did not exist.

Drama scholar **Sandra Shannon**, in her book *The Dramatic Vision of August Wilson*, points out that "Conversely, he envies those people who are not ashamed today to keep traditions such as dancing the polka or celebrating Passover and he (Wilson) finds it painful to consider the campaign by Jews to keep memories of the Holocaust fresh in the minds of their people while far too many African Americans seem embarrassed by any African linkage."

City of Recovered Memory...

Africa plays a vital role in Wilson's work. He takes us to Africa, either by incorporating some visually familiar reference or, in some instances, by invoking supernatural or mystic phenomena. The segment *City of Bones* in **Gem of the Ocean** is a perfect example of this.

The *City of Bones* is the mystical city in the Atlantic Ocean that was built by the bones of Africans who died aboard slave ships bound for the Americas; their corpses were thrown overboard like spoiled meat.

There's *Citizen Barlow*, a young Black man, who comes to a house to be cleansed by *Aunt Ester*. Ester is the 285-year-old – no typo! – the matriarch of the family. Barlow is the seeker and confessant of the play. A migrant from Alabama, he wants to work in a factory, but he steals a bucket of nails, which results in an innocent man drowning rather than submit to an arrest for a crime he did not commit. He insists on seeing Aunt Ester to confess his sin of Black-on-Black betrayal. His mother named him Citizen "after freedom come." But *Solly Two Kings* reminds him that truly to be a "citizen" he'll need to fight to uphold freedom even when it becomes a heavy load.

Solly Two Kings is a 67-year-old former slave and a conductor on the *Underground Railroad*. *Aunt Ester* is also a former slave who is the keeper of tradition and history. She guides Citizen on a lyrical journey of spiritual awakening aboard the legendary ship **Gem of the Ocean** to the City of Bones. While on the excursion, Citizen comes to understand the story of his ancestors and faces the truth about his crime and the innocent man he wronged.

The dialogue between characters is nothing short of symphonic! It swells between *Black Mary* and her policeman brother, *Caesar Wilks*. Also, between Aunt Ester and Solly Two Kings. Director **Chuck Smith** posits that these two had a love affair in motion. On this *City of Bones* trip, Citizen is surrounded by Solly, Black Mary, Eli, and Aunt Ester. It is a communal and spiritual masterpiece. As the play evolves, Citizen inherits the deceased Solly's walking stick, and Black Mary gets Aunt Ester's shawl symbolizing the generational transfer of power and purpose. The transcendent, mystical travel to the City of Bones, said **Smith**, is always an adventure.

Inheritance Lost and Found...

Moreover, it is an adventure with direct ramifications for Black Americans here in the 21st Century. Understanding our past is essential to navigating our future. In the face of the horrors of slavery and *Jim Crow*, Black people employed sermons, prayers, and gospel songs to survive, steel our determination, and succeed. This cultural vitality and continuity can be found in the Blues, Jazz, and Negro spirituals.

Embracing this heritage is also what the late **Zora Neale Hurston** counsels in her masterpiece *Barracoon: The Story of the Last "Black Cargo."* She influenced playwright Wilson. They appear to be cut from the same cloth in many ways, even though they were decades apart.

Writing in their introduction of a new reissue of Hurston's essays *You Don't Know Us Negroes*, **Henry Louis Gates** and **Genevieve West** speculate on the influence Zora would have had on August. "History has borne out Hurston's prediction (that) in the works of so many of her literary heirs, male as well as female, who, taken together since Hurston's literary recovery, have produced perhaps the richest field of fiction in the literary tradition, all indebted one way or another to the poetics and the practices of **Zora Neale Hurston**."

Gates and West, a Hurston scholar, continue the kinship between Wilson and Hurston. "Because of the boldness of her aesthetic theory and the novelty of her political critique, white and Black folks have been 'overhearing' the resplendent voices of the Black experience, within the veil, in a wide variety of ways, of which Hurston no doubt would approve.

In her maestro piece, *Barracoon*, which centers around **Cudjo Lewis**, one of the last living freed slaves to be interviewed by the persistent writer, Hurston brings the full focus on something many of us would choose to avoid. To wit: African chiefs SOLD defeated and captured Africans to White slavers.

As **Alice Walker** writes in the Foreword of *Barracoon,* "Who could face this vision of the violently cruel behavior of the brethren – and the sisters? Who would want to know, via blow- by-blow account, how African chiefs deliberately set out to capture Africans from neighboring tribes, to provide wars of conquest in order to capture for the slave trade people — men, women, children – who belong to Africa? And to do this in so hideous a fashion that reading about it 200 years later brings waves of horror and distress?"

What Cudjo Remembered…

Cudjo Lewis provides Hurston with a perspective seldom voiced. How Black people came to America, and how they were treated by Blacks and whites who greeted them. How Black Americans who were themselves, enslaved people, ridiculed the Africans, making their lives so much harder. Then there is Cudjo's life after Emancipation. His happiness with his newfound freedom helped create a community and build his own house. It's great. But how does one who has become homeless and unemployed fare? Not an unusual question in today's America, but when the person was recently a slave, it's different.

In his book *The Last Slave Ship*, **Ben Raines** also talks of Cudjo. He is a victim of the African Kingdom of Dahomey, one of the most brutal slaving regions in world history. In Africa, a 19- year-old Yoruba named Kossula, Cudjo, came not with a passport but with a slave ticket. Hurston interviewed him when he was 87 years old. The community Kossula founded in Alabama was called *Africatown.* Kossula was not just a knowledgeable Black tapped for a few stories, tales, and colorful phrases, and **Zora Neale Huston** knew this. She did not perceive *Barracoon* as another cultural artifact illustrating the theoretical characteristic of Negro expression but as a singular portrait of Black humanity.

Ta-Nehisi Coates writes in his book *Between the World and Me:* "He is a specific particular, a specific woman or man. Kossula, his wife Abile, and their six children, the host of Africans who founded Africa town, and their shipmates who survived the Clotilda (the slave ship they traveled on)."

None other than **James Baldwin**, in his *White Man's Guilt*, offers that this history – Cudjo's history – is "Literally present in all that we do, and the power of history, when we are unconscious of it, is tyrannical acts. Barracoon is a counter-narrative that invites us to break our collective silence about slaves and slavery, about slaveholders and the American Dream."

Why We Fight Censorship...

This is why those banned books matter. Benighted politicians, whether in Texas, Kansas, or even the *Land of Lincoln*, must not be allowed to decide what our children can and cannot read.

Writers like **August Wilson** do not so much assail the wrongs of the past as they bring them into focus and show how past African Americans addressed them and rose above them. Wilson and his literary forbears challenge today's African Americans to see themselves participating in a historical dialect that shows how best to avoid the mistakes of previous generations. They are a means of communicating and empowering despite seemingly insurmountable odds.

Black writers do not so much portray Blacks as victims of racism, although their circumstances often and accurately appear otherwise – but as capable men and women who, by grasping and valuing our history, will stop wasting rhetoric and energy reacting to unfulfilled lives and missed opportunities and start believing in themselves.

Action Items...

After teasing you with a taste of August and Zora, take a nourishing dive into these Black geniuses:

- Contact Goodman Theatre's Resident Director **Chuck Smith** can be contacted via **Victoria Rodriquez** at <u>Victoriarodriquez@ goodmantheatre.org</u>. The Goodman hosts various events on Wilson's Work. Check with Victoria.

- Watch the introduction to *Gem of the Ocean* by **Dennis G. Jerz** https://www.youtube.com/watch?v=paVFOW9PuL8

- *Gem of the Ocean*- Full play video. (Online access)

- Zora Neale Hurston can be "googled" using such keywords as Their Eyes Were Watching God (2005); *The Gilded Six Bits*, the 2001 film by **Booker T. Mattison**; *Barracoon*; and **Zora Neale Hurston** – *You Don't Know Us Negroes and Other Essays* with an introduction by **Henry Louis Gates** and **Genevieve West**; and at <u>https://wfpp.columbia.edu/pioneer/zora-neale-hurston/</u>

Finally, **August Wilson** and **Zora Neale Hurston** have made us an offer we cannot refuse. Give 'em a shot! And don't let anyone tell you their works do not belong in our schools, in our libraries ... and in our hearts.

STABILITY, CIVILITY
& FRAGILITY...

It's personal.

The violence and the chaos, the shouting and the crying, whether on Chicago streets or D.C.'s Capitol Hill, is not just the stuff of TV newscasts and newspaper headlines.

It impacts us all. As a Black businessman, based in Chicago, with major clients in the public sector, how the Federal Government operates – or fails to operate – is of great importance to me. Whether it's contract delays, slow processing, or nonpayment of invoices, the government's stability and predictability are a big deal. So is the safety of my co-workers and contracted help as they ply our neighborhoods, cataloging and estimating public works that need to be repaired or replaced.

So, we need to take seriously those who warn that American Democracy, as we know it, will come to an end soon unless honesty and peaceful debate are restored to the public square. Closer to home, we need to heed those who know that theft and gunfire will yield only to education and employment.

As to national chaos, journalist **Barton Gellman** has sounded a loud alarm in the January/February 2022 issue of *The Atlantic* magazine. "*Trump and his party have convinced a dauntingly large number of Americans that the* *essential workings of Democracy are corrupt, that made-up claims of fraud are true, that only cheating can thwart their victory at the polls, that tyranny has usurped their government and violence is a legitimate response."*

Gellman further warns: *"There is a clear and present danger that the American Democracy will not withstand the destructive forces that are now converging on it. Our two-party system has only one party left willing to lose an election. The other is willing to win at the cost of breaking things that a democracy cannot live without."*

Gellman's article analyzing the January 6, 2021, attack on the U.S. Capitol draws extensively from the work of **Robert A. Pape**, Director of the U. of Chicago's *Project on Security and Threats* (CPOST). "The last time America saw middle-class whites involved in violence," Pape told Gellman, "was the expansion of the second *KKK* in the 1920s." So, it's about race, not just election results.

"Replacement" Defacement…

Pape's CPOST group analyzed the January 6 rioters and found that other things being equal, insurgents were much more likely to come from counties where the white share of the population was in decline. For every one-percentage-point drop in the white non-Hispanic population, from 2015 to 2019, the likelihood of an insurgent hailing from that county increased by 25 percent. This was a vital link, and it held up in every state. It also recalls the white power chant from the Charlottesville riot of 2017: "You will not replace us!"

In another CPOST nationwide opinion poll, only one statement won overwhelming support among the 8 percent of respondents – a projected 21 million Americans – who claim **Trump** won and **Joe Biden** is illegitimate.

Almost two-thirds of this group agreed that African Americans or Hispanic people in our country "will eventually have more rights than whites."

Gellman humanizes Pape's stark percentages by conducting a lengthy interview with one **Richard C. Patterson**, a retired New York City fire department captain and ardent Trump supporter/Biden denier.

Patterson's background squares with Pape's research, having lived for years in the Bronx, where the 2020 *U.S. Census* counted 20,413 fewer non-Hispanic whites than were enumerated in 2010. As a boy, he grew up in Oakland, CA., where he remembers he applied for an opening at the fire department and, by his telling, encountered the unfairness of affirmative action and reverse racism. "So, no job for the big white kid. The position went to this little woman who I know failed the test."

Later in New York, after a woman successfully filed a discrimination suit against the *FDNY*, Patterson was part of a class being trained to work alongside female newbies. It didn't go well.

"I look at the 2020 election," Patterson said, "as sort of an example on steroids of affirmative action. The straight white guy won, but it was stolen from him and given to somebody else." He explains that Biden may be straight, but that **Vice President Kamala Harris** was on the ticket purely for racial reasons.

So here we are. Part of the rationale motivating this white fireman – and thousands like him – into dancing the Trump Tango is that he thinks he was once wronged by *Affirmative Action*. He sees a Black Vice President as "more of the same." In other words, the violent chaos of January 6 was not just about election results. It was about race, and it was personal.

Closer To Home…

We have a situation closer to home that puts my Black business – and many, many others – in a profoundly menacing bind. It's the violence that besets Chicago neighborhoods. As a Black- owned professional services construction firm, we are dispatching staff to various schools, libraries, and fire stations on Chicago's South and West Sides. There the constant volley of shootings and carjackings continue unabated. We've always been concerned about staff safety as they navigate collapse-prone scaffolds or faulty flooring, but now it's about stray bullets and random crossfire. This puts an entirely different spin on things.

Consider just the Hyde Park area surrounding my alma mater. In Hyde Park the random violence has gone out of control. For example, on December 19, 2020, a Lyft driver picked up two passengers near the University and was shot while stopping for a red light. Or just last November when U of C student **Shaoxing "Dennis" Zheng** was killed. He was just 24 years old, and his alleged killer, just 18, was apprehended while trying to pawn Zheng's laptop computer.

All of which has prompted *University of Chicago* President **Paul Alivisatos** and Provost **Ka Yee Christina Lee** to announce "expanding investments in research and in community-led initiatives and strategies for violence reduction. Crucially, we will develop ways for university members and community partners to drive the directions that this work will take."

Sounds promising, especially with **Waldo E. Johnson, Jr.**, Associate Professor and Deputy Dean for Curriculum at the school's *Crown Family School of Social Work, Policy and Practice*, in the middle of it. Johnson has provided guidance, advocacy, and adherence to the concept of respectful community partnerships. I'm betting he'll be a quiet genius at the forefront of the University's response to these issues.

Anniversary Actions...

As we mark the first anniversary of the January 6 insurrection, we see chaos still surrounds us. It's not only Black contractors that are challenged, but all Black-owned businesses such as restaurants reduced to carry-out and online orders, all the while beset by staff shortages due to *Covid*. We are living in perilous times!

Yet there are positive moves that I – and you – could and should be made to stop the bleeding and begin the healing:

1. Maintain contact with **Trey Baker**, Black Stakeholder at the White House Office of Public Engagement. He can provide the pulse of the Administration's reactions and countermeasures to troublesome issues as they arise.

2. **Congressman Bobby Rush**, proceeding to his final term, can provide info on Infrastructure funding, one of the bright spots on the urban horizon.

3. **Congressman Danny Davis** has agreed to track the nation's new $5.3 billion "*Evidence- Based Violence Prevention Program*" quietly tucked into Biden's infrastructure plan.

4. **Dr. Gary Slutkin** led the effort to engage "*Interrupters*" to stem the tide of violence in Chicago and still backs a focused deterrence approach. In partnership with the *Jewish Community Relations Council* and *Arizona State University*, his Cure Violence campaign recently ran a virtual training session for journalists in Phoenix on best practices for covering violence-related events.

5. To combat future insurrections, let's switch to a public health approach to prevent violent extremism and away from security and intelligence experts with their wiretaps and cultivated informants. In a recent NYT op-ed, **Cynthia Miller-Idriss** of *American University* calls for more social workers, school counselors and

teachers, mental health experts, and religious leaders to debunk online lies … and shortstop the violence those lies engender.

Summing Up…

Speaking of changes in our approach to local violence, when I took up the issue with Bobby Rush and others, I was directed to writer **Francesca Mari**'s suggestions in the *New York Review of Books* June 10, 2021, issue. "The one (point) that needs to be addressed, before we can take on problems that lead people to violence," she pointed out, "are matters such as economic, educational, and racial inequality. If you're not safe, nothing else matters."

That logic squares nicely with conclusions reached by violence scholar **Thomas Abt** in his book *Bleeding Out: The Devastating Consequences of Urban Violence.* Like Congressman Rush, Abt finds that today's urban "gangs" are really "small informal groups that have limited capacity for highly organized crime … They are from neglected and impoverished communities and are formed mainly in response to other gangs."

Abt also echoes Dr. Slutkin's Interruptors strategy by calling for focused deterrence wherein a social worker, community peer, and/or specially trained law officer work in advance with youths prone to violence.

Then again, don't expect the majority of white folks in Kenilworth, Evanston, or the North Shore to get all riled up with these points. Theirs is a different reality. Even well-off, college-educated Blacks may have a different perspective vis-a-vis the root causes of violence. Crime warrants punishment, etc.

But even **Ray Charles** and **Stevie Wonder** could see that, if you have a group of white rioters attacking the nation's Capital, in addition to four

Chicagoans being shot during one recent week on (gasp) Chicago's North Side, mayhem assaults us from many angles. January 6 wasn't so much a mass casualty attack as a recruitment drive for more radicalized Trump supporters. Just as **Dennis Zhang** wasn't murdered by a soulless thug so much as a boy bereft of hope in a world bereft of opportunities most of us take for granted.

Please note this is not some historical, political assessment. This is personal. How does one plan and execute a public works consultancy when the very underpinnings of the public sector are under attack? Or when it's not safe for one's workers to walk the streets?

These are questions that confront us all. It's personal. And the best answer, for now, is to STAY SAFE AND STAY WOKE.

NOW HEAR THESE! OUR TRUE CONCERNS REVEALED BY THE MEDIA MAVERICK, BLACK COWBOYS, AND BEST OF ALL, AUGUST'S ANSWER...

Writing in **N'DIGO** last month, that *Maverick Media Maven,* **Hermene Hartman**, reported on a Black female journalist who complained that a white editor of a major newspaper cut her proposed column so much it was unrecognizable.

That's so Hermene. N'DIGO's editor and publisher rarely misses a chance to promote Black issues and excellence, especially when any powers-that-be attempted to render us invisible. That's why this '*Maverick Media Maven*'(hereafter referred to as M3) started the print edition of **N'DIGO** in 1989 and for a time had it inserted with a major metro newspaper. But as print media fell behind various digital platforms, M3 established this web version and by so doing expanded the reach of Black thought. Alert to the trends and interests of Generation Z, she recently added N'DIGO STUDIO, a podcast-type interview shows that streams anytime at https://ndigo.com/ndigo-studio-podcasts/ and airs weekly on NBC Ch.5. Hartman has managed to pair HipHop with Jazz, young with not-so-young, making for transgenerational attention and appeal.

No, this is not a paean to Hermene nor a self-serving shout-out to my journalistic pal, but an honest response to a well-known fact that needs constant repeating. For decades – no, centuries — Black Voices in America have been stilled, hushed, and tamed. Examples abound but let us consider one with which all are familiar – the ubiquitous Hollywood-produced Western movie.

Black Gunslingers Show Up!

No genre more obscures the existence of Blacks. So indoctrinated were we with **Gene Autry**, **Roy Rogers**, and **John Wayne** that we never knew that, according to the *Smithsonian*, one in every four cowboys was Black. Back in the day, however, young Blacks were encouraged to root for all-White cowboys and pony soldiers as they routed, killed and otherwise displaced the *"Indians"* – our widely-accepted misnomer for Native Americans.

Before 2020 you hardly ever saw a Black cowboy. Only now, like the legendary *Jim Dandy* come-to-the-rescue, **Jeymes Samuel** has co-written and directed a remedy to this Black exclusion titled ***The Harder They Fall.*** By assembling an all-star cast of Black actors including **Idris Elba** and **Regina King**, Samuel has revised forever our collective memory of the Old West. Recently the *Divine Nine* (our coalition of 9 progressive Black Fraternities and Sororities) hosted a special screening to which this *Alpha* and his *AKA* wife attended. It's the first feature film from writer, director, producer and composer Samuel, a British brother better known for releasing his music and accompanying shorts under his pseudonym *The Bullitts.*

Actor **Idris Elba** recently hailed the film to *Indiewire.com* as nothing short of revolutionary for its portrayal of Black people in a region and time that Hollywood had thoroughly white-washed. "What we should be celebrating and what we have been celebrating here today is the impact of the movie on film and on story telling. My daughter is at NYU, she's 19 years old, she comes to see the film and she immediately went back, and it changed her life, because she saw historical figures that she had no consciousness of, in a genre she had no attachment to." He concluded "The ripple effect is going to help cinema (as) film makers diversify their lens a bit in how you tell stories of Black folk." According to **Justin Chang**, NYT.

The storyline revolves around *Nat Love*, a fact-based fictionalized gunslinger and Black cowboy legend born to enslaved parents on a Tennessee plantation in 1854. As a young boy he loses his family in spectacularly brutal fashion, setting up a long-simmering revenge plot. Years later he and his trusted gang find themselves tracking his parents' assassins led by the vicious outlaw *Rufus Buck* (Elba). **Regina King** is *Treacherous Trudy Smith* and **Zazie Beetz** is *Stagecoach Mary*, who in real life was the first Black woman to work for the U.S. Postal Service. **Shawn Carter**, AKA **Jay Z**, works his magic with the film's musical score bringing Hip Hop and Afro-Caribbean to a western film. Not only does "Harder" reinstate Black people to the American Western, but two strong Black women are shown fighting it out — something seldom if ever seen in old Westerns.

August's Answer...

In truth, Samuel's new movie builds on themes already brought to the live stage by playwright **August Wilson**, who adroitly anticipated the widening demand for greater visibility, inclusion, and perspective of African Americans in the performing arts.

Before his death in 2005 Wilson had written 10 plays covering the African American journey, decade by decade, during the 20th Century. The winner of 2 Pulitzer Prizes for Drama, Wilson once visited Chicago's *Goodman*

Theatre at the invitation of Resident Director **Chuck Smith**. My wife and I joined them for dinner prior to the performance of one of his plays, whereupon Wilson kept us in rapt silence, especially after I questioned him about the mission of the Black playwright.

Nothing can come close to what he said that evening, except perhaps for what he wrote in his 46-page jewel of an essay/book *The Ground On Which I Stand*. Therein he outlines exactly how he felt and what his work intends. I didn't record him that night, but he repeated several key points from his book:

- There are and always have been two distinct and parallel traditions in Black art. That is art that is conceived and designed to entertain white society and art that feels the spirit and celebrates the life of Black Americans by designing its strategies for survival and prosperity.

- We can meet on common ground of theatre as a field of work and endeavor, but we cannot meet on the common ground of experience. Where is the Common ground in the horrifics of lynching? Where is the common ground in the maim of the policeman's bullet? Where is the common ground in the hull of the slave ship or the deck of a slave ship with its refreshments of air and expanse.

- Nor do we need the recognition of our Blackness to be couched in abstract phrases like "artist of color." Who are you talking about? A Japanese artist? An Eskimo "A Filipino? A Mexican? A Cambodian? A Nigerian? Are we to suppose that one white person balances out the rest of humanity lumped together as a non-descript "people of color? We reject that. We are unique and we are specific.

- We stand on the verge of an explosion of playwriting talent (Wilson said this in 1996, how prescient!) That will challenge our critics. As American playwrights absorb the influence of television and use new avenues of approach to practice their craft, they will grow to be wildly inventive and imaginative in creating dramas that will guide and influence contemporary life for years to come.

Television and 'the new avenues" of media notwithstanding, Black America would do well to keep alive the benediction of **August Wilson**. Indeed, that is the aim of the Goodman's **Chuck Smith** and **Dr. Sandra Shannon**, president and founder of the *August Wilson Society* (AWS.) Chuck is a childhood friend and Resident Director at the *Goodman Theatre*. Shannon is Professor Emerita of African American literature in the Department of English of *Howard University*, where she is Founder and President of the *August Wilson Society*.

There is no question that the work of Wilson should be studied, taught, and continually reinterpreted. AWS defines itself as a cross-disciplinary learning community dedicated to commemorating the playwright by promoting the studying, the teaching, the performing, the researching, and the ultimate safeguarding of his rich legacy. And what a legacy it is, rendering into poetry and drama the history, decade-by-decade, of African Americans in the 20th Century. Wilson made America and the world more aware of the saga of a people struggling to gain equitable status in a culture they helped build. Through the immensity and ambition of his vision, Wilson crafted a series of linked narratives that not only captured many of the untold stories of the Black experience but increased the presence of African American performers and theatrical talent throughout this nation and beyond. Wilson opened the doors of mainstream theaters to the voices and perspectives of African-descended people, most of them "*involuntary immigrants*" to this country.

Conclusion…

Summing up, we need to face the challenge of Black invisibility. Our invisibility is largely intentional as outlined and reported by Hermene Hartman. But we must respond with innovations such as those employed by Black film director/writer **Jeymes Samuel**, who uses Black Actors to create a blockbuster film about a time largely unknown.

Action Items…

Best of all, we have the legacy of a thought leader, **August Wilson**, who provided a map now kept and communicated by the *August Wilson Society*. I'm no theatre or film critic, but as an advocate for Black Business and a survivor of Civil Rights struggles both won and lost, I beg our larger Black community to support this emergence from invisibility. Here are some good places to start:

- Watch August Wilson's "*The Piano Lesson*" on Netflix.

- Go see Wilson's "***Gem of the Ocean***" at the Goodman Theatre in January.

- Support the *August Wilson Society* and along with Business Leadership Council's **Charles Smith** and myself the AWS pilot program to introduce Black youth to the performing arts. https://www.augustwilsonsociety.org/

- Black Business Scholarships are also being established in honor of Director Chuck Smith for Goodman Theatre Interns.

- See the film "*The Harder They Fall*". Yes, Virginia, there were indeed Black Buckaroos.

BEEN THERE DONE THAT! - IT'S TIME FOR BLACK BUILDERS TO POSITION FOR PROSPERITY!

It's not a matter of IF, but WHEN the *Biden Infrastructure Plan* – perhaps in reduced form – will become law. At that moment, billions of dollars in construction contracts and fees will come into play for Black contractors, engineers, architects, and other professionals. Blacks with hard hats will be summoned to union hiring halls. Black receptionists and payroll clerks will be in instant demand.

Or not.

Much depends on the willingness and ability of minority contractors and their political allies to get their ducks in a row. And do it now, before white-owned construction giants gobble the lion's share, likely behind familiar window dressing and lip service that give an illusion of minority participation.

So what needs to happen? At the risk of sounding like a guy with-all-the answers, allow me to make a few suggestions based on a professional lifetime of dealing with – and succeeding at – these very issues.

Recommendation No. 1: Find a model that works. A Tale of Two Cities...

Rochester, New York is a metropolis of 200,000 with 40% African American residents. **Michael Corkery** of *The New York Times* in an article headlined *Black Capitalism Promised a Better City for Everyone. What Happened?* (9/12/21 NYT) explains that Rochester in the '60s had two corporate behemoths in *Xerox* and *Kodak* that wanted to help. Responding to then-**President Richard Nixon**'s *Black Capitalism* policy, *Xerox* helped create *Eltrex Industries*, a Black-owned enterprise that made vacuums and other parts for copying and film processing.

I visited Rochester twice in the 1970s on behalf of the *National Association of Minority Contractors* (NAMC). These and other promising partnerships between *Kodak*, *Xerox*, and other large companies showed a great deal of potential and promise. But the flame was extinguished over the decades, according to Corkery. *Eltrex* shut its doors in 2011. Among challenges was its dependence on winning repeat contracts from *Xerox* and *Kodak* which were fighting for their own survival in a digital age. Their ability to support the partially employee-owned venture became limited. Today, Corkery concludes, the Black business initiative of that era has all but vanished.

Chicago a Different Story...

On July 23, 1969, our *Coalition for United Community Action* shut down the first of more than $80 million in area construction projects. Our goal was Black jobs. African Americans then were confined to the "wet and trowel" trades among construction unions and all but shut out of electrical, plumbing, sheet metal and HVAC trades. The **Rev. C.T. Vivian** was our leader and the Lords, Stones, & Disciples were our troops. Three seismic developments had their beginnings in our edgy effort.

1. We introduced the concept of Black Contractor Advancement as part of the push for more Blacks in the better-paying trades. It was a twofer, in that more Black Contractors would inevitably "hire our own."

2. **Congressman Parren Mitchell** (D-Md.) created the Black Business Braintrust which advocated for Federal support of Black business.

3. **Harold Washington**, then an Illinois State Representative, assisted Black contractors with legislation helping them obtain the insurance and surety bond coverage required of all contractors bidding on major projects.

The **Reverend C.T. Vivian** was pivotal at this point. The dynamic Reverend, who passed in July of 2020, was Martin Luther King's Lieutenant. Today's activists would do well to consult his memoirs as presented in "C.T. Vivian – It's in the Action" with co-author **Steve Fifer**.

The Reverend made it simple: "We brought together 61 non-governmental organizations and formed the *Coalition for United Community Action*. But the real players, the big-time players, were the gangs. Our concern was how do you move from their usual way of thinking. If you could get them involved so that they became the force, you need to go after the biggies. If you don't have any force that's already bought by *City Hall* or the businessmen, what forces are you going to use to change Chicago?"

"The building trades had all kinds of jobs but if you were Black, you didn't become a full member of any of them," Vivian recounts, "So we had to take on the unions. We did it nonviolently, but all these guys in the unions were afraid, we weren't. They would leave work and work would stop. We stopped half a billion dollars of work right downtown in the middle of the city."

Street Heat and a D.C. Seat...

Earlier, **Rep. Parren Mitchell** and his allies in Congress pivoted on *President Lyndon Johnson's Executive Order 11246* that established requirements for non-discriminatory practices in hiring and employment on the part of U.S. government contractors.

The Mitchell-organized *Black Braintrust* also launched surety bond and working capital lines of credit and loan guarantee programs that greatly helped Black contractors get startup financing and bonds. My construction firm, *UBM*, got its first bond through this **Small Business Administration** program. By 2005 we were the largest Black-owned construction firm in Illinois. **Harold Washington** went on to be Chicago's first Black mayor in 1983 and promptly issued an *Executive Order* that required city contracts to have a minimum percentage of minority business participation.

Based on these actions – beginning with on-the-street pressure that blossomed into *Federal*, *State* and *City* requirements – we live now in a world where minority and female participation is expected as part of government procurement. The *NAMC* continues in operation with chapters around the country with best practices shared via email, rather than face-to-face huddles, during this damnable pandemic.

Where We Are Today...

What's to be learned, then, now that **Joe Biden** is about to roll out a *Build Back Better* program that promises at least $1.5 trillion (with a T!) in new public works nationwide – the largest such program in a generation? The challenge is to be prepared – prepared to bring the heat if Biden's program gets stalled or curtailed by *Democratic* infighting or *GOP* intransigence; prepared to take advantage of past wins but also of growing labor shortages that are about to hit the construction industry. After all, construction unions once allergic to minorities soon may not have enough members to fill manpower orders, much as the *Teamsters* now can't move goods and services due to a shortage of truck drivers. It's worth noting that obstructing Black entry, the unions now have to resort, very often, to non-US citizens to fill the labor demands.

Chicago's *Business Leadership Council,* whose founding leaders **Frank Clark**, **Jim Montgomery,** and **John Hooker** have passed the baton to a younger group, is surely one key player. Leaders such as **Charles Smith, Jim Reynolds** and **Avis Lavelle** have taken up lead roles and are doing a terrific job. But in order to seize current and future business opportunities and future business opportunities, Chicago's Black businesses must better recognize the necessity of having an advocacy group that can interact with policymakers, elected officials, and public agencies. Obviously, the situation now is different than we faced in the 70s and beyond. Tactics change, but now as then, there is a dire need for well-informed leadership capable of navigating tricky and sticky political, legal and cultural issues. *BLC*, or something like it, will be the key to success.

Just as the late **Parren Mitchell** led the *Black Business Legislative* push into the 80s, **Congressman Danny Davis** (D-IL) has committed to creating a *Black Business Bridge* to Biden infrastructure opportunities. He wants to ensure that funds coming into states and cities are fairly distributed, especially among qualified Black enterprises. "Danny" has hosted both in- person and virtual zoom meetings to discuss these issues. Black entrepreneurs and job seekers would do well to tune in.

Getting Prepared...

Some upcoming opportunities will be bigger than many Black firms can handle alone, even with programs in place to assist with financing, technical assistance and bonding. Legitimate teaming with other Black firms and large majority-owned firms will be required. Sophisticated legal services to create bona fide joint ventures and sub-prime entities will be required. Experienced lawyers like **Graham Grady**, **Jim Montgomery** and **Kevin Brown** are among those adept at such intricate combinations. The *Business Leadership Council* can refer the uninitiated to additional law firms and accountancies. At the risk of sounding like a *Boy Scout Troop Master,* I herewith stress the need to BE PREPARED!

Nothing would be sadder than for large project developers/owners to seek waivers to *MBE* participation requirements because there are no Black Businesses able to respond in a timely way to estimating, proposal drafting or payment delays. **Marv Wilson**, founder of *Performance Spectrums* and a peerless organizational guru, has outlined steps to be taken to ready Black businesses for upcoming opportunities.

Wilson counsels' clients on long- and short-term strategic planning; on vision, mission and value development; on internal systems and process development; on leadership development and management coaching. He advises that it is as necessary to work ON the business as it is to work IN the business. This entails everything from business plan development to succession planning. He's someone all Black businesses should know. www.performance-spectrums.com

Sure, the pandemic has forced many to maintain social distancing and limit group meetings. But this is an ideal time to improve business opportunities and operational practices. The *Biden Black Business* train is nearing the station. Time is wasting to get your ticket. It's a ticket of up-to-date info, of organizational readiness, but most of all, of recognition that opportunities on this scale come along but once in a generation. I've been there. It's time to do that.

30TH ANNIVERSARY SALUTE
TO MINORITIES IN CONSTRUCTION

Wednesday, November 3, 1999
Regal Knickerbocker

COMMEMORATIVE PROGRAM BOOK

NAMC
NATIONAL ASSOCIATION OF MINORITY CONTRACTORS

Hall of Famers Edition
44th National Conference

EYES ON THE PRIZE...

While we're dancing the *Pandemic Polka* and watching the *Trump Tax Return Tango*, it would be easy to ignore the *Black Business Ballet* now being choreographed under the **Biden Infrastructure Plan**. That would be a mistake.

The roughly $1.2 trillion infrastructure bill – the largest steel-and-concrete federal spending package in a generation – has cleared the Senate on a rare bipartisan vote and likely will gain House approval this Fall ... one way or the other.

The Biden mega-plan would provide funds to rebuild roads and bridges, expand airports like *O'Hare International*, modernize *Union Station*, extend the *CTA Red Line* and even replace $15 billion worth of lead water pipes in less affluent neighborhoods across the nation. State and local governments will decide where much of these funds get spent. Hereabouts that means *IDOT, CTA, Metra* trains, *PACE* buses, and the *RTA*.

The stakes for Black-owned businesses and construction workers could not be higher. Several in-the-know construction execs predict that nationally there could be $150 billion to $300 billion worth of Black Business Opportunities over the Biden Plan's 10-year disbursement run. It's hard to be more exact because various states and localities have very different minority set-aside programs. For instance, the *RTA*, which funnels tax funds to *CTA, Metra*, and *Pace*, has a 16.2 % goal on contracts under its procurement rules. Illinois does 20%, though many states do far less, pointing to U.S. Supreme Court rulings that have limited outright mandates.

So the overture has begun to this production and the curtain is about to rise. Trouble is, the music is complicated, the script is only partially written and the dance steps are – in a word – tricky.

History Lesson...

What must be done, then, to take advantage of all this? Past being prologue, it might help to look at what we in the trades did leading up to, and following, the seminal *Public Works Act of 1977*. Those stars didn't align by themselves. We worked the corners, convened conferences, met at meetings (often behind closed doors), and otherwise coaxed and cajoled our way to an unprecedented minority set-aside framework, much of which survives today.

Praise be to the late **Congressman Parren Mitchell** for his deft maneuvering among the U.S. Commerce Department, the U.S. Small Business Administration, the National Association of Minority Contractors, and, of course, the Congress of the United States.

But that was 1977. **Jimmy Carter** was in the White House, and Democrats held supermajorities in both the Senate and House. Today we also have a labor-friendly president, but the Senate is evenly split, and Democrats hold a razor-thin majority in the House. Moreover, some of those House Democrats are threatening to take a walk on the Biden Plan unless they first went passage of an additional $3.5 trillion program of social and environmental programs. Republicans are saying no way to that linkage.

But again, history holds some valuable lessons. The *Public Works Act of 1977* was "only" a $4 billion program, but it set important precedents for *Minority Business Enterprises* (MBEs) and fixed percentages of set-asides.

Parren Mitchell (D-Maryland) chaired the House Small Business Committee and wisely set up an informal Black Business Brain trust of which this writer was a grateful member. So advised, Mitchell's committee set in motion the 10% minority business requirement that became part of the Public Works Act. This opened the door for my fledgling *UBM* construction company and many other members of the National Association of Minority Contractors (NAMC) to participate in federal contracts.

But it was easier said than done. Critical to this opportunity was our ability to talk to and gain information from the various agencies tasked to bid and let those contracts … and make sure MBEs got their share. Then and now, however, government agencies are won't to, and often barred from, having direct pre-bid contact with specific companies. However, organizations advocating for Black Businesses can have access and establish a dialogue with agencies. That now betokens the value of today's *Business Leadership Council*, just as back then we rallied behind the *NAMC*. The latter group, by the way, is still going strong. **Curtis Thompson**, the lead representative of the Chicago area NAMC, can be reached at Curtis@Namc-chicago.org.

And one final but crucial history lesson: Get ready to play some Defense! As in the past, there will be some folks who claim any MBE set-aside provisions are nothing by "reverse racism. "Biden's Infrastructure bill is chock full of anti-white racism," shrieked a recent op-ed headline in the New York Post. Author **Betsy McCaughey** trots out the tired, worn-out argument used by white racists that claim anything done to assist Blacks takes away from whites. You know, the old zero-sum game. They act like nothing is owed to those shut out by 400 years of slavery, 100 years of *Jim*

Crow, and the much more recent, systematic exclusion of Blacks from trade unions and Black-owned businesses from lists of qualified bidders. Tell the truth. Enough is enough.

Action Items...

So what's our first move?

- **Charles Smith**, Chairman of the Business Leadership Council, hosts a series of in- person and virtual meetings. He has agreed to dialogue with funded agencies to advance business opportunities for BLC and Black businesses at large. He has already hosted hybrid meetings with *Illinois Transportation* **Secretary Omer Osman**, and with *IDOT* to better link Black businesses with Illinois projects. Contact *Psande@blcchicago.com*.

- **Joseph Williams**, President of the *Target Group*, leads an organization that matches Black contractors with major construction projects. Target also connects Black job aspirants with entry-level and journeyman-level construction jobs. Target under Williams also is planning an unsolicited proposal for a multi-year program to provide management and technical assistance to Black contractors. Included would be pre-apprentice training leading to entry-level positions for Black candidates. The Biden infrastructure package will create some 11 million jobs, generating some $1.5 trillion in earnings for some 647,000 Black hires. Contact *jwilliams@targetgoupinc.com*.

- The federal *Minority Business Development Agency* (MBDA) is tasked with getting the word out and helping MBEs with compliance issues. **Kandice Brown** *KandceBrown5@MBDA.gov* and **Antavia Grimsley** represent this agency of the U.S. Department of Commerce. See *AGrimsley1@MBDA..gov MBDA* will host a national *Minority Enterprise Development* (MED) week

September 19-25 so that both private and government buyers can advise minority providers of products and services. More info at *https://medweek.mbda.gov/*

- **Congressman Danny Davis**, who announced his candidacy for re-election on August 8, has vowed to work with **Senator Raphael Warnock** (D-Georgia) and his staff of the *Senate Committee on Commerce, Science and Transportation*. This committee will have oversight of many infrastructure dealings.

- **Congressman Bobby Rush**, chairman of the Energy Subcommittee of the House Committee on Energy and Commerce, has agreed to designate a staff member to follow up on Black Business opportunities in the new infrastructure program. A major part of the plan is the expansion and modernization of the nation's electrical grid, a huge potential for Black businesses.

Not Just Hard-Hat Jobs..

Of crucial importance throughout is the realization that the 2,702-page *Infrastructure Investment and Jobs Act* won't just create work for those with hard hats and muddy boots. Besides all the architects, engineers, and white-collar estimators, there will be opportunities for businesses providing insurance, legal services, communication specialists, passenger car repair and maintenance, advertising, technology consulting, and public relations. And if Democrats succeed in linking the Infrastructure plan to their even larger proposal for $3.5 trillion in education and social services, you can add lots of teachers and health care workers.

But the passage of federal spending plans, no matter how big, is only the front half of a long battle. After the happy press conferences are over in D.C., the critical back half requires us to work quietly behind the scenes to link our companies and, most importantly, our people, especially people-in-need, to the jobs pipeline. Right now, we need to:

1) Identify which agencies in Chicago will be receiving these funds; 2) Establish communications with the Minority Business offices in each of those agencies; 3) Determine which large firms we can market to, or joint-venture with, if you are a small business or sub-contractor; and 4) Match your business with the location and scope of available contracts and interest.

Summing Up...

Now is the time, while the Infrastructure bill is lumbering its way toward a signed law, for Black businesses to get our ducks in a row. This is especially true while we are in a pandemic. For instance, *MBEs* need to take advantage of the huge savings of time and money made possible by less travel and more virtual meetings. The flip side, of course, is the challenges of managing staff productivity and morale while employees are in a hybrid situation. Not to mention the unpredictable availability of clients (especially those responsible for accounts payable!)

But seriously, the orchestra is playing a grand overture, and the curtain is about to rise on one of the greatest opportunities of our lifetimes. We are like the young **Alexander Hamilton** at the opening of this new, unbounded nation in many respects.

It's time to focus like laser beams on the opportunity that awaits. Like the young man from the West Indies rapped in Broadway's **Hamilton**:

Rise up; it's time to take a shot
Rise up; take a shot, shot, shot
It's time to take a shot, time to take a shot
And I am not throwin' away my
Not throwin' away my shot

JUNETEENTH, JIMMY & RALPH

A swath of white America is locked in curious cacophony over something called Critical Race Theory. Okay. But while some finally come to grips with the darker chapters of their history, Blacks need to hunker down and look inward for survival and direction.

This essay is aimed at wisdom we can glean from classic African American thought.

But first let us dispense with CRT. Two months before Loser Don lost to President Joe Biden, the creep whose business lackey is now under indictment by the New York States Attorney had a federal Directive issued to cease and desist all training on critical race theory or white privilege.

The Office of Management and Budget explained the "President" was concerned about exposing federal employees to "un-American propaganda." Certain training on racism is divisive … false and demeaning, it claimed, and federal agencies were to identify all contracts or spending on this training and come up with a plan to stop it." Thankfully Joe Biden reversed this order in February, but by then the perfidious pony was out of the barn. The lie about CRT became marching orders for Trump's tricksters and continues to spread like wildfire.

Critical Race Theory is simply an analytical tool to uncover the role of racism throughout American history. But to some white people the fact that white supremacy was overtly used to infect America's system of power with self-serving racial privilege is too much to handle. CRT unravels the American myth, argues New York Times columnist **Charles Blow** in a June 13 piece. Properly applied, CRT challenges the long-standing narrative that white America had crafted about the country and it unveils truths that it has tried to hide or erase.

In recent weeks Tennessee, Texas, Oklahoma, Iowa, and Idaho have passed laws on what can be taught in public high schools. They seek to change public education by banning the expression of CRT-related ideas. Even if this censorship was legal in the narrow context of public primary and secondary education, it is antithetical to educating students in the American tradition of free expression.

During the same week that the U.S. made Juneteenth a national holiday, Texas precluded any teacher from explaining the state's own history of enslavement lest students feel "discomfort, guilt…anguish". You cannot have it both ways! You get a holiday but cannot get informed about it in the classroom. That is crazy!

Juneteenth Remembered

On June 19, 1865 Union Army General Gordon Granger released the following Order No. 3: "The people of Texas are informed that, in accordance with the Proclamation from the Executive of the United States, all slaves are free. This involves an absolute equality of personal rights and rights of property between former masters and slaves and the connection heretofore existing between them becomes that between employer and hired labor. The freedmen are advised to remain at their present homes and work for wages. They are informed that they will not be allowed to collect at military posts and that they will not be supported in idleness either there or elsewhere."

Harvard professor and historian **Annette Gordon-Reed** in her book *On Juneteenth* states "All over the South, but in Texas, particularly, whites unleashed a torrent of violence against the freed men and women and sometimes whites who supported them that lasted for years"

This is *deja-vu* all over again! The government issues a directive benefitting Blacks followed by white backlash. No matter. The end of slavery has been celebrated by Blacks for over 100 years and this year finally became a national holiday. Yet today the public schools in many states, teachers are being barred by state bans on any discussion about the origins and purpose of the holiday.

That Juneteenth has been designated a U.S. federal holiday has been met with mixed reaction. **Kaitlyn Greenidge,** a contributing writer for The New York Times, recently worried that the holiday recognizing slavery's end will be co-opted and commercialized, witness Walmart's quick marketing of Juneteenth tee shirts. "But mostly I am sad because when a holiday becomes co-opted like this, those who can gain a sense of self and solidarity from celebrating it often lose it. The agency that comes from deciding your own traditions – a cold water toast, a watch night – become lost to a corporate calendar and mega stores selling you Juneteenth cookout check lists. You can lose sight of the possibility that exists in marginated histories which has been the space to imagine a better world."

Kevin Young, Director of the National Museum of African American History and Culture, states "we might count Juneteenth among those things Black people have long enjoyed that white folks don't know about' When Juneteenth becomes a holiday, will it remain Black? We at the museum are keenly aware that history should not just be the record of what happened, it should also be a record of how we remember what happened and how, too often, memory and testimony have been ended in favor of fear and fantasy." African Americans should not have to bear the burden of this history alone. Nor should Black achievement be something that only African Americans celebrate.

JIMMY, JIMMY, JIMMY

No discussion of how America selectively remembers its history can be complete without acknowledging the work of the late James Baldwin.

Eddie Glaude Jr. in his 2020 book *Begin Again: James Baldwin's America and Its Urgent Lessons for Our Own*, performs a huge literary feat in capturing the essence of James Baldwin in less than 250 pages. Yet Baldwin was given a tough time during the 1960s and '70s, largely because he was not accepted by Black nationalists of the time. Baldwin died in 1987, but Glaude gives us a here-and-now two-fer. He translates and interprets the oft-times oblique Jimmy, while simultaneously connecting the dots between the author's positions and the Black condition of today.

In 1985 Baldwin noted that America had become quick to congratulate itself on the progress it had made with regards to race, and that the country's self- congratulations came with the expectation of Black gratitude. (This was particularly evident among white liberals following the election of Barack Obama.)

As Baldwin put it, "People who have opted to congratulate themselves on their generous returning to the slaves their freedom, which they never had the right to endanger, much less take away. For this dubious effort… they congratulate themselves and expect to be congratulated.

Glaude argues "What is happening today isn't unprecedented. It's just uniquely of OUR times. We have to understand our own anger and disappointments and figure out how to pick up the pieces, to hold off the temptation of HATE and despair and to fight the battle once again." He continues "We need a third American founding to begin again without the insidious idea of the Value Gap. This gap continues to get in the way of a New America. We need an America where 'being white' is no longer the price of the ticket. Instead, we should imagine the country in the full light of its diversity and with an honest recognition of our sins. It is worrisome that there is a deep sentiment in some quarters of this country for nothing more than a return to American life before Trump. I find this feeling dangerous because it is not merely a response to the damage Trump has wrought on the country – and on the American psyche – but also more subtly a reaction to all the long-standing and difficult questions Trump's presidency has brought into view"

Ralph to the Rescue

The other essential Black thinker in any discussion of CRT and white supremacy is **Ralph Ellison**. His 1952 masterpiece "Invisible Man" has been translated into fourteen languages and has never been out of print – testimony to its relevance in today's racial reckoning. The book chronicles the path of a young Black man whose successful search for identity ends with the realization that he is invisible to the white world. Like Baldwin, Ellison disappointed some Black nationalists. Critics agree that the influence of Invisible man on American literature is incalculable. Ellison states in his prologue, "So my task was one of revealing the human universals hidden within the plight of one who was both Black and American, not only as a means of conveying my personal vision of possibility, but as a way of dealing with the sheer rhetorical challenge involved in communicating across our barriers of race and religion, class, color and regions."

Adam Bradley, in the NYT's readily accessible **"T Book Club"** series of online discussions, guides us with amazing clarity and passion through the Invisible man's labyrinth. The historic context of this classic is useful in appreciating Ellison's genius. The Civil Rights movement of the 1950s and 1960s had its genesis in The Great Migration, the move North of

6.5 million Black Americans from the South. This created large Black communities in New York's Harlem and Chicago's South Side. In the early 1900s Black migration increased dramatically with the beginning of WWI in response to the demand for factory workers in the North. While the move did not bring social justice to Blacks, it did provide some social, financial and political benefit and it established the issue of race in the national consciousness.

Neither space nor my scholarship allows for an adequate assessment here of the brilliance of Ellison's work. Bradley, however, gets it done in the "T Book Club". Let one example suffice regarding *Invisible*: "The novel is set in the past but has resonance in our time. There is surreal, symbolic and insistent realism in Ellison's approach to systematic racism and white supremacy then and for our moment."

Totaling Up

With all these warnings and analyses, where do we find ourselves? **Adam Serwer** in his new book *The Cruelty Is the Point: The Past, Present, and Future of Trump's America* provides a compass. "The conditions of America today do not resemble those of 1968; 1868 offers a better example. The story of that awakening offers a guide and a warning. In the 1860s, the rise of a racist demagogue to the presidency, the valor of Black soldiers and workers and the stories of outrage against the emancipated in the South stunned white Northerners into writing the equality of man into the Constitution. The triumphs and failings of this anti-racist coalition led America to the present moment. It is now up to their successors to fulfill the promises of democracy, to make a more perfect union, to complete the work of reconstruction."

Serwer continues: "There has never been an anti-racist majority in American history; there may be one today in the racially and socioeconomically diverse coalition of voters radicalized by the abrupt transition from the HOPE of the Obama era to the CRUELTY of the Trump age. All political coalitions are eventually torn apart by their contradictions, but America has never seen a coalition quite like this."

"If a new president and a new Congress do not act before the American people's demand for justice gives way to complacency, or is eclipsed by backlash, the next opportunity will be long in coming. It would be unexpected if a demagogue wielding the power of the presidency in the name of white man's government inspired Americans to recommit to defending the inalienable rights of their countrymen. But it would not be the first time."

As for this writer, I agree with my main man Ta-Nehisi Coates that Serwer is essential reading, but what do we do with this information at this time?

Action Items

1. Petition colleges and universities to set up Webinars to consider points raised herein. Follow the model used in the "T Book Club" video series of bringing scholarly and practical approaches to the table.
2. Expand on the AKA Medical Trailer Model. The sorority did the unthinkable recently by fielding a walk-in trailer for purposes of mammograms, blood pressure tests, Covid19 shots and blood donations
3. Fund N'DIGO to create an information hot line to educate the Black community on how to restore K-12 education/learning lost due to Covid remote and hybrid classes
4. Create alternative educational sites to discuss white supremacy coupled with Black political action to compensate for the lack of same in classrooms and workspaces.

5. Tune in WVON (AM 1690) at 10 a.m. on Thursday July 15 for a first-ever discussion of Black Community Impacts of white print media bias.

Regarding No. 5 above, it would be easy to despair with all the attacks on the Black community. Yet the resilience of our leaders is all the more encouraging. While contemplating this effort, Business Leadership Council member Hermene Hartman forwarded a recent op-ed from the July 10 *New York Times* about the white media and the Black community. Now BLC member Melody Spann-Cooper of WVON has committed to assembling mainstream media representatives to take them to task. This all happened without planning meetings and conference calls. It stems from an undying love for Black People.

References:

1. "On Juneteenth" by Annette Gordon Reed
2. "Begin Again" by Eddie S. Glaude Jr.
3. "Invisible Man" by Ralph Ellison
4. The New York Times Style Magazine "T Book Club": "A Conversation on 'Invisible Man'"
5. "The Cruelty" is The Point by Adam Serwer

GASLIGHT FIGHT – "DON'T BE BAMBOOZLED BY GOP VOTING REFORMS"

A knock-down, drag-out battle over voting rights – and the future of our Democracy – is being waged this year between Republicans who still control many state legislatures and Democrats who control Congress … but by the slimmest of margins.

Say you didn't know? That's no surprise. We're all being *"gaslighted"* by a well-oiled GOP smoke machine into thinking that our Republican friends simply seek to tidy up ballot box security following a one-time easing of rules to accommodate voting during the *COVID-19* pandemic.

That's a lie – a whopper almost as big as the Big Lie that you-know-who would have been reelected last November but for massive vote fraud in key states. Like the easily fooled wife of a murderous husband in the old *Gaslight* play and movie, we're being asked to see one thing but believe another.

The best analysis of what's actually going on is laid out in a report titled "A Democracy Crisis in the Making" recently issued by *Law Forward*, a non-profit watchdog reachable at https://lawforward.org/.

Here's their description of what's hidden within the "reforms" being promoted and passed by various state legislatures:

"Among this group, one set of consequential proposals has flown under the radar. They involve efforts to alter basic principles about how elections should be administered and put highly partisan elected officeholders in charge of basic decisions about our elections."

"In 2021, state legislatures across the country — through at least 148 bills filed in 36 states — are moving to muscle their way into election administration, as they attempt to dislodge or unsettle the executive branch and/or local election officials, who traditionally, have run our voting systems. This attempted consolidation would give state legislatures the power to disrupt election administration and the reporting of results beyond any such power they had in 2020 or indeed throughout much of the last century."

"These are substantial changes that if enacted could make elections unworkable, render results far more difficult to finalize, and in the worst case scenario, allow state legislatures to substitute their preferred candidate for those chosen by the voters. American democracy relies on the losers of elections respecting the results and participating in a peaceful transition of power. If instead, the losing party tries to override the will of the voters, that would be the death knell for our system of government."

It's All About Black Votes…

Paul Krugman's recent op-ed in *The New York Times* seconds this analysis in a column headlined "The Banality of Democratic Collapse." "However, it plays out," Krugman concluded, "the GOP will try to ensure a permanent lock on power and do all it can to suppress dissent."

This GOP offensive is more than Looney Tunes out of the Trump music mayhem manual. How did we get here and how do Black people survive and prosper while white America goes through an identity crisis? Another question that baffles me is Where are the GOP's good guys? Is **Mitt Romney** alone?

Make no mistake. It was 2020's historic, kick-ass magic pulled off by Black voters in Georgia and other key "swing" states that is causing Republicans to change the rules, or at least try. What **Stacey Abrams** and her crew did in getting the first Black Senator elected' and in capturing both Georgia Senate seats is, well, unbelievable. Black turnout also pulled Michigan and Pennsylvania over the finish line for **Joe Biden**.

Do The Math...

Black Americans represented 50% of all Democratic voters in Georgia but are just 33% of that state's population. **Stacey Abrams**, who ran for Georgia Governor in 2018 and received more votes than any Democrat in Georgia history parlayed that energy to bring home the bacon for Biden. In Michigan, 20% of Democratic voters were Black though only 14% of the population. In Pennsylvania we were 21% of all Democratic voters though just 12% of that state's population, reports Rashawn Ray of the Brookings Institution. In response to these victories secured by unprecedented Black voter turnout, the backlash from Republican-led states has been equally unthinkable.

Under the pretense of voter fraud and election cheating, various lawmakers in 47 states have introduced over 360 bills with restrictive provisions. Arkansas, for example, advances two bills that tightened the state's voter ID requirement. The old voter ID law allowed voters who arrived at their polling place without valid identification to vote a provisional ballot if they signed a sworn statement attesting that they were registered to vote. The proposed bill eliminates this option and requires voters who show up without identification to return to the county clerks' office by the Monday following the election with qualifying identification to have their vote counted. Georgia, Iowa. Arizona, New Hampshire, Texas. Florida and Michigan are also pushing such restrictive rules. There are 28 such bills of this type in 18 states, according to the *Brennan Center for Justice. www.brennancenter.org*.

Federal Pushbacks…

On the bright side, Democrats in Congress have crafted **HR 1** (*For the People Act*) and **HR 4** (*The John Lewis Act*) to counter these state legislative assaults against Black voting. **HR 4** attempts to reverse the 2013 Supreme Court rulings that limited the 1965 Voting Rights Act. **HR 4** reestablishes pre-clearance by the Federal government for states showing discriminatory voting rules. HR 1 would roll back many laws suppressing Black votes. The 818-page bill would affect gerrymandering, campaign spending, and the release of ten years of tax returns for president and vice president candidates.

But **HR 1** is running into broad opposition. It is a well-intentioned effort but has little chance of passing as written, a case of trying to do too much in too little time. Its Gerrymandering section is opposed even by members of the **Congressional Black Caucus**. Because there is little chance the bill will pass in its current form, Democrats face a clear choice. They can wage what might be a symbolic fight for all the changes they would like. Or they can confront the acute crisis at hand by crafting a more focused bill, one that aims squarely at ensuring all eligible Americans can vote and that those votes will be counted.

The New York Times editorial board agrees, "If Democrats can find 50 votes for reform, they should not postpone necessary interventions in the illusory hope of a bipartisan breakthrough, nor allow Republicans to filibuster. American history is sometimes narrated as a gradual expansion of participatory democracy as workers and women, and Black people gained the right to vote. Unfortunately, the reality is less flattering. Participation has expanded, and it has contracted. Democracy has strengthened and waned. The gains in the second half of the 20thh century are now eroding. As a result, there is a narrow window of opportunity to intervene."

It's All About The Benjamins...

Why does all this voting suppression matter in our current space, here in Illinois, where Democratic majorities reign supreme? Let us count the ways. If you have a family in Chicago, the violence visited in our neighborhoods is combated by funds flowing from the state and Federal governments. If you're a parent with children in public schools, federal policies and funding affect their education. And so on with Black business, which is dependent on the responsiveness and funding from federal agencies ranging from the *Small Business Administration to the Department of Health and Human Services.* So your vote matters down here on the ground, and it's in our best interests to understand the issues and play solid DEFENSE against this onslaught leveled at the Black vote.

Like the Watergate tapes that caught Nixon, a leaked conference call has shed light on the GOP's overall strategy. **Jane Mayer** of *The New Yorker* magazine tells us "a private conference call on January 8th between a policy advisor to Senator Mitch McConnell and the leaders of several prominent conservative groups including one by the Koch Brothers network—reveals the participants 'worry that the proposed (Congressional) election reforms garner wide support not just from liberals but from conservative voters too."

Aha! The behemoth bucks of the Koch brothers appear to be aligned with others to fight against the *For the People Act.* It's not clear that they care one whit about Black people. They want to protect the anonymity of their financial contributions and continue having **Mitch McConnell** and even quasi-Democrat Joe Manchin follow their directions. Mayer further recalls that "**Nick Surgey**, executive director of *Documented*, a progressive watchdog group that investigates corporate money in politics, told me that it made sense that McConnell's staffer was on the call because the proposed legislation "poses a genuine threat to McConnell's source of power within the Republican Party, which has always been fundraising."

Watch This One…

The New Yorker piece by **Jane Mayer** warns what kinds of "*gaslighting*" loom ahead. "Kyle McKenzie of the Koch Brothers "conceded the legislation's opponents would likely have to rely on Republicans in the Senate, where the bill is now under debate, to use "under the dome type strategies," meaning legislative maneuvers beneath Congress's roof such as the filibuster to stop the bill because turning public opinion against it would be incredibly difficult."

That makes sense because average workaday Democrats and Republicans are both against billionaires buying elections. Thus, we have it. **The Koch Brothers** et al. are backing Republican opposition to **HR 1** and **HR 4** to protect their billions of "*benjamins*". The New Yorker does us a huge service to expose this portentous political partnership.

The laws that enable Black people to fight voter suppression, increase turnout, and repeat the stunning victories in Georgia, Michigan, and Pennsylvania are in jeopardy! The Koch brothers and other financial behemoths would sacrifice these rights to maintain their dark money status and sway Republican lawmakers. But their "under the dome" strategy will not work against the will of an informed and active Black population. Gaslighting may be a tried-and-true form of psychological manipulation, but if we spot the reason and reach of this anti-Black attack on our vote, we will not be bamboozled. We will vote.

Action Items...

1. Push for **Election Day Registration**. Twenty-one states and the District of Columbia have enacted some form of same-day registration.
2. Redistricting starts later this year. Get involved in understanding the maps at the local level.
3. Register others and volunteer to get out the vote.
4. Protect eligible voters from improper purges from the voter rolls.
5. Protect against deceptive election practices.
6. Research your local election dates and guidelines and distribute them manually and online.
7. Double check your voter registration status.
8. If you plan to vote by mail, request your ballot immediately.
9. Host a *Virtual Voting Party* to go over ballot measures.
10. Consider working the polls.
11. Make sure everyone in your household has a ride.
12. Stay in line and avoid insults and taunts.

The above rare recommendations from the *ACLU* and the *Brennan Center*. However, #9 has application and urgency in between elections. A virtual meeting to discuss where we are and how to support and defend the Black vote is necessary.

Boycott? The Koch Brothers own the makers and suppliers of products and services we buy every week. Investigate products manufactured or distributed by the **Koch Brothers** and consider boycotting them as long as they attack Black votes.

Congressman **Danny Davis** has agreed to host a virtual Town Hall meeting to discuss the status of **HR 1** and **HR 4** in both the House and Senate. He will also recommend actions to educate our community about who's behind opposition to these needed bills and what we can do to defend the gains we have made over the last 50 years. So, stay tuned for more information. Meantime, ignore the gaslight. Save the vote!

RAOUL'S RICHES: UNMASKING THE MYTH OF WHITE SUPREMACY

Black playwright August Wilson once observed that "Those who would deny Black Americans their culture would also deny them their history and the inherent values that are part of all human life."

"There are, and have always been, two distinct and parallel traditions in Black art," the late Wilson said in his seminal 1996 speech titled "The Ground on Which I Stand" . "That is, art that is conceived and designed to entertain white society, and art that feeds the spirit and celebrates the life of Black Americans by designing its strategies for survival and prosperity."

Now comes Raoul Peck to once more exceed these high expectations. Peck is the award-winning Black documentarian who explored James Baldwin's life in his 2016 film "I Am Not Your Negro."

This year he's out with a powerful documentary titled "Exterminate all the Brutes" – a gut- wrenching broadside against historic white hypocrisy now showing on HBO Max or at https://www.hbo.com/exterminate-all-the-brutes/episodes.

It's a film comprised of archival drawings, illustrations, historical documents selected and shown at a rapid clip with sound effects and spot-on musical accompaniments. One powerful device Peck uses is to have the characters

(Black, White, Indigenous) whether good, bad or ugly, looking straight out into the camera, wide eyed providing a seldom experienced eerie emotion.

Before jumping into the four-part docuseries, however, it's useful to review how Raoul Peck was drawn into the evolution of the lie that is white supremacy. His earlier bio-doc on James Baldwin was the springboard. Critic Robert Ito of the N.Y. Times marvels how Peck reminded us that "Baldwin called Whiteness a 'metaphor for power' and called out this country's legacy of racism in the bluntest of terms."

"Baldwin is one of the most precise scholars of American society" Peck agreed in an interview. "If you didn't understand the message, that means there is no hope for you." Peck does us a huge favor by illuminating Baldwin's association with Medgar Evers, Martin Luther King Jr. and Malcolm X. He examines the common thread among them and the short window of time in which they were all killed.

After producing the award-winner about Baldwin, Peck was exhausted. However he was bothered with the next logical question: How and why did these policies and practices originate? What started Eurocentrism and white supremacy and who were the enablers and spreaders of these notions?

We get Peck's answers in "Exterminate all the Brutes," a four-episode sweep across 600 years of Western Civilization.

"The story that he tells is a vast one," reviews Richard Brody in the April 9, 2021 issue of The New Yorker. For Blacks it is the prime story of the millennia, "that of white supremacy, or more specifically, whites' presumption of supremacy. A presumption that as he (Peck) makes clear, continues to this day, to be asserted with violence and justified with lies" (Think January 6 at the Capitol.) "What is more, working with historians, Peck puts the very writing of history at the core of the story.

He understands history as the victor's record of events and sees American national mythology as a fiction that depends on an assumed racism."

"This foundational myth of the "Discovery" of the West's indigenous people becomes a tale of Western superiority and of white European-justified domination up to and including the extermination of indigenous people and the cultivation of cleared land by way of enslaved Africans."

The New Yorker's Brody begs the obvious question — How one can have the audacity to state that they DISCOVERED a land which, upon their arrival, had over 100 million inhabitants.

Film-maker Peck, adds the Times' Ito, evokes some crucial historical connections that rarely appear in popular culture. For instance, in the myth of the 18th Century's overlapping ages of ostensible enlightenment and revolution, Peck emphasizes that the French and American Revolutions sought freedom for whites, all the while promoting the subjugation of Blacks, whether at home or in their colonies. This running deceit is artfully dramatized by Peck using authoritative voice-overs and heart-rending dramatic scenes, using real or fact-supported reenactments.

Peck connects a Transgression Trio of African slavery, Native American genocide and the Nazi Holocaust. He traces a connection between Nazism and the rhetoric, symbolism and violence of the current day's white supremacist. His stated goal is to create a matrix for future study and to inspire activism leading to change.

Peck's "Exterminate" even gives Donald Trump his due, showing how the former president is a here-and-now "ghost" of slavery. Though officially ended, the ghost lives on in the many complex forms of institutional racism. burdensome.

Imagining the Reverse

Peck agrees there is no such thing as alternative facts, writes Ito. But he recognizes the selective nature of all historical narratives and the power of controlling the remembered images. He probes deeper truths in some scenes by asking viewers to imagine what history might have been if things had gone in a different way.

Exterminate All the Brutes also delivers some media magic. In one scenario Columbus and his cohorts are killed on the beach by the indigenous people of Haiti. In another we're shown white children being captured and enslaved by Black slave masters. This role-reversal is a powerful gut-punch. It's one thing to see Blacks killing white people. But to see the systematic, intentional power of Blacks over white slaves, headed for what we know was the Black slave's future, this sets the mind racing. How would YOU like this, white America?

Side Lessons

Once you view the documentary, an excellent guide toward appreciating its making would be to watch the conference recently hosted by The Lincoln Center in New York. https://www.youtube.com/watch?v=w7OQ_Yn8ptI

Participants joined from Paris, Uganda, California and New York. Attending were Roxanne Dunbar Ortiz, Mahmoud Mamdani and, of course, Raoul Peck. Among topics considered are the film's potential impact … and the fate of white Eurocentrism. Some consensus likelihoods emerged:

A. There will be a huge shift in consciousness as a result of this film.
B. There is compelling honesty in the work coupled with the credibility of the storyteller, giving the opus greater impact.

C. Converting 600 years into 4 hours was a hellacious accomplishment, providing those of limited attention span a mammoth opportunity to learn.

D. HBO, aiming a series of this type can help future generations fight ignorance and false narratives, especially with people glued to their phones.

E. With the Trump fiasco still in fresh memory, with immigration surges and white Americans feeling their back up against a demographic wall, the timing of "Exterminate" could not have been better.

F. The world is changing and the U.S. is changing. It could easily be that the next generation, with its majority minority population, will evolve a new world historical narrative with elements of this film as one of its pillars.

Exterminate All the Brutes is a gift that keeps on giving. It's like Muddy Waters singing "Mannish Boy" or Luciano Pavarotti singing "Nessun dorma". It's so nice you'll want to watch it thrice!

Peck stated that his goal is to provide a framework for future study and to allay the ignorance and disinformation invading the Black community. Given the polarization and racial tension now abounding, understanding some of the original elements of our national discontent is crucial. Are not Republicans now asking President Biden to withdraw the Education Department's proposal that true Black History be taught in the schools? Are not 39 Republican lawmakers led by Senate Minority Leader Mitch McConnell demanding that Biden drop what they call a "politicized and divisive agenda" fixated on the country's "flaws?"

This challenge is also aimed at "The 1619 Project", a feature launched by The New York Times in which Nikole Hannah-Jones and others reframe the county's history on slavery and its effects, plus the unsung contributions of Blacks after slavery.

Wrapping Up

There comes along once or twice in a generation a seminal artistic gem that empowers, enables and informs African Americans. "I Am Not Your Negro" was one of these. Now Exterminate All the Brutes steps onto the pedestal. HBO has done something that was inconceivable two or three decades ago in making these films available and accessible. This is especially true during the pandemic afflicting the country, when we're all too tempted to stare at cable TV of dubious significance, Do yourself a favor and sample Raoul's Riches.

INFOCALYPSE NOW!

Every so often a new way of thinking joins forces with a new way of communicating so that things long assumed to be true can no longer be taken for granted.

Martin Luther would have been an obscure 16th Century heretic were it not for the newfangled printing press. More recently we can fairly ask if there would have been an Arab Spring without the ubiquitous cellphone…or a Donald Trump presidency without Twitter and Fox News?

That latter nightmare ought to remind us that these recurring intersections between new technologies and potent ideas can doom us to disaster as well as draw us to discovery.

Now comes author **Nina Schick** with a timely warning titled *Deep Fakes and the Infocalypse: What You Urgently Need to Know.*

Schick zeroes in on the phenomenon of calling the truth something different. She borrows the term *"Infocalypse"* – defined as the dangerous and untrustworthy information ecosystem within which most humans now live – from a 2016 coinage by media theorist Aviv Ovadya.

This is the brave new world of doctored "deep fake" videos, of calculated misinformation, and of a highly partisan news ecosystem that tramples old rules that used to separate fact-based journalism from opinion-laced rhetoric.

Georgia On Our Mind

Schick's *Infocalypse* is a particularly useful tool for African Americans trying to understand the huge amount of humbug swirling around today's racially charged events. I've been using it of late to cut through the smoke still clouding attempts at Black voter suppression in the State of Georgia.

You may remember that, following unsubstantiated claims that Trump, not Joe Biden, won Georgia and its pivotal electoral votes, the state legislature there passed Senate Bill 202. It recently was signed into law by Governor Brian Kemp.

The New Georgia Project, founded by Stacey Abrams, promptly called it the "Voter Suppression Bill." Her group filed suit in U.S. District Court, arguing that the new law violated both he First and Fourteenth Amendments to the U.S. Constitution.

The law enacts many new restrictions, such as eliminating Sunday voting, shortening the early voting period, limiting the number of ballot drop boxes, and prohibiting non-poll workers from giving food or water to voters waiting in line.

This Georgia drama continues to spawn subplots. Major League Baseball pulled its scheduled All-Star Game from Atlanta and is sending it to Denver. Delta Airlines, Coca-Cola, Home Depot, UPS, and other large Georgia companies have issued tepid statements against the law with language like they "support the right to vote for all."

It's a tightrope walk for these companies, because Black groups are threatening more, such as eliminating corporate contributions to

Republicans who support suppressing the Black vote. Several Black leaders have gone so far as to advise these corporations to pull out of Georgia altogether if the law is not repealed.

Meanwhile, a backlash came from Republican lawmakers shouting that they will eliminate all tax breaks and subsidies now going to companies who publicly oppose the law. Black groups countered by threatening to boycott sponsors of the recent Masters Golf Tournament played in Augusta, Georgia.

Ironically, this year's Master's made Lee Elder an Honorary Starter. He was the first Black golfer to play in golf's most fabled U.S. tourney. Was the honoring of Lee Elder an attempt at balancing the scales?

So, whose "truth" is really the truth? Georgia's governor stated there was nothing discriminatory about the new law. "It expands access" to the polls, he claimed, and follows similar "reforms" underway in Texas, Arizona, and other states.

Yet to most eyes, the Georgia law is the exact opposite of expanding access. Question: How did we come to call what we plainly see, by the name of something else?

Big, Noisy Lies

Nina Schick tackles this question straight-on. Though it was published weeks before the Georgia law blew up front pages and newscasts everywhere, the book points to the rise of Trump as Exhibit A of the all-enveloping Infocalypse.

"Nowhere is this more apparent than the elevation of a man who is perhaps the embodiment of the Infocalypse – Donald J. Trump – to the White House," she writes.

Schick pointedly adds that "populist leaders are normalizing and perpetuating our increasingly crowded information ecosystem", raising the question of "whether this will lead to a tipping point when Western political systems and society can no longer cope. Will robust political debate and societal progress be possible if our shared sense of reality collapses into a ceaseless domestic information war?"

Trump, Schick argues, is not just a symptom of this new, dangerous era, but is "making the crises of trust worse. Dominating the information ecosystem using his outsized influence to spread copious amounts of false information, including deep fakes and cheap fakes. He is actively feeding the partisan polarization that reduces everyone's willingness to find common ground. It's no accident that the United States has been gripped by societal unrest."

Doubtless Schick would have applied these same measures to the January 6 Capitol riot more-or- less instigated by Trump, or the litany of official excuses surrounding the ongoing epidemic of Black lives lost at the hands of white police.

According to a *Washington Post* database, Trump made over 18,000 false and misleading claims during the three years leading up to the 2020 presidential campaign.

Schick says the truth, however, is often drowned out by "a tactic academics call censorship though noise. It is a classic tool of disinformation. By flooding the zone with so much information that no one can keep up, confusion and distraction ensue."

Divide And Conquer

Trump has also brought America closer to the tipping point by using information warfare to entrench partisan polarization in American society.

Yet while reinforcing the partisan divide suits Trump's political objectives, it makes the United States weaker.

If Americans are too busy fighting one another, they cannot respond to existential threats that require bi-partisan solutions…like the Infocalypse.

Distrust and polarization normalized in our information systems mean it doesn't take much for violence to spill over into real life. In the Infocalypse, Schick argues, violence can spread faster and become more and more difficult to control.

Breanna Taylor, George Floyd, Atatiana Jefferson, Daniel Prude and Daunte Wright Consider that violence visited on Black people by white police. On May 25, 2020, George Floyd was murdered by a Minneapolis policeman. In April of 2021, a white policewoman kills a Black man just a few miles away, claiming she mistook her gun while reaching for a non-lethal taser.

And the list grows: **Daniel Prude** in Rochester, New York; **Breanna Taylor** of Louisville Kentucky; **Atatiana Jefferson** in Fort Worth, Texas; **Daunte Wright** of Brooklyn Center, Minnesota; **Marvin Scott** of McKinney, Texas; **Jenoah Donald** in Hazel Dell, Washington; **Xzavier Hill** of Goochland County, Virginal; and so on.

The Infocalypse will continue to evolve despite the 2020 election results, Schick posits, and that is the real challenge.

"I have told the story of the Infocalypse through one of the most dangerous actors, Trump," she writes. "But ultimately the Infocalypse is bigger than Trump. If Trump left office tomorrow, the Infocalypse would not leave with him.

"Unfortunately, the current state of American politics makes it difficult to see how the bi- partisan effort that is needed to ward off the worst effects of the Infocalypse can be mustered. And that is the real tragedy. If a whole society mobilization against the corrupt and dangerous information ecosystem fails, we all lose."

In the meantime, Black people continue to be under attack. Republican state legislators in several "red" states are sponsoring a blizzard of voting restrictions against Blacks, according to the Brennan Center for Justice.

Like my University of Chicago basketball coach, the late Joe Stampf, once told me: If someone hears the same lie often enough, he or she would soon believe it. "All humans," Schick explains, "are vulnerable to what psychologists refer to as the 'illusory truth'…the longer someone is exposed to something, the more likely he or she will believe it, even if it is fake.

"We are facing a future in which all information is untrustworthy because the environment in which it exists has become so corrupted. To avoid a permanent "fxxked up dystopia", Schick urges that "we need to understand, defend and fight back."

Summing It Up

Our information ecosystem has become untrustworthy and dangerous. Our society is becoming more familiar with disinformation, misinformation, imagined conspiracies, and "fake news."

What to do? Schick recommends several antidotes, ranging from fact-checking to self-imposed information Rules-of-Expression.

Other useful truth-finding tips are coming from Stacey Abrams, The New Georgia Project, the ACLU, Brennan Center for Justice, and the Southern Poverty Law Center.

Misinformation and polarization, a dual threat accelerated by Trump and now perpetuated by his "base" Republicans, make it more difficult to gain a democratic consensus.

Example: a federal "For the People Act", which tries to counter Georgia-type voter restrictions, has passed the House...but is stalled within a narrowly divided Senate.

Action Items...

1. Form a study group to discuss the "For the People Act;"
2. Petition high schools and colleges to initiate curricula around polarization in the U.S.
3. Support the Brennan Center, ACLU, and the Southern Poverty Law Center.
4. Read Nina Schick's *Deep Fakes and the Infocalypse: What You Urgently Need To Know.*
5. Google *Say Their Names*, a work in progress which gives the names, dates and age of Blacks killed by law enforcement.

And one last thing, about the coronavirus pandemic. It is overwhelming Black life in the United States. We all know that had it not been termed a "hoax" by you-know-who, more Black people would be alive today.

Blacks are three times more likely to get infected than whites and twice as likely to die from the virus. Trusted information is an absolute necessity. We are now moving into a "fxxked-up dystopia." Nina Schick gives us fair warning. Take it!

REPARATIONS REVISITED

Reparations, that upsetting-to-many relative of affirmative action, has burst onto America's front pages again, this time with a dateline right here in the Chicago area.

The City of Evanston on March 22 authorized the payment of some $400,000 in grants of up to $25,000 each to Black homebuyers and rehabbing homeowners. It is the historic first installment of a larger $10 million Local Reparations Fund set up in 2019 to redress the north shore suburb's history of racial steering and redlining seemingly aimed at segregating Blacks into a confined section of town.

But right away several Black leaders cautioned everyone to hold their applause. They pointed out that eligibility is restricted to those with an ancestor who lived in the suburb between 1919 and 1969, that the grants may be used only for tightly defined housing transactions, and even that applicants first pass credit checks. Funding for this program is to come from annual cannabis taxes.

"What we have here," said Ald. Cicely Fleming, the only City Council member to vote against the disbursement, "is a housing program with the title reparations." Others caution that the disbursements for housing repair and mortgage assistance primarily benefit banks and financial institutions, who they consider entities directly responsible for redlining and other discriminatory practices the program seeks to address, according to The Washington Post.

Be that as it may, this first disbursement of real money under the name "Reparations" calls for an in-depth discussion of what these programs ought to entail, why they are necessary and, most importantly, how they can be applied coast-to-coast – not just in municipalities with a guilty conscience about past discrimination.

A Nation's Original Sin

No one is better at directing this discussion than Ta-Nehisi Coates. He's my go-to young writer/journalist/thinker and author of a must-read explanation *The Case for Reparations* in the June 14 issue of *The Atlantic* magazine. It's a case of paying Black people "something" in return for 250 years of slavery, 90 years of Jim Crow, and 60 years of separate-but-equal.

Historic precedents abound. Coates cites the 1783 case of the freewoman Belinda Royall, who was kidnapped as a child and sold into slavery. She spent 50 years as a slave before her master fled Massachusetts, allowing her to beseech the Massachusetts legislature for financial assistance.

Belinda was granted a pension of 15 pounds and 12 shillings, to be paid out of the estate of slaveowner Isaac Royall. It was one of the earliest successful attempts at petition for monetary redress. On a wider scale, Quakers in 18th Century New York and New England demanded that "membership be contingent upon compensating one's former slaves."

So, it was not out of nowhere that in 1987 an umbrella organization emerged called the National Coalition Of Blacks for Reparation in America (N'COBRA). Many questions need thoughtful answers…though likely won't get them without determined advocacy.

"Broach the topic of reparations today," Coates observes, "and a barrage of questions inevitably follow: Who will be paid? How much will they be paid? Who will pay?" "Perhaps after a serious discussion and debate," Coates writes, "we may find that the country can never fully repay African Americans. But we stand to discover much about ourselves in such a discussion — and that is perhaps what scares us. The idea of reparations is frightening not simply because we might lack the ability to pay. The idea of reparations threatens something much deeper — America's heritage, history, and standing in the world."

The early American economy was built on slave labor, Coates explains after laying out the data. "The Capitol and the White House were built by slaves. President James K. Polk traded slaves from the Oval Office. The laments about 'Black pathology,' the criticism of Black family structures by pundits and intellectuals, ring hollow in a country whose existence was predicated on the torture of Black fathers, on the rape of Black mothers, on the sale of Black children.

"Black nationalists have always perceived something unmentionable about America that integrationists dare not acknowledge," continues Coates. "That white supremacy is not merely the work of hot-headed demagogues or a matter of false consciousness, but a force so fundamental to America that it is difficult to imagine the country without it.

"Some ask, 'Won't reparations divide us?' Not any more than we are already divided. The wealth gap merely puts a number on something we feel, but cannot say – that American prosperity was ill gotten and selective it its distribution. What is needed is an airing of family secrets, a settling of old ghosts."

Then this zinger: White resistance to reparations is "fear masquerading as laughter," and a way of "ignoring not just sins of the past, but sins of the present and the sins of the future," Coates writes.

Acknowledgement The Key

The late Congressman John Conyers introduced H.R. 40 in 1989, but the bill was referred to committee and did not see the light of day. Conyers re-introduced the bill in every Congress until his death. Now Congresswoman Sheila Jackson Lee is taking the lead. She held recent hearings on H.R. 40 – hearings that explained in detail the four things the bill does:

1. It acknowledges the fundamental injustice of slavery.
2. It establishes a commission to study slavery and the subsequent racial and economic discrimination against freed slaves.
3. It studies the impact of those forces on today's living African Americans.
4. A commission would then make recommendations to redress the harm inflicted on living African Americans.

Reparations and H.R. 40 have been used by many interchangeably. That is unfortunate. H.R.40 funds a study and makes recommendations. Reparations would provide actual restitution for previous harm.

Matthew McCarthy, CEO of the Ben and Jerry's ice cream chain, is one of the few corporate types to acknowledge past injustice and support a Conyers-style reappraisal and redress. 'None of us living today owned slaves or created the legacy of over 400 years of racism," McCarthy has written. "However, we are the only ones who can do anything about it. Recent events have shown us what ignoring our past means to our present. H.R.40 is our best chance to come to terms with the full story of our country's founding."

And yet, no Republicans have signed on to H.R. 40 even though 160 Democrats have done so as of this writing.

Other institutions have begun the difficult work of acknowledgement and redress. For instance, Georgetown University announced they will try to make reparations to the descendants of slaves held by the university more than a century ago.

In 1838, some 272 of its domestic servants were sold into the Deep South plantation system so as to relieve a Georgetown budget crisis. Lately Georgetown has engaged in a long-term project to more deeply understand and respond to the university's role in in the injustice of slavery and the legacies of enslavement and segregation in our nation.

Meanwhile, Harvard University has launched a $5 million program to study and react to its early involvement in the slave trade. The University of Virginia has organized a consortium (Universities Studying Slavery) that brings together over 40 colleges across the country and the world to share resources about the role of slavery and racism in their histories and its impact today.

And now we have Evanston, Illinois, which may be the first to ante-up real money, for payment directly to Black families, rather than just commission commissions and talk-the-talk. Said Kam Howard of N'COBRA, "Most other commissions file resolutions and then allocate funds for them, but Evanston set aside the resources up front."

The Way Forward

So where are we? Reparations are due African Americas for slavery and the support the U.S.

government provided that practice. Answers are needed: Who pays? Who decides eligibility? Who settles the issue of which Blacks deserve funding? How will the funds be managed?

A good place to seek answers now comes from A. Kirsten Mullen and William A. Darity Jr in their book *From Here to Equality: Reparations for Black Americans in the Twenty-First Century.* The authors see today's racial wealth gap as the most robust indication of the cumulative economic effects of slavery and latter-day white supremacy.

A national trust fund should be established, they argue, to which eligible Blacks could apply for grants for various asset-building projects, including home ownership, additional education, start- up funds for self-employment, or even vouchers for purchase of financial assets.

An additional possibility is the use of the fund to assist in developing endowments for historical Black colleges and Universities. Regardless, all uses of funds must be directed at eliminating the racial wealth gap. They also argue that the invoice should go directly to the U.S. Congress, not piecemeal to state or municipal jurisdictions, or more crucially, to politically influenced local courts.

Passage of H.R. 40 would be an important first step. Immediately it would establish a congressional commission to investigate slavery and its multi-generational effects, plus the feasibility of reparations. It will have 18 months to issue a report.

Who Gets And How Much?

As for how much is owed Black Americans, the closest thing to a dollar estimate has been provided, ironically, by a long-ago Confederate functionary trying to explain slavery's economic value. He said, "Our slaves, directly and indirectly, involve a value of more than four thousand million dollars".

That four billion dollars compounds to $2 trillion, or $9.3 trillion, or a whopping $42 trillion by the year 2019, depending on whether you compound interest at 4, 5 or 6 percent.

With approximately 40 million Black Americans in the United States today, the per capita amounts would come, respectively, to about $50,000, $225,000 or $1,050,000.

One strategy recommended by Mullen and Darity to generate equitable distribution of Reparation funds would be to designate a portion of the funds for competitive applications, with priority given to applicants with lower wealth or income.

Applications might include proposals to launch a new business or pursue a new invention. A professional trustee team would judge which proposals merit funding. A National Reparations Board would be established as the civil agency responsible for day-to-day management and execution of the program.

None of this is unprecedented. The federal Office of Redress Administration carried out the mandate of the Civil Liberties Act of 1988 to provide reparations to Japanese-Americans who were incarcerated by the federal government during World War II.

Next Steps

President Joe Biden has voiced support for the study proposal in H.R. 40, but has stopped short of saying he would sign the House version in its current form. Vice President Kamala Harris supported H.R. 40 when she was in the Senate, but lately has not committed.

Based on the activity taking place in the colleges and universities and the momentum surrounding H.R. 40, the Reparations study and funding is real. Darity and Mullen argue for billions of dollars funding over decades. What follows is a call to Black educators, Black business, HBCUs, churches, non-profits, community organizations and those interested in social justice to get informed, get involved and stay WOKE!

Information sources:

1. N'COBRA- National Coalition of Blacks for Reparations in America National Coalition of Blacks for Reparations in America (NCOBRA) (ncobraonline.org)
2. William A. Darity- *From Here to Equality* https://www.kirkusreviews.com/book-reviews/william-darity-jr/from-here-to-equality/
3. Georgetown U. https://www.georgetown.edu/slavery/#:~:text=Georgetown%20Reflects%20on%20Slavery%2C%20Memory%2C%20and%20Reconciliation%20Georgetown,legacies%20of%20enslavement%20and%20segregation%20in%20our%20nation.
4. Universities Studying Slavery: Universities Studying Slavery (virginia.edu)
5. *Harvard and the Legacy of Slavery,* Tomiko Brown-Nagin, Radcliffe Dean: Initiative on Harvard and the Legacy of Slavery — Harvard & the Legacy of Slavery

Action Items

1. Join the zoom meeting with Professor Erik Gellman, U of North Carolina-Chapel Hill, to discuss Reparations and the book *From Here To Equality.* Register with *N'DIGO* for a mid- summer date.
2. Join Congressman Danny Davis in a Zoom meet to get an update on H.R. 40 and recommendations on participation. Date and time pending.
3. Petition Senator Dick Durbin to provide an update on the Senate version of H.R. 40 and what actions should be taken to register support.
4. Charles Smith, leader of the Business Leadership Council. Host an elected official and university officer zoom meeting to explain potential business opportunities resulting from H.R. 40 becoming law.

5. Petition Congressman Bobby Rush to form an advisory committee in the formation of the National Reparations Board called for by Darity and Mullen and seek to volunteer on same.

Borrowing from Mario Puzo's *The Godfather* – This is an offer you can't refuse!

RIOTS IN BLACK AND WHITE

On March 4 the Congress of the United States was forced to adjourn early after security officials received information about another planned attack on the nation's Capitol. This was to eliminate a possible repeat of the January 6 debacle, only this time it was a false alarm.

How has it come to this? How could the highest governmental forum of the world's most powerful nation be forced to cut short its deliberations – again — under threat of assault by a rag-tag domestic mob?

Now comes **Kathleen Belew**, a University of Chicago historian, with a plausible explanation in her book *Bring The War Home, the White Power Movement, and Paramilitary America*. She traces today's *White Power* movements back to the war in Vietnam, to its unmasking of government incompetence and its seeming legitimation of violence as a political strategy. Her Exhibit A is the fanaticism behind the 1995 bombing of the federal office building in Oklahoma City.

"The Oklahoma City bombing," Bellew writes, "stands as the fulfillment of the revolutionary violence waged by the white power activists. Gulf war veteran **Timothy McVeigh** carried out the bombing in connection with other activists, read and distributed the novel that had structured the violence of the ORDER, chose a building that white power had targeted since 1983, the year they declared war on the state, talked about stealing weapons from the military post; and saw civilians as "collateral damage" in a war upon the federal government. Bellew continues "His action was the work of a post-Vietnam War Paramilitary white power movement that was structuring militia violence and supposedly "lone acts of terrorism" in 1995."

But despite the horror of Oklahoma City, where 168 died, the hard fact that militant White Power was only just beginning to flex its ugly muscles was strangely placed on the shelf.

Racism's Disappearing Act

Left unfinished, unexplained and unconfronted, it was inevitable that the movement would only grow in the years following 1995. White Power was readily legible as a coherent social movement, yet for years it was largely narrated and prosecuted as a series of scattered actions by inexplicable "lone wolves" motivated not by ideology but by madness or personal animus. Recent events, however, show it should have been recognized as producing, supporting and deploying a coherent world view. And that view poses a radical challenge to our treasured liberal consensus around racial and gender equality, around support for crucial democratic institutions including the vote, the courts and the rule of law.

Instead, there was a seeming disappearance of the movement in the years after Oklahoma City. This vanishing act was, in effect, engineered by the white power activists themselves, but permitted and furthered by government actors, prosecutorial strategies, scholars and even journalists. Their unwillingness to confront the ugly new reality left open the possibility of new waves of action. Even as prolonged wars in Iraq and Afghanistan shaped a new generation of camo-garbed white power activism, this new activity would largely evade public understanding despite the warnings of watchdog groups. That is, until it broke into mainstream politics in the 2016 presidential campaign and election.

Outright racism and a need to re-establish white supremacy were major motives behind the January 6 Capitol chaos instigated by the pro-Trump mob. **Thomas Edsall** of *The New York Times* fairly asks "How toxic is the combination of pessimism and anger that stems from a deterioration in standing and authority"? How hard is it for any group, whether it is racial, political, or ethnic, to come to terms with losing power and status? What encourages desperate behavior and a willingness to believe a pack of lies?"

Also, in the Times, **Bart Bonikowski**, a professor of sociology at NYU, argues that "What makes their actions all the more dangerous is a self-righteous belief, reinforced by the President, that they are on the correct side of history as the true defenders of democracy, even as their actions undermine its core institutions and threaten its stability". And Andrew Cherlin of Johns Hopkins U. observed that white supremacy and rank racism are prime motivators, and they combined with other elements to fuel the insurrection: a groundswell of anger directed specifically at elites and an addictive lust for revenge against those they see as agents of their disempowerment.

The Pathology of Racism

These socio-political analyses work. However, racism is the key constant here in understanding why and how this kind of violence is possible. Another explanation would be the pathology though which racism creates these conditions. An individual experiences their standing in society as relative and comparative. So sometime the gains of other groups feel like losses to whites. Whites in the last 60 years have seen minorities gain more political power and economic and educational opportunity. Even though these gains are grossly exaggerated, whites perceive a loss in status.

The United States had a Civil War over slavery in the 19th century and subsequently a continuous history of structural racism and white oligarchical rule until the 1960s … and in many aspects until the present. Trump supporters who rioted in DC share the belief that Trump is a hero.

Trump did not find the mob, the rioters found him. The white mob consisted of veterans, law enforcement officers, teachers, realtors, elected officials and at least one that knocks your socks off. **Fred Klein** was a State Department Trump appointee with top secret clearance. He was among those charged by the FBI for his role in the January 6 sedition. While diverse, most had anti-Black goals that glued them together.

Obscured in that day's mayhem was the trauma endured by two groups of Blacks in the middle of the riots – the African American congressional staff and the Capitol Police on duty January 6. Luke Broadwater of *The New York Times* reported under the headline "Black officers fought a different battle. The racist slurs hurled at Black officers were especially painful."

Blow-by-Blow

Capitol Police Officer **Harry Dunn** reported the following: "The bigotry and trauma experienced that day were enough to intimidate anyone." Now that he is talking about his experience, he says other Black officers have told him that they too, experienced racist slurs from the rioters. "I didn't really get a sense things were turning bad until they found the pipe bomb at the RNC in the afternoon," remembers Dunn. "The crowd started growing. These were terrorists. They had weapons and they were attacking us. They had flags that said "COME AND TAKE IT" with a picture of a gun. You know these guys are fricking armed. And I'm thinking 'I got my gun pointed at these guys and I can't concentrate on one person. But 100 people could concentrate on me. How long is it before I get shot?'"

"The MPD Metropolitan Police were holding the line so valiantly. They fought their asses off. The rioters didn't just come through the doors, they came through the windows. We were outmatched. There were downed officers behind me and I'm like " I have to hold this hallway. Y all not coming through here' They said" we're coming" ." This is our house, We're taking over" That's when I said" We've got dozens of down officers here. Why are y'all doing this. Get out. It was a group of OATH Keepers and they appeared to be concerned. "Officers are hurt?" That's when one guy said "We're doing this for you" and showed me his badge. He was an officer! But they didn't get through me . Only one person attempted to get through me and he met the floor. They 're saying Trump is our is our rightful president. Nobody voted for Joe Biden. So I said" I voted for Joe Biden. What? My vote doesn't matter? A woman responded "this n word voted for Joe Biden. Everybody that was there started joining in "this n word ' It was over 20 people. We were all in this war but we all had different battles than everybody else fought . I said to my buddy ' I got called n word a couple dozen times today. I'm looking at him . He's got blood on him. I've got bloody knuckles . that's when I said ' Is this America?"

Black congressional staff were deeply troubled by a replica noose and gallows ominously erected outside the Capitol and a man carrying a Confederate battle flag. The mob that attacked the building included undeniable symbols of white supremacy and violence against Black people. Black staffers, many of whom marched to promote Black lives against police brutality, watched as a diminished Capitol police force was overtaken by a white horde, in some cases opening doors and taking selfies with insurrectionists inside the building.

On a call with *Congressional Black Associates* (CBA) and the *Senate Black Legislative Staff Caucus*, frustration was shared. **Jim Saksa, Jessica Wehrman** and **Lindsey McPherson** for *Roll Call* report that Some talked about having descended form slaves who built the Capitol in which they now work and a feeling of being betrayed by the institution that now put them at risk. Aides with the CBA and SBLSC want accountability and they also want to build a stronger relationship between Capitol Police and

Black staffers. These staffers are hoping to better understand what Black officers are facing in the aftermath of the insurrection.

Herline Mathieu, president of CBA, stated "Unfortunately, as Black staffers, our grievances existed long before the attack on the Capitol. For us the haphazard response of law enforcement was a slap in the face, which also causes concern for our safety in our work environment moving forward."

On Black "Riots"

In July 2015 **Dylan Roof**, a white teen, killed nine African Americans in Bible a study group at *Emanuel African Methodist Church* in Charleston, South Carolina. Roof, like his January 6 Capitol Cousins wanted to start a race war. **Issac J. Bailey** chronicles this story in *Why Didn't We Riot: A Black Man in Trump Land*. Bailey, an award-winning journalist, author and scholar, reminds that in writing about Roof, his editors allowed him to be as harsh as he chose. At the same time, they cut any negative references to white police killing Blacks. Bailey continues "Make no mistake, this level of thinking isn't the sole dominion of Trump supporters and white conservatism. White liberals here often demand it too, including a friend who told me I was turning an ally into an enemy for speaking forcefully about yet another white police officer shooting yet another Black man. He votes for Democrats. He preaches racial equality. He was more angered by my refusal to accept the death of an unarmed Black man at the hands of the police than by the killing itself."

Sound familiar? It can be exhausting being Black in this rhetorical place, which is why sometimes we've whispered when we should have roared. We have acquiesced when we should have said "Hell No!" that's why maybe Black People should have rioted after what Roof did and what the cops did, because it seems to be the only way to get white people to pay attention. We should have made it clear just how angry we are, and how angry we have long been. We should have cared less about white comfort, more about equality. But fighting racism nonstop in a place that uses our tax dollars to honor the men who raped our ancestors can feel futile. Having to fight for racial equality against our white neighbors who want to look the other way frustrates like little else. Listening to supposed allies explain it away leaves you tired. Bailey continues:

"The word "riot" conjures up images of "mobs" or" gangs" of Black people stalking the streets with baseball bats, staring down police in military gear and throwing Molotov cocktails. I'm not talking about that. I'm talking about a COMMUNAL SCREAM. I'm talking about a public declaration of Black Anger, the kind that scares those in power, scares white people, scares not a few well off, comfortable Blacks. I'm talking about asserting our right, our moral duty, to not sit quietly, to no longer substitute calm for justice. We should not have allowed the police to go back to policing as usual without a reckoning. We should have demanded an independent oversight of such incidents that isn't led by law enforcement officials. We should have said we would not relent until these officers were stripped of their badges and batons. White people have been rioting against Black people since before the founding of he country, calling it "proper 'and "natural ' and "God ordained" even as they insisted Black people should not riot too. Throughout our history when white people rioted, they killed scores of Black people, burned Black Businesses, overturned elections in which Black people had emerged has victors and purposefully targeted Black people who found a way to become wealthy and educated despite the long tentacles of Jim Crow."

Bailey seems to call for righteous, nonviolent riots that are persistent, strategic and self- sustaining.

Action Items:

As is my practice, the following are recommended. There is a clear and present danger that white power could erupt at any time, targeting Black institutions, people or assemblies. The following organizations provide survival literature, defensive devices and training models to resist.

1. *Lawyers Committee for Civil Rights Under Law; Brennan Center For Justice; American Civil Liberties Union; Southern Poverty Law Center.* A visit to their respective websites may be as vital to your health as wearing a mask.
2. Secure the book –*Why Didn't We Riot? A Black Man in Trump Land* by **Issac J. Bailey**. It's 175 pages of mandatory reading for all.
3. Establish a *Zoom* conference session with others to consider the Bailey analysis and recommendations.
4. Secure the recording of the *Harper Lecture* of **Kathleen Belew**, in which she discusses her book. Available in April. More info: 773-702-8360
5. Establish an intergenerational *Zoom* conference with high school, college scholars, fraternity and sorority activists and with elders which can share lessons learned, strategies and tactics toward Black Protection in today's environment.

Final Warning

The breach of the Capitol was fomented by a leaderless resistance that included veterans, law enforcement officials and other white supremacists. They can strike again without warning. Black people can be targets. This essay is aimed at Individuals, community leaders, journalists, business organizations and educational institutions. Review the books and materials contained herein to protect gains made (Georgia's recent Senate elections despite attacks on Black voting) and the prevention of surprise attacks (*Emanuel AME Church* in Charleston.) There is much to do toward Black survival and progress against the white power threat. Government alone can't do it all, as January 6 made clear.

AGE OF WISDOM, AGE OF FOOLISHNESS

With apologies to Charles Dickens, his best-of-times/worst-of-times comparison of London and Paris during the chaotic early 1800s does not hold a candle to what Black America is going through right now.

Just when we find ourselves in the driver's seat — or at least upfront with one hand on the wheel – our precious cargo – the children who will determine the future of our people – are being turned away and cut loose to fall by the wayside.

Just when President Joe Biden, his bid for the White House rescued by the Miracle of South Carolina, begins appointing Black and pro-Black cabinet offices. Just when he begins signing executive orders that reverse the race-baiting orders signed by his unlamented predecessor. Just when things start looking up, we learn that millions of Black schoolchildren are free-falling down an educational pit from which they may never fully recover.

That pit is called "remote learning" . . . and it is not working. Now that the early, panicky weeks of the COVID-19 pandemic have turned into tedious months of closed schools and at-home computer screen frustration, the data could not be more clear ... or more frightening.

Black students and educators are between a rock and a hard place, especially in large urban school systems that serve tens of thousands of low-income families and have remained entirely remote since March. Public schools in Washington. D.C., with a 59% Black enrollment, is testing four months behind in math and one month behind in reading. Virtually no second grader started this school year reading at grade level.

Falling Further Behind

Abby Goodnough in The New York Times reports one difficulty is that, while kids generally listen to their grandparents, older caregivers are often overwhelmed and uncomfortable with technology and can provide limited oversight and support. Then there's the lack of wire or Wi-Fi connectivity in so many apartments, especially public housing with its ubiquitous cinderblock walls.

Laura Meckler and Hannah Natanson of The Washington Post report on a McKinsey & Co estimate that the shift to remote is setting white students back by one to three months and Black students back three to five months. John King Jr., president of the Education Trust, worries that "We should be very concerned about the risk of a lost generation of students." Lost? How else to describe the thousands of kids who, for one reason or another, are AWOL day-after-day from their "remote" classes. Research finds children in high poverty districts missed an average of about 12 days of remote classroom time this past spring compared to eight days at low poverty schools.

As for the very young, Chicago Public Schools reported enrollment among Black pre- kindergarteners had dropped by 44% and nearly 30% for Hispanics, both far larger percentages than for whites and Asians. As for teenagers, we know that applications for federal student aid were down 16% this fall as were submissions to the Common Application, a portal used by hundreds of college aspirants. The Healio.com website reports that the number of Blacks in medical school, previously an upward trend has been reduced due to the Coronavirus.

Getting Personal

My take on this unfolding disaster is not without self-interest. As a Black businessman, as a lifelong advocate of Affirmative Action, as an advisory board member of Chicago's Urban Prep network of charter schools for young Black men, I am deeply concerned about COVID-19's impact on the employability and career chances of Black students. How will this setback impact the potential of African Americans to begin careers as engineers, architects, estimators, and skilled tradesmen? Will opportunities we fought so hard to win in my industry be wiped out in a toxic cloud of educational failure due to — what? — anti-viral precautions?

What is to be done?

Here's where we need to play our Best of Times card and remind the new powers-that-be in Washington how they got there. Besides the Miracle of South Carolina, in which a flailing Biden candidacy in the primary was resuscitated by Rep. James Clyburn and his Afro-Democratic legions, there were the follow-up twin victories in the Georgia U.S. Senate runoffs. Those victories give the Biden presidency a narrow Senate majority and, presumably, a flock of key TRIUMPHS!

For one thing, how about organizing a nationwide effort to provide high-intensity tutoring and summer school programs for students most impacted by the "remote learning" fiasco? Right away such an undertaking will be met with a chorus of "Who's going to pay for that?" After all, it would cost tens of billions of dollars to reach all students who will need remediation at a time when school districts are already struggling for basic needs. The McKinsey study estimates it would cost $42 billion @ $1,600 per student for vacation academies over summer break to serve small groups.

But let's not wait for summer schools. Right away we need the Biden Administration and Congressional Democrats to do something about "remote learning" so there will be more than a remote chance that key academic subjects are learned. For starters, the emerging economic stimulus program needs to include state-and-local education funding comparable to the "Warp Speed" program that boosted research and development of anti-virus vaccines.

At the local level, some of these federal resources should be used to have teachers spend one day each week contacting students they are most worried about and working with community organizations to provide tutoring and other supports. Last summer a Milwaukee elementary school held an online tutoring program pairing teachers and college students, many of them Black, with 30 mostly Black children for up to 4 hours of one-on-one video instruction each day. They made 2½ months progress in one month. Additionally, school staff needs to visit homes, deliver supplies, troubleshoot software glitches, and generally touch base.

Besides outside help, Black families need to take virtual school seriously. The elephant in the room, according to education experts like Jack Schneider at U. Mass, is that "Children in a stable home situation, where parents have sufficient resources, will stay engaged in an online environment, whereas children whose temperament, socioeconomic status or home situation is not compatible with the academic environment will fall further behind. The damage done to school children with scarce resources is likely to be irreparable. The best thing to do is to offer everyone a 'do-over.'

Twindemic

Joining COVID-19 is Black youth violence. You cannot rail against remote learning and ignore it. Whereas many have blamed the spike in crime on the virus, emboldened criminals, gun proliferation and a change in policing appear to be a primary cause that Black murder has increased by 95% in Milwaukee. 55 children were killed in Chicago in 2020. 18 were murdered in Chicago on May 31. Police interaction has changed. Heather Mac Donald (Wall Street Journal) reports a Chicago Detective "Every day you have to decide to get out of your patrol car and do something or do nothing. Carjacking is already up 135% in Chicago in 2020 and spilling into the suburbs. In Chicago proper, there have there been 144 carjackings through January 31, with 144 guns recovered. The murder of George Floyd and calls for "defunding the police have led to a 'cop conundrum."

Black citizens need the assurance of police protection, while police are taking a hands-off approach. One sad example – CPD arrested a Black 14-year-old. responsible for much of the carjacking in the 8th ward. The teen was on electronic monitoring at the time of his arrest! One may ask why to bring up this in a "best of times/ worst of times" essay. You cannot talk of addressing Black educational needs, without recognizing the treacherous environment Black youngsters must navigate.

The Way Forward

So we find ourselves at a crossroads. Black Business would like to employ, train and mentor young professionals in construction, finance, insurance, and related areas. Yet we see the supply of prepared candidates is being threatened. Yet these are also the "best of times," as Dickens might describe if only we approach the problem with wisdom and end quickly the foolishness of the past 4 years.

The table is set. Recently President Biden chose as his Secretary of Labor Boston Mayor Martin "Marty" Walsh, a former leader of the Boston Building and Construction Trades Council, an umbrella group for unions. At last here's a key presidential advisor with intimate knowledge of the issues we've been working on for decades. When we started with our Coalition for United Community Action back in the 1960s, Black contractors and tradesmen had to force a shutdown of publicly-funded construction sites across Chicago just to get the attention of local leaders. Now we have a voice in the Oval Office.

Now's the time to press our Senators and Black Congressmen, as well as our personal relationships within the Biden administration, to advance our positions. The U.S. Small Business Administration has still-relevant yet underutilized programs which I advanced, with others, back in the day. Locally I am calling on Charles Smith, Chairman of Chicago's Business Leadership Council; Chairman Emeritus Jim Reynolds; Tim King, CEO of Urban Prep; and Gary Slutkin, of Cure Violence, to develop proposals to help students up and out of the remote learning pit.

The need is now. The time is right. Black businesses are facing a brain drain, unable to engage educable candidates to take the good-paying but highly technical positions we have. We need resources directed to Black education over the next 12 months, not the next federal budget cycle. Educators and business leaders with personal connections should seize on the new Administration's encouraging openers and urge them to act, and act quickly, on our proposals.

To that end let Charles Dickens' opener from A Tale of Two Cities be our closer: "It was the best of times, it was the worst of times, it was the age of wisdom, it was the age of foolishness, it was the epoch of belief, it was the epoch of incredulity, it was the season of light, it was the season of darkness, it was the spring of hope, it was the winter of despair."

GLEE, GRIPE AND GRIEF

The rule of law. It's both sword and shield for Americans, especially African-Americans who would otherwise stand naked before powerful but malevolent forces out to do us harm.

Then again, it also helps to have some change in your pocket. For example: Alpha Phi Alpha, the first Black fraternity, was founded on December 4, 1906. In recent weeks Congressman Danny Davis and I raised funds for the Georgia U.S. Senate race of Alpha brother Raphael Warnock. We requested and received donations in denominations of 1906. In poured donations of $1,906, $190.6 and $19.06. It is a delight to be a part of the victory of the first Black senator from a deep red southern state. No praise is sufficient for the outsized role that Stacey Abrams played in getting out the vote. Her genius and commitment are unbelievable.

Where was the rule of law, though, the next day? Where was security when a rabid mob of white thugs took over our nation's Capitol? Might there have been collusion between rioters and those in charge of protecting our most hallowed halls? How would the police have acted if protesters were Black.? And what was Devious Don's role in inciting this insurrection? Would not a real president stop promoting falsehoods and deal instead with the deadly global epidemic that has killed more than 19,000 folks right here in Illinois?

Amid this cacophony, however, are two important issues we can't afford to ignore, both involving law and money.

Intent on Harm

Following the police murder of George Floyd in Minneapolis, the state of Oregon designated $62 million of its $1.4 billion Federal COVID-19 relief money to provide grants to Black residents, business owners, and community organizations. As reported by John Eligon of The New York Times, one Mexican-American and two white business owners are suing the state arguing that this set-aside for Black residents discriminated against them. After some $50 million worth of grants were awarded a court has frozen $8.8 million pending the court outcome.

The $62 million, mind you, is just 4.5% of the state total. But national affirmative action foe Edward Blum is underwriting one of the two lawsuits, claiming it's all about preventing racial exclusion. This is the same Blum who underwrote a group of Asian students in their suit against Harvard's admission program. Walter Lega, a plaintiff in one of the Oregon suits, is a white electrical firm owner. He's claiming a special fund for Blacks is not warranted and he's joined by the white owner of a logging company. The other suit involves a Mexican-American owner of a coffee house.

In 2019 Black Oregonians received just four of the 984 loans that the Small Business Administration issued statewide according to the Portland Business Journal. Oregon has other programs to assist other minority groups, including a $10 million fund aimed at undocumented Latino immigrants and one created by Portland officials to aid a district of largely Asian-owned businesses, reports Eligon.

I'm no lawyer, but the case against Black grants seems spurious at best. These are COVID-19 related funds and Blacks are disproportionately victims of the disease, with infection rates eclipsing those of Latinos, Asians, and whites. Black-owned businesses have shut down at a rate of 41% compared to 31%for Latino-owned, 26% Asian and 17% white, according to a Stanford University study. Blacks have a disproportionate share of the virus and a sound argument can be made that we're entitled to proportionate relief.

"The idea that in this case – a lumber company could use the 14th amendment as a weapon to prevent the descendants of slaves from receiving an economic benefit in a time of disaster – is utterly inconsistent, "observed Clark D. Cunningham, a professor of law at Georgia State University."

Don's Parting Shot...

There is another legal assault against Black people that has received little notice amid the recent cacophony ... yet has the potential to do long-lasting injury. No surprise here. Like a thief in the night, the Trump Administration has sought repeatedly to steal away advances made by Black people over the past 50 years. In this case, his Justice Department has submitted for White House approval, a change in how it enforces Title VI of the Civil Rights Act, which prohibits recipients of federal funding from discriminating based on race, color, or national origin.

The change covers housing programs, employers, schools, hospitals, and other organizations and programs, according to reporters Katie Benner and Erica Green of the NYTimes. The Justice Department would continue to monitor intentional discrimination but would no longer consider "disparate impact" on minority or other groups. Disparate impact takes into account patterns of behavior, policy, and action and that results in damage to Black people even though it is not done intentionally.

The proposed changes affect loans, grants, contracts, educational institutions, mortgages, real estate development, and other activities receiving federal funds. Entire business plans would be upended. The incoming Biden Administration could not immediately reverse the move, but a new attorney General could put its implementation on hold.

The Bigger Picture

So, where are we? The wider context of race in America is a good vantage point. Juliet Hooker, in her contribution to the anthology "Grief and Grievance: Art and Mourning in America," writes that "The other feature of the (often unconscious) conflation between whiteness and the political rule is the complex distortion of historical narratives about white supremacy. On the one hand, there is a reflexive desire to relegate racism to the distant past in order to deny white subordination in the present, combined on the other hand with a simultaneous nostalgia for unchallenged eras of white dominance."

"The public remembrance and reverence for symbols in the U.S. South," she continues, "in the name of supposedly non-racist appeals to 'tradition' illustrate this dynamic as does the slogan 'Make America Great Again.' … When white vulnerability (real or perceived) is politicized, it results in moments of profoundly dangerous consequences."

Juliet Hooker nails it! The white mob riot at the Capitol was, indeed, a dangerous consequence. Our mission now is to ensure any follow-on insurrections do not succeed, be they in the streets or in America's courtrooms.

Action Items…

The incoming Biden team at the Justice Department led by Chicago area native Attorney General Merrick Garland is a good start. So is Associate Attorney General Vanita Gupta and Assistant Attorney General for Civil Rights Kristen Clarke. A native Chicagoan and dynamic friend and advocate, Minyon Moore, is on the Biden transition team and Advisory Board. Moore worked wonders in the Clinton Administration, orchestrating the "mend it, don't end it" strategy to save affirmative action from legal challenges.

We must monitor their efforts and contact them when needed. Our Congressional representative's offices – esp. Sen. Dick Durbin and Reps. Bobby Rush and Danny Davis — should pass along the key appointees' office and email addresses. Take it from someone who has worked these corners in the past, newly appointed officials are rarely omniscient and welcome information on issues that affect Black people.

The following organizations should be contacted to obtain the status of the lawsuits and regulatory threats mentioned above … and to determine how these advocates can be supported:

Lawyers Committee for Civil Rights Under Law (www.lawyerscommittee. org); NAACP Legal Defense Fund (www.naacpldf.org); National Center for Youth Law (http://ylc.org); and National Women's Law Center (http:// NWLC.org). Their contact information can be found online. Their offices have a file of cases that can be of use to our local organizations.

My favorite young Black thinker and writer, Ta-Nehisi Coates, sums it for me. "The first white president in American history is also the most dangerous still, by the fact that those charged with analyzing him cannot name his essential nature because they too are implicated in it." Coates goes on: "One must be able to name the bad bargain that whiteness strikes with its disciples- and still be able to say that it is this bargain, not a mass hypnosis, that has held through boom and bust."

I ask NYTimes Op-Ed contributor Roxanne Gay to close us out: "This is America. This has always been America. If this were not for America, these (riots) would not have happened. It's time we face this ugly truth, let it sink into the marrow of our bones, let's move to action. With everything that took place on Wednesday, it was easy to forget that Jon Ossoff and Raphael Warnock won their senate races in Georgia. Their victories were gratifying and cathartic, the result of solid campaigns and the hard work of organizers on the ground. The easy narrative will be that Black women and Black people saved this country and they did. And they should be celebrated. But the more challenging narrative is that we now have to honor our salvation by doing something with it."

WANTED: BLACK BUSINESS VACCINE!

Calendar 2020 is speeding into history amid so many scary headlines that it's hard to know where to focus.

Can Deadbeat Donald pardon himself in advance? Will he leave office voluntarily? Does SCOTUS know better than epidemiologists whether it's a good thing to have crowded churches and synagogues? Why are Asian students challenging Harvard's affirmative action program? Will the Georgia Senate runoff tilt toward Democrats? Who's going to take – or take a pass on – the newly approved COVID-19 vaccine?

All these items scream for attention. But the most urgent question for African Americans is the coronavirus. Even if all the above were resolved in Black Americans' favor, it would be of little value if most of us are ill with an incurable disease … or dead. Though selective "at-risk" personnel are already being inoculated, experts predict that, due to the complexity of its manufacture, distribution, and storage, folks will still be lining up for shots in the third quarter of 2021. So a hoped-for "herd immunity" likely won't be achieved until a year from now.

Business Blues...

One too-often overlooked aspect is how Black Business is doing in this uncertain and murderous milieu. According to **Rodney A. Brooks** in the July 17 *National Geographic*: "COVID-19 has pounded Black-owned Business particularly hard. Research at the U of California Santa Cruz and a report by the *National Bureau of Economic Research* found that 41% of Black-owned businesses, some 440,000 enterprises have been shuttered by COVID-19 compared to 17% of white-owned businesses."

These businesses tend to be barber shops, supply stores, food providers, bars and other retails outlets. Why so vulnerable? The disparate impact of the virus is deeply rooted in historic and economic injustice. Racial disparities in healthcare wealth, employment, wages, housing, income contribute to greater susceptibility to the virus.

Black businesses tend to cater to Black consumers, many of whom have been hit hard by the COVID-19 shutdowns. Black unemployment rose to 15.4 % in June. The riots and looting following the death of **George Floyd** made a bad situation worse. For instance, thieves *FED EX* and *UPS* stopped deliveries to the entire neighborhood.

Builders Among The Bluest...

Construction contractors – my neck of the business woods – face a triple threat. Contracts have had to undergo many changes due to delays caused by *COVID-19*. Pretending things are normal is a big mistake. Early in the epidemic, virus-related hospitalizations among unmasked and un-distanced construction workers spiked four-fold in Texas according to Helio News. For Black professional services firms, trying to service public- and private- sector clients whose employees are "working remotely" has prompted management chaos. Internally there's the challenge of overseeing staff at a distance. Then there's the inability of many public agencies to pay invoices on time (if at all) what with drastically reduced tax revenue.

Looming large in construction contracts is the term "*Force Majeure*" which in simple terms means unforeseen circumstances that prevent someone from fulfilling a contract. The pandemic has created a legion of unexpected consequences in executing contracts. Allow me, then, to describe the situation of three Black-owned businesses struggling now to survive and compete in the Chicago area.

Company A is an architectural firm, well established with an expanding client base. The firm is a tenant in a downtown office building that has been closed due to virus spread … and closed without adequate notice nor a plan for situational entry. Several office staff asked to work remotely or from an alternate site, which became chronic no-shows. And who could blame them? One architect had to stay home to take care of a sick relative; another administrative staffer had to mind two-grade school children whose classes had "gone remote;" a third stayed away because he didn't want to ride public transportation and did not have a computer at home.

So here's a Black professional with assignments on the books, projects to complete, clients to see, and payrolls to meet. All these functions have been interrupted, and ironically, just as the virus is presenting fresh opportunities. The firm would have been well-positioned to help public agencies reconfigure their offices to accommodate returning staff who now must maintain social distancing and 40% maximum attendance. Everything from coat closets to ventilation systems needs to be re-thought.

Company B is a 7-year-old Black-owned professional services firm specializing in operations management, procurement, strategic planning, project management, and facility assessment. The company's founder is unique in the construction industry – a former senior executive with Chicago Public Schools, city purchasing officer, and leadership with the Department of Aviation. In other words, an owner with more public and private sector relationships than almost all Black-owned companies. Yet because of the virus he currently lacks staff and resources to take advantage of those relationships. An excellent collaborator with larger prime construction firms, Company B's owner is challenged as never before with client development, staff management, project delivery, and corporate financing. As with Company A, opportunities abound … if only the simplest of business procedures had not become so impossibly convoluted.

An Insider's Tale…

My own company, **Comprehensive Construction Consulting**, is a 12-year-old Black- owned and operated construction management and engineering firm. We have a Business Plan, an Implementation Plan, and a Succession Plan. All are tuned to develop younger Black Professionals, for careers in construction management, and all were developed in part by a professional Organizational Consultant whom I'll call "W." A younger leadership team is in place, and yet, even with the digital savvy of youth, their resilience and flexibility are tested constantly as they respond to client issues in a timely manner and make nimble adjustments.

An example: Our company hosts an annual breakfast for clients, team partners, and industry leaders. Figure 80 attendees. Figure the Cook County Board President as invited main speaker with her staff making follow-up presentations. Q and A follow. Now figure-in COVID-19. Suddenly the event had to convert to a Zoom meeting. We pulled it off with 90 "virtual" attendees but only with a lot of help from Consultant W and a whole lot of patient stick-to-itiveness.

But all is not "peachy keen." To complement our existing team (and capture some of the road, highway, and tollway business ahead) the firm needs a young engineer that can navigate highly technical "engineer speak." But identifying, securing, and onboarding such a person during this pandemic has been a challenge, even for our highly capable HR manager.

Both Sides Now...

Black firms face great difficulty during the *COVID-19* era and many will not survive. Not so with many large publicly-traded (not to say white-owned) corporations. According to The Washington Post, "between April and September, one of the most tumultuous stretches in modern history, 45 of the 50 most valuable publicly traded U.S. companies turned a profit. Despite their successes at least 27 of the 50 largest firms held layoffs this year collectively cutting more than 100,00 workers. Further, the 50 largest firms companies averaged a 2% revenue growth over the first nine months of 2020. Conversely, small business revenues sunk 12% over the same period, according to data collected by software provider *WOMBLY.*

The **George Floyd** murder and subsequent racial reckoning have prompted some large companies to focus on helping Black businesses. While there is much to investigate what their annual Black Business spend is, they have publicized the following: *Facebook* $200 million; *Google* $175 million; *Netflix* $5 million. This is to be saluted. Successful Black businesses need various forms of assistance to navigate this pandemic and funding from these behemoths is part of the remedy. Recently the national *Business Roundtable,* a gathering of our nation's largest corporations, put it this way: "White family wealth in 2019 was eight times that of a typical Black family and five times that of a typical Hispanic family. These longstanding systemic inequities can have a compounding negative effect across generations, and the trends will not reverse unless all of us – government, business, and civil society – take steps to ensure that every American can participate fully in the economy."

What To Do?...

In that spirit, I am proposing a *"Private Sector CARES Program"* not unlike the public sector's *CARES* (aka Stimulus) Act that can include loans that are forgiven if certain milestones are reached. The funds can come from the *Facebook*, *Google*, and *Netflix* commitments ($400 million) plus others to follow, that would fund Black business creation and expansion in areas with the largest Black populations. Chicago ranks 2nd in the top ten.

So let's say $40 million would be directed to Chicago Black Businesses. Who's at the table? Who will decide on eligibility and funding priorities.? I propose our Business Leadership Council take a major role in this endeavor. I propose that **Charles Smith**, Vice-Chair of the BLC, convene a *Zoom* meeting with representatives of these 3 corporations to discuss the following:

1. What is their annual spending with Chicago area Black Businesses and how are those businesses to access opportunities?
2. Establish a private sector CARES Program to provide management and technical assistance to Chicago area Black Businesses.
3. Fund an "executive loan" program to provide engineering and other executives to work for 1 year or more to identify and coach staff of Black Businesses.
4. Fund a Virtual Shepherding Program for Black Businesses.
5. Fund a study of leadership and management practices during COVID and of preparations for the exit from COVID. Where are the opportunities?
6. Mentor new businesses that emerged just before COVID. Explore strategies for survival.

One crucial take-away from this proposed BLC meeting with corporate funding sources will be BLC's role in establishing, advising, and delivering the *Private Sector CARES Program*. A logical first step would be an assessment survey, to be completed within 6 months, to match prospective funding with areas of greatest need and most promising outcomes. This could be a collaboration between the BLC and Chicago-area university business schools.

The *COVID-19* pandemic is accelerating a Great Dividing between global corporate haves and local business have-nots. Black business is on the wrong side of this dire and politically unsustainable equation. Chicago's corporate and Black leadership can lead the way to solutions. Let's do the work!

THE BIG LOSER GETS WOKE'D!!

"Don't make no waves, don't back no losers" was the unofficial motto of Chicago politics back in the heyday of "Hizzoner" the late Mayor Richard J. Daley.

Fact is, more than 70 million Americans just violated that cardinal rule by voting to reelect the current White House occupant, one of the biggest LOSERS in U.S. political history. But make no mistake, the 77 million Americans who voted for the ultimate winner – former Vice President Joe Biden — were set up to do this thunderous thrashing by Black voters. Our Brothers and Sisters not only rescued Biden's candidacy in the Democratic primaries but put him over the top in the November 3rd general.

This was accomplished thru the virtue of *attention*, which is the process of concentrating on specific information while ignoring the noise of other, extraneous information. In so doing we escaped the vice of *distraction,*the specialty of our soon-to-depart president.

Donald Trump's web of distraction for a time ensnared us all. For months I'd puzzle over why so many white Christians believed he was sent by God; why so many threatened with COVID-19 refused to wear masks; why violent white supremacists earned praise rather than punishment.

What I know now, in the afterlight of the Nov. 3 vote, is that the antics of Loser Trump and his Republican enablers were simply *distractions*– highly addictive distractions – from what really matters in our lives. Some intriguing theories are emerging about this. One is that Loser Trump provided those from poorer or working-class backgrounds with an element of fantasy that allows them to "travel" to places – Trump Tower? Mar-a-Lago? — they may never go. Another theory is that working-class whites, convinced they have been betrayed and cheated by elite globalists, could with Trump gain a measure of revenge. In other words, they were distracted.

Caroline Framke, TV critic at Variety magazine argues: "Trump was the host of a reality show that revolved around the fact that he... is the only person whose opinion matters. It's still under- appreciated just how effectively he's transformed the presidency into a national 24/7 experience. It's not just that he has hawked his own steaks at press conferences; held government events at his self-titled hotels etc. He knows how to get and keep people's attention in such a way that envisioning life without his presence becomes impossible."

As the election night (week? month?) unfolds, it's understandable that, for many, the only real emotion you can muster is exhaustion. The Trump show has been the all-consuming TV production of all time. For a man obsessed with attention, validation and how many viewers he has at any given time, his entire administration has been a Trumpian fever dream come true.

Barack Obama emphasized this point campaigning for Biden. "You're not going to have to think about the crazy things they said every day," declared our sorely-missed former president. "You're not going to have to argue about them every day. It just won't be so exhausting."

Then again, it didn't help that MSNBC and CNN, which also keep close track of ratings, would routinely spend 15 minutes of every 30 minute "news" program criticizing something Loser Trump said. Like the legendary Oscar Wilde once suggested: "There is only one thing in the world worse than being talked about, and that is not being talked about."

What Really Matters

The challenge now is to set aside the attention theft by Loser Trump and to focus on what really counts for African Americans. Our most immediate issue is the COVID-19 pandemic. It's been proven that Blacks are three times as likely to be infected as whites. This is due, in part, to housing, jobs and other social determinants, but there are other, more immediate factors.

Prisons are releasing a number of inmates due to coronavirus outbreaks and the released are bringing the virus back to their communities. There is chaos surrounding testing, contact tracing, mask wearing and social distancing. And now we have the prospect of a vaccine and all the complications that attach thereto.

Pfizer says its vaccine is more than 90% effective in preventing the disease among volunteers in its trials. That level of protection would put its two dose vaccine on a par with highly effective vaccines like those for measles.

Yet there are questions about vaccines for Black people. There's the undersized level of Blacks participating in the trials and whether that will be carried over into the distribution phase. Moreover, some such as shut-ins may be unable to get a vaccine while others simply refuse it. And under the best of circumstances, it takes time to make enough vaccine and even more time to distribute it. Besides, no vaccine protects everyone who receives it.

Who Gets Vaccinated?

Then there's the matter of who ought to get the vaccine asap … and who can wait. Alison Galvani of Yale and Jan Medlock of Oregon State argue that we should, instead of trying to protect those facing the greatest danger, vaccinate first those most likely to transmit the virus. Molly Gallagher of Emory University suggests we might improve outcomes – reduce the amount of mortality and reduce the amount of transmissions — by prioritizing certain groups.

Evidence shows college students and young adults are significant transmitters but less likely to suffer complications. So if a vaccine proves effective for all ages, saving the most lives could mean prioritizing children and young adults even though they're among the least likely to suffer harm.

Laura Matrajt, a Seattle-based expert in the mathematics of public health, calculated that if there was only enough vaccine that is 60% effective to cover 30% of the population, we'd face a choice. Giving it to younger people would minimize symptomatic infections and non-ICU hospitalizations, whereas giving it to older people would minimize ICU hospitalizations and deaths.

Keep in mind, however, that racial minorities have borne a disproportionate burden from the disease. Ought not the distribution schedule address that imbalance? African Americans need to understand this triage over who gets saved. We need to be part of the conversation.

Fighting Irish Folly

Then there's the simpler matter of responsible behavior. Some 5,000 Notre Dame students recently stormed the field after their football team beat Clemson U. This not only violated coronavirus protocols but broadcast a terrible example to millions. It was later reported the N.D. coach told players beforehand that their fans would swarm the field if they played well and won.

The school appeared to condone the emotional display because stadium security stood aside when the crowd rushed on. The administration, under fire for allowing this madness, gave a weak admonition to students that grades would be withheld until they were tested. Not very convincing one month after the school's president was spotted without a protective mask, glad- handing pols at a crowded White House reception.

Lacking exemplary behavior by our president(s), we all struggle to stay safe today without stunting our tomorrows. One of the toughest trade-offs has to do with our schools. Should we go all remote or return to our classrooms? Is there a "hybrid" middle course? What are the pros and cons? These questions are especially crucial for Back students.

The pandemic has revealed how crucial are childcare and early learning, instructional methods and traditional after-school supports. The crisis has also laid bare the economic and racial disparities that hinder equal access to these essential public goods. Childcare is a critical support for working parents but beyond the reach of many cash-strapped Black families.

With so many schools closed due to COVID-19, there is an opportunity now to make more progress on the digital divide – the gap between students who have access to the Internet and those who do not. A divide also between students who are taught to use technology in active creative ways… and those who stick to shopping and gaming.

Then there's the vexing trade-off between remote l and in-school learning. My son Tim King, leader of a highly successful charter school network here in Chicago, recently laid out the case for in-school in a Chicago Tribune submission.

For the young Black men at his Urban Prep schools, he reminds, far more is at stake than grade point averages or college entrance exams. Classrooms and school gyms are safe, supportive environments. Out on America's streets, homicide is the leading cause of death for Black male teens, while suicide is the third-leading cause and rising. One in three Black men will be imprisoned in his lifetime compared with 1 in 17 white males. Black male unemployment is higher than in other groups. They are more likely to face excessive force from police. The high school dropout rate for Black males is 41% higher than for white males.

In Chicago, the local data is worse. So far this year more than 3,000 people have been shot, resulting in 550 deaths of which 75% were Black males. Remote schooling, imposed here on charters by public school board edict, will have reverberations for years to come, King argues. Rigorous in-person instruction is desperately needed to counter these grim statistics, adding that every year of education increases positive life outcomes.

Action Items

Clearly the country is not prepared for the latest surge in COVID-19 infections/hospitalizations and Black folks are the most imperiled. Since we don't yet have a "seat at the table," let us create tables of our own! Here's three ideas for action:

1. Media marvels Hermene Hartman, Melanie Spann-Cooper could join with Dr. Claudia Fegan (Cook County) and Dr. David Ansel (Rush Hospital) to create a Zoom meeting place, and later, a social media hotline. This would inform and report on how Black people can survive and prepare for the current pandemic and upcoming winter weather and Holidays.

2. BLC leader Charles Smith might convene a Zoom session with educator Tim King; violence expert Dr. Gary Slutkin; along with a WVON designee. The purpose would be to address the challenges of educating Black students in a pandemic. Confront

the trade- offs between health risks in class and violence on the streets.

3. The results of these events should be summarized in a position paper reflecting the best thinking of Black business leaders, health professionals and seasoned educators. These should be submitted to Mayor Lori Lightfoot and County President Toni Preckwinkle.

Final note: This writer was just in a Zoom meeting with Alpha Phi Alpha brother Raphael Warnock, a Georgian who faces a January run-off election for the U.S. Senate. We will be in touch with voter suppression fighter Stacey Abrams and raising money and manpower to rescue the Senate from the Big Loser's lieutenants. Ignore distraction and join us at https://warnockforgeorgia.com/

BLACK HOPE AND HEALTH

The New York Review of Books asked 18 writers to comment on what's at stake this November in its pre-election edition dated Nov. 5, 2020. Each member of this high-powered panel of progressive thinkers offered his or her unique take, yet all were emphatic in their severe disappointment with current U.S. leadership ... or lack thereof.

Some were downright scary.

Yale historian Dave Blight argued: "We are about to experience a presidential election, perhaps the first since 1860, when it is possible that millions on each side will not find defeat acceptable.

... We are essentially two political tribes fighting a cold civil war that may determine whether or not our institutions can survive the strife fomented by a pandemic, racial reckoning, the death of a transcendent Supreme Court justice, and the re-election campaign of our homegrown authoritarian president."

In preparation for this election, Blight asserts, the incumbent and his lieutenants have dragged up "voter ID laws, reduced polling places and days, felon disenfranchisement, voter roll purges, restrictions on mail- in voting, an evisceration of the Voting Rights Act of 1965 and a constant rant about 'voter fraud' without evidence."

"The Republican Party has become a new kind of Confederacy," argues Blight. "It has weaponized the truth and rendered it oddly irrelevant. It has brought us almost to a new 1860, an election in which Americans voted for fundamentally different versions of a pro-slavery or an anti-slavery future"

Others in *The New York Review of Books* assembly worry about why the Russians favor Donald Trump and why does he let them? National security writer Thomas Powers suggests that, if Trump loses, he ought not have access to classified information as have previous former presidents. He argues Trump's relationships with Russian oligarchs, banks, intelligence agents and Vladimir Putin are *that* suspect.

Black author and essayist Darryl Pinckney reminds that the Proud Boys and other militarized ultra-right groups are readying themselves while too many voters and non-voters take it for granted that everything will work out. But how can they be complacent about an administration that has put a muzzle on the Centers for Disease and Prevention (CDC) in the midst of a pandemic?

Benighted Believers

Nothing drives the polarization home as much as the cult-like craze of some of Trump's supporters. The New York Times devoted its entire Sunday Oct 18 opinion section to examinations of Trump's damage to the democracy. Yet true believers like John L. Schilling, a Pennsylvania retiree, reacts in a subsequent letter-to-the-editor: "I find that Mr. Trump honestly connects with us people more than any other president since Ronald Reagan. He has done much that was beneficial for the country with little positive coverage from the media and despite considerable obstruction. When he speaks, he speaks to us not over our heads in platitude or political speak. He produces results and runs the country well."

That kind of groundless misperception is un-deserving of comment, other than to say it demonstrates a complete addiction to the lies the president sells. The fraught question of the moment is how many Mr. and Mrs. Schillings are still out there?

According to the Pew Research Center there are now 30 million Blacks and 30-plus million Hispanics now eligible to register and vote. In 2008 63.6 % Black voter turnout went on to elect Obama with turnout being 61.6% in 2016. One in 10 will be generation Z (Americans who will turn 18-23 next year). Consequently the eligible voters will be younger and more diverse.

It's possible that the stars will align to bring a Joe Biden victory. But a number of things have to happen: Black voter turnout will not yield to suppression; state governors will honor their oaths and bring out the National Guard, if necessary, to combat the Proud Boys, "Boogaloo Bois" and Oath Keepers bent on intimidation; transportation will be provided to reach newly-distanced polling places; and the social distancing and masking required by various pandemic protocols will not deter voters.

The Health Factor

Regardless of who wins the election, one thing is certain. The coronavirus will remain a serious threat to the country and African Americans will continue to be victims of its wrath. It has been well documented that Blacks comprise an outsized percentage of those infected and deceased.

So let us take a slight detour from election boulevard to survival street. Coronavirus will be felt by African Americans for decades to come. Blacks have been hit with many social setbacks, it's true, but trying to improve Black health in the midst of a global pandemic, of resurgent racial turmoil and of this screwy election? That's unheard of!

I have advanced on these pages that the mistrust Black people have for any vaccine, coupled with the inability to include African Americans in ongoing scientific trials, will make for a long time before we overcome this pandemic and its after-effects. Moreover, the sheer logistical complexity of vaccine distribution will push its availability many months away. Even if we have a change in the White House, the pandemic will continue to threaten and injure Black people disproportionately.

Coronavirus has been a moving target since it was first identified. Just as we've learned that many parts of the body are points of vulnerability during the virus' active phase, we've found that many symptoms linger for weeks or months even after tests come back negative. The good news is that there is much that can help one feel better. However, this requires continued access to health care … and that begins with good information.

Healio.com, a valuable health information website, reports on a meeting of minorities in cancer research. At an AACR forum Dr. John D. Carpten discussed the killing of George Floyd and its psychological effects on the Black community. He describes the weeks following Floyd's death as emotionally, spiritually and psychologically draining. The virtual meeting of the AACR group illustrates just how far Black health care is behind, further demanding immediate and continual attention.

The monthly online journal Nature Medicine (**nature.com/nm**) also reported on a recent event with useful action items. An August posting describes a meeting of health professionals discussing how racism and police brutality affect the lives of Black patients. Physicians share how to discuss racism with their patients and how physicians and their organizations can work toward health equity. Their overriding conclusion: Black people need us now.

One way to help eliminate racial disparities in health care is to address the social determinants of health – the conditions of places where people reside, learn, work and play. The focus should be on equity as individuals may require different resources and tailored services to live the healthiest lives possible.

What we have here, then, is an unprecedented "Twin-demic." We must mobilize not just to ensure a fair and uncorrupted election, but beyond that, to defeat a spreading contagion that is killing Blacks at a disproportional rate due to social and economic factors all-too familiar.

Let us close, though, with some personal upside. My wife and I went for early voting and it was efficient, encouraging and energizing. Imagine a socially distanced crowd with 6-ft. marks on the floor, jugs of hand sanitizer, courteous staff. It was one of City College's finest moments. If it wasn't illegal, I'd do it again ... all the way to November 3.

COVID CONUNDRUMS

In the midst of the coronavirus caterwaul, we get yet another surge of madness mayhem. The governor of Michigan is targeted for kidnapping. Our Chief Executive, aka the Dismal Demon, gets COVID-19 as the infection spreads among White House staff and guests. Meanwhile, Twitter moves to limit the spread of Trump's erroneous tweets.

Amid this rhetorical rubble, stirs an understandably uneasy African American population. Many are concerned that our historic back-of-the-bus treatment will extend to the upcoming distribution of anti-viral vaccines now under development.

Think of it. Blacks are only 13 % of the U.S. population yet account for 30% of COVID infections and 26% of deaths. As a vaccine is developed various trials are required to examine the side effects, the safety, and any ethno-specific adverse reactions. Then there's the inevitable obstacle to a fair distribution among minority populations. Already, leading pharmaceutical companies report difficulty to recruit minorities to participate in the ongoing vaccine trials. According to the PEW research group, Blacks comprise only 3% of volunteers for vaccine trials. This should not surprise. With so much disinformation swirling around, including that being tweeted from our ditsy White House, many African Americans are doubly prone to avoid the vaccine trials. Besides our understandable mistrust of the system, many are preoccupied with the exigencies of day-to-day survival.

Mistrust no mystery

For generations Black people have known about the Tuskegee Experiment where Alabama Black men were infected with syphilis in order to confirm research that would go on to benefit primarily white people. (See James Jones, author of *Bad Blood.*) Then there was Henrietta Lacks, the Black Baltimore woman who, while a patient at Johns Hopkins Hospital, had a sample of her unusually strong cancer cells removed without her permission. This led to one of the most enduring cell lines in research history, with no economic benefit to Lacks. (See Rebecca Skloot, *The Curious Life of Henrietta Lacks.*) Once it was common for Black-frequented healthcare facilities like Cook County Hospital to note race on donor forms so that Negro blood did not go to whites. Blood was segregated well into the 1950's and in Louisiana until 1972. Then there was Dr. J Marion Sims, the Father of Modern Gynecology, who performed experiments during the 1830s … mostly on Black female slaves, without anesthesia.

Compounding the situation for many is the not-so-simple matter of day-to-day survival. It's true there has been a decline in robberies and store burglaries due to store closings and shelter-in- place. Yet there has been a spike in violent shootings and killings in Black neighborhoods across major US cities. "We're surrounded by murder and it's almost like your number up" said one Kansas Black woman, doubtless speaking for many.

Schools, libraries, recreation centers and public pools have been closed. Nonprofits, churches and recreational sports leagues have scaled back. Mentors, social workers and counselors have been hampered by social distancing. Summer jobs programs were cut. Violence intervention workers are banned from hospitals. Group therapy programs that were one-on-one are now online. Without jobs and support activities. violence prone neighborhoods are experiencing a pandemic within the pandemic.

Police have pulled back in some cases due to the George Floyd and Breanna Taylor protests, not to mention social distancing requirements. Black students told to stay home for "remote learning" are increasingly exposed to street violence. For example a leading Charter high school for Black young men established a hybrid schedule of ½ time spent in class and ½ remote. During one remote home session, a promising young man was shot and killed at his residence.

Programs That Work

So how can Black America, saddled with historic distrust and struggling to survive, start winning its own distinct battle with COVID-19? Rev. Paul Abernathy of Pittsburgh's Neighborhood Resilience Project is teaming with researchers from Duquesne and Pittsburgh Universities to develop a manual for communities on arresting decline and sustaining progress in Black neighborhoods. As quoted by writer Jan Hoffman in The New York Times, Abernathy argues "we cannot talk about vaccine without acknowledging the other epidemic—our kids aren't being educated and food lines are longer. Hope is gone. That makes volunteering for the vaccine trials more meaningful right.? Telling them that, they will say 'Are you kidding me?' My house got shot-at last night. And you want to talk about Covid?"

In Chicago other models are being tested. Heartland Alliance, with its READI program, combines transitional jobs with behavior coaching and service for men at risk of gun violence. Children's Home & Aid Society's "Choose 2 Change" program has had success reducing violent crime, arrests and contact with the criminal justice system. Their model relies on mentorship with community advocates and group behavior designed to address trauma. Black Women Organized for Power (BWOP- CHICAGO) is using zoom meetings and social media to organize and set agendas.

Testing the Testers

Still the problem remains: How to recruit more Blacks to participate in ongoing COVID vaccine trials so that the results will detect and reflect any Black anomalies? The esteemed epidemiologist, Dr. Anthony Fauci urges that African Americans be involved in Phase 3 trials now starting.

During Phase 3, thousands of participants receive an inoculation – either an experimental vaccine or a harmless placebo – so as to compare whether a vaccine prevents infection. Researchers must then wait until subjects have been naturally exposed in their communities. This process can take six months or more, even a year or longer, if the tested vaccine is to meet federal Food & Drug Administration standards before reaching the market.

Careful site selection is important. Some argue that drawing participants from communities where transmission is high can reduce risk to the tested volunteers because they would be more likely to catch the virus anyway. But this rationale ought not exploit at-risk populations vulnerable to the virus, ethics experts warn. These socioeconomic and racial disparities need especially to be taken into account when performing so-called "challenge" studies, wherein volunteers are deliberately infected with the virus after being inoculated with an experimental vaccine.

This inevitably recalls Tuskegee, Henrietta Lacks and others, and it immediately raises the question of: What if something goes wrong? What's the recourse? The Wall Street Journal's Peter Loftus and Susan Pulliam report the U.S. Government has paid out $4.4 billion in the past to compensate for damage caused by experimental vaccines for diseases ranging from flu to polio. Any future payouts for injuries due to COVID-19 will be paid out under an updated program known as the "countermeasures injury fund" set up to cover vaccines like flu, anthrax and Ebola. The new fund has a tougher threshold for proving a relationship between an injury and the vaccine. It also has a shorter statute of limitations, no avenue for appeals and doesn't pay damages for pain or suffering like the older vaccine compensation program.

Sarah Rubenstein of The Wall Street Journal Online cautions "Federal law does not require researchers to compensate participants harmed in such trials. It merely requires that their consent forms spell out whether compensation will be available for research-related injuries in trials that involve more than minimal risk."

LIFT that "viral load"

So where are we now? Blacks need to get accurate information on vaccine trials, on fairness in the final vaccine distribution and on insurance protection for vaccine malfunctions. All the while we must guard against the pandemic's fallout of violence as we examine and then implement proven Community Advocacy models.

But it all begins with good information, and that can be hard to find in the shadow of a chief executive who has mocked the wearing of masks and who, because he managed to get himself infected, now claims to be "immune" to COVID-19. (He isn't.)

So ignore the White House for now and instead dial-up your favorite Internet search engine and try some of these keywords:

New England Journal Medicine; American College of Physicians; Fauci; National Medical Association; Sherman Silverstein Lawyers; Georgia Clinical and Transitional – Community Engagement Program; NAACP Legal Defense Fund; Lawyers Committee on Civil Rights Under Law; Health and Medicine Policy Research Group.

And one bit of final, personal advice: stay in touch with your healthcare crew. Know who or where to call if and when you're hit with symptoms. Have an action plan. I am fortunate because my docs are close friends, golf and dinner partners, all-around go-to guys. They have kept me healthy over the decades with flu and pneumonia vaccines, shingles vaccines and the rest. Their counsel on the hoped-for COVID-19 vaccine is this: "Wait until the politics are out of vaccine effectiveness." Based on that, I'm playing it safe … and will check back on November 4.

PROMISING RESPITE! MOVE TO REPEAL CALIF PROP 209 AIMS TO UNDO PROVEN INJURY

Black America has a lot riding on the top-of-ballot contest between Joe Biden and the incompetent incumbent. But on Nov. 3rd save some attention for a bottom-ballot referendum question out in the big, bell-weather State of California. Its outcome may be just as important to you, your children and to your children's children.

We're talking here about a new referendum that would repeal California's infamous Proposition 209. Passed by referendum in 1996, that amendment to the state's constitution bans affirmative action "on the basis of race, sex, color, ethnicity, or national origin in public employment, public education, and public contracting."

Its passage 24 years ago effectively reversed the affirmative action goals used in the University of California Admissions Process to benefit Black and Hispanic Students. A subsequent review by the U.S. Supreme Court agreed that rigid racial quotas are indeed out of bounds. But SCOTUS tempered this by allowing public universities and governments to bend admission and hiring standards if they could show a "compelling interest" in diversity, and then apply "strict scrutiny" to their modified selection process. Faced with holding mandated public hearings and complying with more red tape, many colleges and governments simply scrapped affirmative actions and reverted to their old "if you're Black, get back" ways.

So, what has been the ultimate impact of Proposition 209?

Damage Proven

This very question has been debated in forums – from barbershops and hair salons to highbrow academic conferences. Now comes some actual, 100% data that shows dramatically the damage done to a generation of Black and Hispanic young Californians.

Zachary Bleemer, a doctoral candidate in Economics at the University of California Berkeley is the author of the first research of this kind. He assembled an anonymized database of every student who applied to eight campuses in the University of California system from 1994 to 2002. He included their high school grades, demographics, income and SAT scores. He tracked what colleges they attended (whether in California or elsewhere), along with their academic majors and degrees. For those in California, he also tracked what courses they took and how much they earned in the job market for years after graduation to age 30.

The results, released this summer, are staggering, depressing and infuriating. Read it at https://cshe.berkeley.edu/sites/default/files/publications/rops. cshe.10.2020.bleemer.prop209.8.20.2020.pdf

Reports Bleemer:

"The total enrollment of Black and Hispanic students at the University of California declined by about 800 students per year after 1998. This was the result of the university's eight campuses all ceasing implementing race-based affirmative action as a result of Proposition 209. (Minority) applicants sharply shifted way from UC's more selective Berkeley and

UCLA campuses, causing a cascade of students to enroll at lower-quality public institutions and some private universities.

"Proposition 209 set off the most massive reshuffling of college students in US. History, as it upended the admission process for hundreds of thousands of students in both the UC and CSU systems," wrote Teresa Watanabe of the L.A. Times of Bleemer's work.

"Suddenly all of these universities stopped using this policy. It seemed like a great opportunity to understand what affirmative action was doing for thousands of students in California. And the answer looks bleak for those students."

In other words, students who would have enrolled at the flagship campuses before the ban attended less selective universities in the system. This in turn pushed out other Black and Hispanic students who moved down the ladder of selectivity. Those at the bottom lost their grip entirely and exited the system altogether.

The Injury heaped on Black California Students could not have come and worse time in terms of missed opportunities. California in the late 1990s was on the brink of an explosion in technological wealth build. Degrees from the states' premier universities were tickets to Silicon Valley positions.

Bleemer concluded that "Ending UC's affirmative action polices did not lead the university's (minority) applicants to earn higher grades in challenging courses, but it did cause them to be less likely to earn STEM degrees and any graduate degrees." Wages were also diminished.

Some opponents of affirmative action have posited a "mis-match theory'" that Black students have been hurt by preferential admissions being unable to compete with academically superior classmates. Bleemer disagrees: "If Black and Hispanic students had benefitted from enrolling in less selective universities, they would have been more successful in rigorous math and science course there. They were not. Instead they were less likely to earn bachelor's degrees in a science or engineering field as well as less likely to graduate overall compared with Black and Hispanic students before Proposition 209. They are also less likely to earn graduate degrees."

California seems to have set back a generation of Black and Hispanic students, pushing them down and out of the University of California system and helping to widen the racial wealth gap with seeming little offsetting benefits for other students.

Prop 209 Aftermath

What Bleemer's data doesn't show, of course, is the way Proposition 209 emboldened the anti- affirmative action crowd nationally, leading to a spate of like-minded challenges and court cases. One suspects that Ward Connerly, the Black businessman on the UC Board of Regents who led the push for 209, had this "pin action" in mind from the get-go.

Connerly (referred to as "scum uncle Tom" by Noble John of Black News Weekly) is the ideological cousin to Supreme Court Justice Clarence Thomas, who got into Yale Law School on Affirmative Action and has since railed against it. Affirmative Action had been Supreme Court challenged in the past, it's true, (1974 DeFunis; 1976 Bakke) but Prop 209 opened the floodgates: 2003 Grutter; 2016 Fisher; and 2019 on behalf of Asian Students against the Harvard University Admission Program.

Justice Thomas (Mississippi Congressman Bennie Brown hung the "Uncle Tom" label on Thomas) in the 2013 Fisher v University of Texas, opined that UT Austin's admission policy amounted to discrimination and compared the school's admission program to slavery and segregation. Say what? Sounds like those old-time slaveholders who argued that slavery was a "positive good" that it "civilized Blacks and elevated them in every dimension of life."

Likewise Ward Connerly of Prop 209 fame has stated that Affirmative Action is bad for all. He joins this curious Thomas fraternity in arguing that race-based preferences are bad and that it reinforces inferiority in Black beneficiaries of the programs.

One Man's Experience

I beg to differ. My path is an argument in favor of saving – and expanding – affirmative action as an antidote to that other, non-viral disease that plagues America: historic, structural, systemic White racism. Let me explain.

In 2004 Federal Judge James B. Moran ruled that Chicago's Affirmative Action Ordinance regarding MBE (Minority-owned Business Enterprise) utilization could continue with some adjustments that the City provided. This program has enabled many Black firms to start up, expand and prosper. Initially started by Harold Washington and honed by Richard M. Daley, Chicago's program allowed the creation and development of my UBM, which employed over 100 people and became in 2004 the largest Black owned construction firm in the state of Illinois.

Later it allowed UBM alumni to form another company, CCC, to find a profitable niche and develop the next generation of Black construction professionals. But for this writer, the benefits of affirmative action go beyond providing jobs or earning profits. Affirmative action has empowered me to "Pay it Forward," to graduate two sons from Georgetown University, with one completing GU Law. And further, it blessed one son with the entrepreneurial spirit to start a network of Charter Schools aimed solely at educating young Black men.

That's why I know it a really big deal that the California University System Board of Regents recently endorsed unanimously Proposition 16, the upcoming constitutional amendment that will erase and replace Prop 209. Doubtless the social unrest prompted by the murder of George Floyd in Minneapolis helped cause this change-of-heart.

Moment for Change

Those ongoing protests, amplified recently by a similar death-by-police killing in Kenosha, WI, are prompting many changes-of-heart. White Artistic Directors in theatres, both small and large, are resigning to give their positions to Black Directors in order to provide spaces for Black artists, playwrights and interns.

Adidas and Google are crying "Mea culpa" for ignoring Black upward mobility in their organizations and are committing big dollars to various non-profit African American causes. Black Lives Matter has become a rallying cry equal to "We Shall Overcome " of days past.

But in it's own quiet, superlative way, Zachary Bleemer's new study on the hurtful impact of Proposition 209 is a compelling call-to-action. Every educator, elected official and social advocate should read this document.

Simply stated: The 24-year affirmative action ban by California's public universities knocked out Blacks from even applying for college and depressed Black wealth-building at a key moment in the West Coast technology boom. Bleemer has connected these dots beautifully.

CARPE DIEM

Truly, now is the perfect time to advance some specific proposals advancing Black educational issues. White police pump 7 shots into a Kenosha Black man, and a Antioch, Illinois white boy Trump acolyte shoots into crowd, killing 2. LA Clippers coach Doc Rivers goes on a tear about whites killing Blacks. Major League Baseball and NBA players cancel games in protest to Black deaths There can be no better environment to advance a Black Educational initiative. I'd lay odds 8 to 5 that there will be hand wringing and "what can I do?" by some well-meaning, guilt- ridden managers of the purse … but ultimately they will be responsive to doing the right thing.

Here are some key "asks."

> College Admission- parlaying California's Prop 16 change, allow and/or utilize the use of Race in college admissions. Extra credit can be provided for African American applications, fitting within the "strict scrutiny" guidelines of the Fisher/UT at Austin Supreme Court case.

> Persistence Partner Program- Establish a mentor / protégé relationship with Black College students and two (2) adults with time and passion for their success. Two mentors provide continuity in the event one mentor is conflicted. These mentors would guide, counsel and LISTEN to the Black students on campus or online so as to aid in course completion and life management. (This especially if "distance learning" drags on.)

> Computer Contributions- whether on line or in class, Black students will need laptops and broadband access. Apple, Adidas, JP Morgan Chase, Netflix, Amazon, Microsoft, Airbnb, Nabisco, Gatorade all have joined in supported Black Lives Matter. That being the case, donating to Black education is a no brainer. Petitioning these behemoths for hardware and IT assistance in this social climate is not too much to ask.

These are just a few from my "to do" list. Do not let this opportunity pass. It may not come again for another 50 years. And do stay up a bit later on election night, not just to cheer the presidential results … but passage of California's Proposition 16. Momentum also matters. Like they say at the UNCF: Opportunity is a terrible thing to waste!

CRIMINAL JUSTICE, CORONAVIRUS AND THE COURTS

There are over 2.3 million Black people in jails and prisons in the United States.

That terrible fact, explained in detail by Michelle Alexander in her book "The New Jim Crow", becomes even more ominous now that the COVID-19 virus is racing through prisons and jails across the land.

Alexander shows the many parallels between mass incarceration and Jim Crow. The most obvious is illegal discrimination. Like Jim Crow, mass incarceration marginalizes large segments of the African American community, segregates them physically (prison, jails, ghettoes) authorizes discrimination against them in voting, employment, housing, education, public benefits and jury service.

Ta-Nehisi Coates, a writer and thought leader among the next generation of Black leadership, explained the connection in a recent edition of The Atlantic Magazine: "The Blacks incarcerated in this country... hail from communities that have been imperiled across the deep and immediate past and continue to be imperiled today. Peril is generational for Black people in America. And incarceration is our current mechanism for ensuring that the peril continues. Incarceration pushes you out of the job market, disqualifies from feeding your family with food stamps, and allows for housing discrimination based on criminal background checks. Incarceration increases your risk of homelessness. Incarceration increases your chances of being incarcerated again."

An African American need not be accused of a crime to become snared into the criminal justice web. Sarah Stillman of *The New Yorker* recently chronicled the path of Rosyln Crouch of New Orleans, La. This Black mother of 12 had a 4-year-old material witness warrant out for her arrest in Orleans Parish. Material witness warrants allow law enforcement to arrest and jail someone who hasn't been accused of a crime — and may even be a victim of the crime in question — in order to insure her testimony. In 2016, an Orleans Parish Prosecutor had requested a warrant for Crouch, to compel her testimony in the trial of a man accused of shooting one of her friends. Why not home arrest or a monitoring bracelet?

The incarceration situation is made insufferably worse by the coronavirus. At Louisiana's Elaine Hunt Correctional Center some 85% of the women (65% Black) have tested positive for the coronavirus and 2 inmates have died. Closer to home, Chicago Blacks have accounted for 56% of COVID-19 deaths though we are only 30% of the city's population.

Race and Coronavirus

The New York Times lodged a Freedom of Information Court Petition which forced the Centers for Disease Control and Prevention (CDC) to provide greater specificity on coronavirus infections and deaths according to race and ethnicity. Why have Black people have been disproportionately affected by the coronavirus.

A closer look leads us to the same old same old: decades of spatial segregation; inequitable access to testing and treatment; and now we learn – the withholding of racial/ethnicity data from reports on virus outcomes

"There's nothing different biologically about race. It is the condition of our lives "says Dr. Camara Phyllis Jones MD, PHD"

This disease has traveled the country across hundreds of counties in urban, suburban and rural areas and across all age groups. Yet Black people have been nearly twice as likely to die from the virus as white people.

I've long wondered what the motive is for withholding the race of coronavirus victims. Was it inefficiency? Further investigation shows that CDC depends on reports from local and state sources. The hospitals and medical departments have been so overwhelmed that they've not gotten timely reports to the CDC. Not only is race and ethnicity missing from over half of the CDC reports, so are potential likely sources of individual cases. Fully 43% of Black workers are employed in service or professional jobs that can't be done remotely compared to one in 4 white job holders.

Doubtless this accounts for some of the Black virus burden. The problem is there was no one there! This is significant because earlier we were told that preexisting conditions — asthma, obesity, high blood pressure, etc. — were the main causes of death to Blacks. Not that simple.

CDC information was wrong! Some say the lack of transparency and the gaps in information highlight a key weakness in the public health surveillance system. But here's the thing. CDC states that the gaps in their data are because of the nature of the national system which depends on local agencies. Think about this: the CDC asks state and local health agencies to collect detailed information about every person who tests positive. But it cannot force local officials to do so. Or upgrade their gear, apparently. One reason the virus among Blacks is going unreported and hence unattended is that many local and state agencies still use FAX machines to convey test results to CDC.

Black Lives Matter?

Another reason could be that states may be so eager to "open up" their economies that they intentionally withheld the number of cases. And if it's mainly a Black problem, who cares? Now that race-accurate data is beginning to flow to-and-from CDC, we can see that factors beyond prior health issues are causing African Americans to have an outsized number of virus illness. Among them are: having to leave home to work; leaving and returning to a crowded apartment; using crowded public transportation; going to a crowded work place. All of this besides a lack of healthy food options and access to health care.

Those of us fortunate enough to be able to work remotely can't even fathom these things! In June CDC estimated that the true tallying of virus infections was 10 times the number previously reported cases. That difference in the reporting of cases explains some portion of the race and ethnicity disparities, but clearly there have been significant miscounts in the number of deaths and cases.

It should come as no surprise that the daily routine of many Blacks places them at risk. Using public transportation, living in crowded quarters, working on society's crowded and hectic "front lines." For example, Black workers make up about one in nine members of the workforce but one in six of all front-line workers. They are disproportionately represented in grocery, convenience and drug stores (14.2%); public transportation (26%); trucking/warehouse and postal service (18.2%); health care (17.5%); childcare and social service (19.3%). In the near term this protects them from job loss, but it exposes them to greater likelihood of infection, write Elise Gould and Valerie Wilson of the Economic Policy Institute.

A case for the Courts?

The 6th amendment to the Constitution guarantees certain rights of all criminal defendants:

1. Public trial
2. Speedy trial
3. Right to a lawyer
4. Right to an impartial jury
5. Right to know who your accusers are
6. The nature of the charges against you.

Ought not the virus now racing through our prisons and jails trigger long-overdue litigation to end once and for all the injustice of mass incarceration?

Judge Jed S. Rakoff, writing recently in *The New York Review of Books,* observes" the most immediate need is how to address applications from incarcerated prisoners seeking to be transferred from jail or prison to home confinement. Prisons are potentially fertile ground for the spread of coronavirus, since social distancing is not practical, sanitary conditions are less than ideal and medical assistance is limited. This is made all the worse by the scourge of mass incarceration which has led to overcrowding in a great many prisons"

The Judge further states there are two inmate categories seeking parole. Those awaiting trial found to be substantial flight risks or dangers to the community, and those who have been convicted and are now serving their sentences yet are seeking permanent or temporary release because of old age, medical history, etc. Both categories are at a higher risk of death from COVID-19.

Then there are the drastic physical constraints that the virus has imposed on the operations of our Courts. Trial-by-remote-video makes it hard for parties, especially jailed defendants, to contact their counsel and vice versa; the public has a right to be present but Judges working remote and not in courtrooms won't accommodate this. Bringing all affected parties before the judge is all but impossible for those having limited technology access; in a Zoom hearing even, an experienced lawyer can't get a feel for what arguments are persuading the judge and which are not; personal interaction between judges and lawyers is absent -a big loss to the defendant; many parties in civil cases rely on briefs and dispense with oral arguments. This would be unfortunate… only at oral argument does the judge get to ask questions of counsel.

Rakoff worries further "If Juries can reconvene by July of this year, their absence since March will be an inconvenience. If by then, restrictions such as groups of 50 or more can be lifted. If it goes well past July and for months to come, it is still dangerous for 12 people to gather together in tight quarters to hear and discuss civil and criminal cases, it is not easy to see how constitutional right to jury trial can be met. Our system of Criminal Justice is being materially compromised by the corona virus pandemic in ways both obvious and subtle." (This week the Leighton Criminal Courts reopen in Chicago, so we'll see)

A modest" to do" list

As is my habit, let's close with an achievable "to do" list:

1. Public Health Officials must identify who is at risk and who has been exposed through testing and contact tracing;
2. Public Health Interventions must involve members of these at-risk communities – including the jailed –so they are tailored to meet their respective needs;
3. Transportation must be provided for non-car owners to and from testing sites;

4. Place matters, too, so officials need to review zip codes with higher COVID-19 cases and dispatch testing there;

5. Community leaders in areas hardest hit by the virus need to be included in policymaking, especially discussions about re-opening.

And here's a 6th suggestion for extra credit: Interruption and Intervention are needed to "stop the bleeding."

First on my list of interrupters is the renowned epidemiologist Dr. Gary Slutkin, founder of Cure Violence. Then there's the ACLU, Illinois Health Matters; West Side Justice Center; Cook County Physicians Association; and the Cook County Bar Association, to name a few. These organizations should be funded in the negotiations BLM is having with major corporations.

Now is the moment to address longstanding issues. The fallout from George Floyd's murder has many corporations committed to contributing to NAACP Legal Defense Fund, to ACLU, and to Bryan Stevenson's Equal Justice Initiative, each of which is worthwhile and effective. There needs to be collaboration with local Chicago area advocates like those listed above.

In a subsequent opus, we are going to examine what kind of Black Business Spend does Apple, Amazon, Adidas, Microsoft and the other business behemoths do. Will they do the hiring and support the development of Black professionals that are needed in their respective organizations? That and the $1.5 trillion infrastructure spending bill passed recently by the U.S. House. It will be closely monitored.

The Floyd killing, the relentless COVID-19 epidemic coupled with the logorrheic Presidential drivel has wounded America. Correcting the imbalance of Black incarceration, coronavirus infection, along with Reporting transparency can contribute to the Country rising like a phoenix from the ashes.

REV. C.T. VIVIAN'S CHICAGO CONNECTION

A key advisor to Rev. Martin Luther King Jr, the Reverend C.T. Vivian passed into eternal life at the age of 95 on Friday, July 17, 2020, the same day as another "Lion of the Movement" Congressman John Lewis (D- GA) at 80 years old.

Rev. Vivian, born in Peoria, Illinois, is especially revered in Chicago for his yeoman support of us locals in opening up the construction trades here.

"CT" as his friends called him, met MLK after the 1955 Montgomery Bus Boycott and helped organize the first Freedom Rides, which triggered federal intervention against racial segregation in the Jim Crow South.

Many may remember when TV news showed him waving a finger at Sheriff Jim Clark of Selma, Alabama, at which point the Sheriff punched him, cameras rolling, for the world to see.

This fracas more-or-less turned a local voter registration drive into a national crusade. CT was one of the first to lead restaurant sit-ins and was jailed for his efforts to get African Americans the right to vote.

Vivian continued to work with SCLC after MLK's assassination in 1968. His life's work would prompt President Barack Obama to award C.T. Vivian the Medal of Freedom in 2013.

Construction Reform In Chicago

Yet few notices of CT's death have pointed to the extraordinary leadership he demonstrated here in Chicago during the late 1960s and early 70s. It was Rev. Vivian who convened the effort to challenge racism in the area's construction industry.

It's no exaggeration to say that hardly any Black, Hispanic, or female union-scale construction workers entering the market after 1971 would have their job if it were not for C.T. Vivian.

It was CT who convened and created here the Coalition for United Community Action, an assembly of 60 organizations aimed at social and economic advancement for Black people.

The Coalition targeted the Chicago construction trade unions and the AGC (the association of predominantly white-owned general contractors) that negotiated union agreements.) The Coalition's twin goals were to get more Blacks into the trade unions and get Black contractors into federally assisted construction projects.

CT's biggest accomplishment was managing the agendas, priorities, and personalities of what was known as the 12 Main. Primary among them were the three LSD: The Conservative Vice Lords, The Black P Stone Nation and The Black Disciples. It was the first and only time that these highly competitive "teen nations" worked together to achieve positive outcomes. Imagine Jeff Fort, Bobby Gore, and Larry Hoover meeting with CT and the other 8.

Why involve organizations commonly referred to as "street gangs?" Because this was the rough- and-tumble Chicago construction industry, not some school board, or genteel, white-collar service sector.

LSD was our troops. We sent as many as 400 out to a construction site to outnumber and – if need be – out-muscle the union hard-hats. C.T. Vivian's nonviolent, patient, persistent leadership somehow made it work.

Other members of the 12 were Calvin Morris (Operation Breadbasket), Sally Johnson (Allies for Better Communities), David Reed (Valley Community Organization), Meredith Gilbert (LPPAC), Robert Lucas (Black Liberation Alliance), Fran Womack (The Coalition), Robert Taylor (Welfare Rights Organization), AI Dunlap (The Coalition), Curtis Burrell (KOCO) and yours truly, Paul King, Jr. of the West Side Builders.

This group met almost daily, often as early as 6 a.m., and its members never disclosed the active construction site that was to be targeted for closure that day. C.T. Vivian was the Catalyst and Convenor.

Shutting It Down!

On July 23, 1969, CT led the first construction shutdown – a HUD-financed project on West Douglas Blvd. It would be the first of $80 million in idled projects to follow.

Once we got everyone's attention, it was CT's fearless negotiating style that came into play. He was not loud, just persistent in driving a point home. He gave each of us a voice and a role to play, for he possessed a paternal passion for leadership development.

Another big asset was his ability to shift gears, bantering with white union leaders on one side, then abruptly taking us to challenge the white general contractors. We knew they were united against us…but also that they really didn't trust each other.

Lastly, CT's seminary and church sermon preparation put him in good stead in challenging Mayor Richard J. Daley, who chaired subsequent formal negotiations between the unions, the AGC, and our Coalition. He was concise, even-tempered, and patient.

When CT testified at hearings held by the U.S. Department of Labor here in Chicago, he came armed with statistical data supporting our claims. Much of that information was researched and developed by the Chicago Urban League.

The CUL was not in the Coalition because some of our tactics were offensive to CUL supporters. But we worked confidentially and cooperatively…and would have been dead in the water without CUL to back us up.

CT later testified in Washington D.C. and submitted written testimony to the Senate Labor Committee. His focus was Black jobs, but he also turned me loose to advocate for Black contractors.

So how could a Civil Rights minister develop the prescience and genius to go up against an industry that accounts for one out every six jobs in the country?

Troublemakers!

Professor Erik Gellman does us a favor with his recent book "Troublemakers – Chicago Freedom Struggles though the Lens of Art Shay." Gellman quotes Rev. Vivian with this terse explanation of what it's about, then and now: "Because culture has closed (young Blacks) out, they needed to find a way to get in and …. rebuild their own community."

Gellman explains that our Coalition "sought to pressure the Office of Federal Contract Compliance to hold accountable firms that received these federal dollars but did not practice "affirmative action."

As CUCA's protests spread, Chicago representatives of a dozen federal agencies responded by forming the Federal Ad hoc Committee Concerning the Building Trades, whose research confirmed Blacks' blatant exclusion from the building trades except three.

Nine unionized industries had labor shortages, it found, but they nonetheless continued to discriminate. To many observers inside and outside the CUCA, a revolutionary restructuring of institutional racism in employment seemed possible. "In the summer of 1969," one federal official remarked, "the Black community in Chicago was better organized than anywhere in the country."

Chicago Defender editor John Sengstacke agreed, declaring there was "more compact unity behind (CUCA) on this issue than there was behind Martin Luther King in the struggle for integrated housing in Chicago."

Professor Gellman provides a scholarly, well researched testimony to the brilliance and wisdom of C.T. Vivian. Gellman continues "In the summer and fall of 1969, they (CUCA) deployed to dozens of construction sites across Chicago, where they shut down several hundred million dollars' worth of federally funded construction projects."

Photographer Shay captured one of many confrontations as hundreds of young Black men showed up to take over a construction site. They coerced white workers and foremen to leave the site, making threats, but avoiding violence.

Citing President Johnson's 1965 Executive Order 11246, they declared that all 19 of Chicago's building trades and its principal training facility, the Washburne Trade School, maintained racially exclusive barriers to unions and jobs.

Gellman has a TRIFECTA here! Accurate description of what actually took place, how he is able to capture the pulse of what was discussed, the challenges and the victories is a research masterpiece.

The photographs of Art Shay are off the chart. To see one of the Black P Stone nations reading James Baldwin is one thing, but to see that phenom in a book is a pleasant surprise. Gellman does a masterful job with his notes. For those interested in further study and lessons learned —And especially for Black Lives Matter Activists: "Troublemakers" is a good place to start.

For Additional Reference Material, the Chicago History Museum is the place to go. The contact is Julie Wroblewski. She is in charge of a collection of documents provided by yours truly that are available to investigate and assess the contributions of C.T. Vivian and the Coalition he led.

Closer to home and hearth, I wrote a book, "Reflections on Affirmative Action in Construction" – a copy of which I especially treasure because CT signed the title page as as follows "To Paul King, a tireless worker and a friend I never hope not to have."

And one other thing: In November 2010, CT was initiated into ALPHA PHI ALPHA Fraternity, the first Black Fraternity, founded in 1906, of which I am a Life Member. Into that same line of Atlanta initiates was another icon, the Rev. James Lowery, along with a very special hero of mine, my son Tim King. At Tim's Urban Prep Charter Schools, young Black men continue to, in CT's words, "find a way to get in."

Rest in peace, C.T. Vivian, for your work lives on.

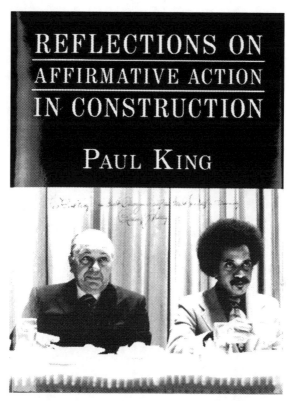

REFLECTIONS ON AFFIRMATIVE ACTION IN CONSTRUCTION

PAUL KING

Published in 2009, this book documents the Protests, Politics and Progress that are the inspiration for this current collection of Black Brainworks.

Rev. C.T. Vivian and Paul King at the 1972 National Association of Minority Contractors (NAMC)/MOVE Conference in Chicago.

BLACK INJURY RECOGNIZED; NOW WHAT?

The murder of George Floyd by white Minneapolis policeman Derek Chauvin has unleashed a torrent of protests across all 50 states and even some worldwide.

Two very different things about these protests jump out: 40 percent of the demonstrators are non- Black; and one in 10 is a Generation Z'er (born in 1995 or later).

Black author and thought leader Ta-Nehisi Coates notes that "significant swaths of people and communities that are not Black, to some extent have some perception of what Black pain and suffering is." He adds "George Floyd is not new. The ability to broadcast it, and the way that it was broadcast, is new."

Makes sense. But why? The generation Z kids saw Barack Obama, a Black dude, as their President way before they could vote. Yet they also saw the litany of white-inflicted Black death go on and on. Erik Garner, Freddy Gray, Trayvon Martin, Breanna Taylor, Tamir Rice, Ahmaud Arbery, to name a few.

Jelani Cobb of *The New Yorker* posits that Floyd's death and the agonizing, protracted manner in which it occurred, caused the different kind of reaction. Fully 71 percent of white Americans now say that racial discrimination is a "big problem." Across the globe, what many people saw was not in and of itself astonishing. That it was happening in America was.

Suddenly Confederate statues are coming down. Aunt Jemima is coming off pancake boxes, along with Uncle Ben's rice and maybe even Ms. Butterworth. Black NFL players are demanding that a quarterback blackballed for kneeling against social injustice during the national anthem be rehired. Nearly two-thirds of Americans now say that the NFL owes Colin Kaepernick an apology.

So, the time is ripe for real change. Yet our history tells us that real change isn't that simple. Some compare the George Floyd protests to the civic unrest of following the 1968 assassination of the Rev. Dr. Martin Luther King.

But in some ways the Floyd killing has had even more impact. There's the serial nature of all the recent deaths-by-police, the reach of cable TV and digital media, plus the graphic videotaped brutality of the Floyd killing.

Even so, Black America needs now to take a lesson from 1968. The time is now, while the pain still burns and our cries echo in the streets, to convert our anger into lasting gain. Let me explain.

Let Pain Beget Gain

In 1965, well before the MLK assassination, Lyndon Johnson coined the phrase "affirmative action." Something was needed to redress the effects of Black enslavement, Jim Crow and urban removal. LBJ issued Executive Order 11246, which banned discrimination on federally funded projects. This opened the door for Black contractors.

But it took the April 1968 murder of MLK to move public support behind what happened next here in Chicago. On July 23, 1969, The Coalition, led by Martin Luther King lieutenant C.T. Vivian, used both the Presidential mandates and growing public sympathy to shut down a federally funded construction project on West Douglas Blvd. It was the first of over $80 million in closed projects to follow.

"You can work in our community, but not without us," was the motto of The Coalition. As a local leader, I helped recruit the Lords, Stones and Disciples along with everyday Blacks seeking construction jobs. We also formed the West Side Builders Assn. – the perfect vehicle when President Richard Nixon later embraced affirmative action, albeit under the very Republican name of "Black Capitalism."

Affirmative Action was the basis of our success. Lyndon Johnson knew it was not enough simply to stop discriminating. Extra effort was needed and that was Affirmative Action.

But here's the lesson: We found that protests, however loud and heartfelt, were not enough. They are a start, but the formula for lasting gain has four P's: PROTEST, PROCESS, POLITICS, and PROFITs.

Back then, protests led to negotiations, meetings, organizing and finally – engagement with elected and appointed public officials. Our opponents were the construction labor unions and the Association of (white) General Contractors (AGC).

Another important event taking place was the formation of the National Association of Minority Contractors (NAMC) in Oakland, CA. Shortly thereafter, Congressman Parren Mitchell (D-MD), created the Congressional Black Caucus Business Braintrust. I was a member of both. Process. Politics.

The negotiations with the unions and the AGC were chaired by none other than Mayor Richard J. Daley. That led to the Chicago Plan, which had goals and timetables to bring Blacks into all 20 trade unions. To cement and spread our gains, we testified at Congressional hearings in Washington and in Chicago.

It's About Being Black

But battles won hardly mean the war is over. Affirmative Action came under attack almost immediately with the complaint that, because it was race-specific, it was "reverse discrimination", which unfairly harmed whites.

So, the courts have been filled with challenges. Our Constitution does not deal directly with race, only that all deserve "equal protection." And so, lawyers are still scrambling to put a name to our "disadvantaged class."

This is what is so fascinating about George Floyd's case. There's no hemming or hawing about whom we're talking about here. The protests aren't about "minorities," or small-and- disadvantaged companies, not even that annoying euphemism "of color."

The reaction to Floyd's killing is unapologetically, unashamedly, about the systematic oppression of Black people. Sad that it took a real-time televised murder and weeks of multi- ethnic marching, but here we are.

Reviewing the trek from '68 to now, the utility and value of Affirmative Action is more important than ever. But it must be defended, and it is due to the efforts of dedicated advocates such as Lawyers Committee for Civil Rights under Law, the contractors of NAMC and, of course, the Civil Rights giants NAACP and Urban League. Together we've mounted defense- after-defense against disingenuous attacks on basic fairness.

Given this background, where do we go with the energy generated by the George Floyd murder?

My favorite expert on the subject is my friend Rev. Dr. Bernard Lafayette, Jr, who once marched with MLK and with my late sister, Claudia. Bernard has been training young activists in nonviolent social change. He traveled to Ferguson, Missouri to advise protest leaders there. Here's how he explained it to *The New York Times*:

"Mainly they need training. They need to build coalitions. I prepare folks to take different roles in the movement. You cannot do everything. People have different roles. The other most, most important thing, you got to get people who are ready to register to vote.

"You must have people in power who represent you. You've got to be negotiating and talking to the people who will make decisions. You cannot just put it out there and be screaming in the air. The air cannot make the change."

My own two cents is that Black Lives Matter will need to establish dialogue with various police departments. A first step would be to have an intermediary (preferably an attorney) establish one with the NYPD Guardian's Association, a group of 1,000 Black officers. In Chicago, former members of the once active Afro-American Patrolmen's League should be contacted.

These groups were formed because Black police knew Black communities were being treated unfairly, just as Black patrolmen were getting the worst shifts and assignments. Before talking to mayors or police superintendents, talk first to the men and women on the front lines Having confidential, trusted, one-on-ones with these professionals should guide BLM's approach to the higher-ups. The troops know where to get points on the board.

One thing BLM negotiators will quickly discover is that "Defund the Police" is a political and pragmatic non-starter. Black policemen are, for the most part, the most recently hired and apt to suffer most from any reduction of the ranks. Moreover, few supporters will be found to support an axe-like chop of policing given the needs in Black communities.

Better to have social workers and /or mental health professionals added to 911 call responses, both to calm potentially violent situations … and add a witness to rough-and-tumble situations.

As for politics, let us not underestimate the leverage now swung by Black leaders such as Congressman James Clyburn (D-S.C.), whose support likely turned the tide for Joe Biden in the former vice-president's bid to unseat you-know-who this coming Nov. 3.

South Carolina Congressman James Clyburn breathed life into Joe Biden's presidential campaign.

Lyndon Johnson was able to launch affirmative action, in part, because the assassination of John F. Kennedy caused a groundswell of sympathy that, in the elections of 1964, secured not just the White House, but extraordinary majorities for Democrats in both Senate and the House.

What will the killing of George Floyd deliver? That depends on whether the BLM movement has learned well the recent history of our struggle, the art of turning sudden rage into lasting gain, and maybe more importantly – the deft application of those Four P's.

TIME FOR A TIMEOUT

"Hey Chicago, you want some of this?" he asked me.

Michael Jordan and I had met a few times in Chicago, but I was surprised he remembered me. And there he stood by the clubhouse of South Ocean Golf Course south of Nassau in the Bahamas, shaking one of those purple velvet Crown Royal bags jangling what turned out to be black $100 casino chips. South Ocean is on the southwestern end of New Providence, about 13 miles from City Center.

This was in his playing days, after he bought his huge house on Paradise Island Bahamas, where he could vent his competitive fire on any number of golf courses. My little place was between his and the golf course.

"Only if you're giving them away," I responded to his challenge. I knew nothing about his golf game but was all too aware of mine. We did agree, however, that my Bahamian golf buddy and I would trail his group in our golf cart for a few holes just to check out his game.

The first hole was a 500-yard par 5. MJ was on the green in 3, then 2 putts for par. The second hole was a 420-yard par 4. He took a driver and then a 5 iron and was on in 2 (for non-golfers, that's like Clarence Carter – "He be strokin'"!)

After seeing this, I told my Bahamian friend that's enough, and we drove to the 10th tee to start our own round. The capper on this story is that the two local Bahamian golf hustlers who were playing with Michael sought us out after the round and showed us that same Crown Royal bag full of $100 casino chips.

"I wouldn't try him on the basketball court," one said, "but I got him here."

Several takeaways from this tale are:

1. unexpected opportunities
2. triumphant teaming
3. lessons learned and
4. battles won.

And a real discovery is that in turbulent times to step back, retreat to your personal space (whatever or wherever that may be) and take time to refresh both body and soul.

Go Dancing With MJ

So, allow this writer to request a break in the action. A pause. A timeout from our historic struggles with the coronavirus, with police brutality, with white indifference and with what's-his- name in the White House, to consider what I term a Magic Media Moment.

Better late than not at all, I offer a personal review of the recent documentary about Michael Jordan's final championship season with the Bulls – *The Last Dance.*

ESPN teamed with Netflix to create five two-hour episodes about Jordan and the Bulls. It covers the years they won the NBA championship in 1991, 92, 93, 96, 97, and 98 (two three-peats).

The personalities, personal dramas, and athletic excellence of these Bulls displayed in this documentary are a perfect antidote for the overwhelmed, exhausted mind.

The 10-hour odyssey covers footage of practices and team travel largely filmed by a camera crew that was embedded with the Bulls for their final season together. This was a brilliant maneuver crafted in part by Jordan's business manager David Falk.

The insider footage was part of a planned documentary about the Bulls. Much of the material had been archived by the NBA League, but distribution required approval by the Bulls, NBA and Jordan.

Mark Stein of *The New York Times* observed, "No other luminary in league history has managed what Jordan just pulled off. "His Airness" made the NBA stash exclusive behind the scenes footage of his Chicago Bulls' sixth and final title run in '97-'98 for nearly 20 years. Then had the 10-part documentary that he finally blessed attract an audience of 4.9 million to 6.3 million for each serving."

Critics call the series weak journalism and inaccurate history, a criticism that pales in the face of the huge TV audience. Another shrewd Falk business move was to position the documentary so as to engage a new generation of viewers who had never seen Jordan play...but would be drawn into buying his branded Nike sneakers.

Wesley Morris of *The New York Times* commented, "You could call these 10 hours a walk down memory lane, but that would be like calling the Mardi Gras a parade."

Men With A Plan

For a basketball enthusiast, the 1991-98 era was the essence of team play based on a well-designed plan. The Bulls' triangle offense had all five players touching the ball, whether or not Jordan ended with the score.

Scottie Pippen was the ideal wing man and Dennis Rodman was a tenacious rebounder. The series may not only be a last tango, but it also ended the surprise factor of crisp passing giving way to wide-open 3-point shots. They all do it now…or at least try.

Michael Jordan had a record 10 scoring titles that are not likely to be topped. His discipline and single-minded focus caused some people to wince. Jordan, for instance, did not engage in political or polarizing matters regarding Black issues.

Example: Harvey Gantt, a Black former mayor of Charlotte, North Carolina, was running for the U.S. Senate in 1990 to unseat racist Jesse Helms. Gantt and other political leaders asked for Jordan's endorsement. He refused. Jordan's ambition was to achieve unimpeachable, unparalleled excellence in his chosen career. Everything else was a potential distraction.

Michael Jordan's basketball brilliance eclipsed some of his leadership faults, according to *New York Times* labor writer Noam Scheiber. Jordan showed little mercy when berating his teammates.

The series quotes Jordan challenging a teammate: "I'm going to ridicule you until you get on the same level as me. And if you don't get on the same level, then it's going to be hell for you."

Today's experts and workplace gurus warn against such Jordan rules where and whenever stars exhibit demeaning talk to lesser talents. They would refer to them as "toxic workers" or "superstar harassers".

Jeff Van Gundy, then New York Knicks coach and now NBA TV game analyst, is quoted as saying, "He was so freakishly talented, driven, and hardworking that notwithstanding his behavior, the net contribution to the team still exceeded that of any basketball contemporary. You'd have to be that level of great to lead that way."

The documentary gives ample nods to Scotty Pippen, Dennis Rodman, Steve Kerr and coach Phil Jackson. Pippen injured his left ankle in 1997, but continued to play hurt, helping the Bulls win their fifth championship.

He was considered the best wing man of all time. Yet in the final year of a seven-year contract, he was the sixth highest paid player on the Bull's team and the 122nd highest paid player in the NBA. Given his contribution, Pippen deserved better, and the film shows his disappointment.

Dennis Rodman at first glance appears to be a nut job with multi-color hair. But he was a rebounding machine. And the perfect ball-getter for missed shots, which he'd pass the ball out or put it back in for two.

What Dennis brought to that team was the glue. He played his role as hard as anyone could possibly play it. Rodman could be a terror and distraction to opponents and teammates alike in his successful quest to becoming the rebound leader in the NBA for the Bulls in '95 and '96. It's an example how Rodman's eccentric personality often overshadowed his greatness as a player.

Bulls guard Steve Kerr provides a great interview for ESPN and Director Jason Hehr. Now head coach for the Golden State Warriors, Kerr was the ideal role player for Jordan, Pippen, Rodman, et al.

Steady as a rock, Kerr tells a tall tale in the documentary. He was asked about his recruitment coming out of high school. "Very little," he recalled. "About the same attention I was getting from girls."

Yet Steve is immortalized for his buzzer-beater in the 1997 NBA Finals vs Utah. With the score tied at 86, Jordan passed the ball to Kerr with scant seconds on the clock, enabling him to hit the game-winner for the championship. That was the same year Kerr won the All-Star Game 3-point contest.

We see not just the talent, but the teases and tantrums of the Bulls' star players. Also recognized is coach Phil Jackson's prodigious psychology and patience. Jackson never appears rattled by the crazy activity surrounding his team.

The University of North Dakota alum would be called by many the "Zen Master" after taking over from Doug Collins in 1989. Tex Winter, another coach and Xs and Os genius, worked with Jackson to develop the triangle offense in which three players kept the ball moving in a virtual triangle. Teamwork and controlled intensity. Phil Jackson's college majors were philosophy, psychology and religion.

Back To The Struggle

Let us return now from the athletic triumphs of yesteryear to the here-and-now issues of race and rage. Let us see if triangular teamwork and laser-focused intensity can achieve for our people the success earned by the Chicago Bulls of yore.

Like theirs, my professional achievements have been no solo act, but a triangular affair not unlike Phil Jackson's studied approach. I founded our UBM construction company with two excellent, honorable and mutually complimentary partners – Sandra Dixon Jiles (MBA) and Sham Dabadghao (Civil Engineer).

We started in 1974 and by 1984, when Michael Jordan came to the Bulls, we were well on our way to employing 100+ staff and becoming, in 2004, the largest Black-owned construction company in Illinois.

Key partners included the Near North Insurance Agency, which provided the various liability and performance guarantees that too often stymie fledgling minority-owned contractors.

But the most important psychological thing Near North CEO Mike "Mickey" Segal provided us was use of a skybox at the old Chicago Stadium for Bulls games just when Jordan and his team were beginning to make waves.

It was a nest for networking – the secret sauce of doing business in Chicago. Often, we could invite 16-18 guests to enjoy catered food and drink, not to mention a perfect view, down low over the Bull's bench.

Ten years later, when the new United Center opened in 1994, UBM had been involved in the new stadium's construction and we were able to lease our own skybox.

Keep this in mind when you hear the rants of haters opposed to affirmative action, to SBA(8a) set-asides and to MBE utilization requirements. These are the programs that helped UBM be successful enough to purchase a 20-seat skybox in the United Center.

Talk about timing: The Bulls had won three titles by '94 and were poised to win three more. All the while our UBM team entertained friends, clients, vendors, and many, many Black high school students. Many of the latter experienced, perhaps for the first time, a bright and shining future previously unimaginable. Skybox? They had been to the Mountaintop!

Let us prepare, right now, for the Championship Challenge, the presidential election. It is scheduled, date certain, for Tuesday, November 3, 2020. This election is more critical to Black people than any in recent memory.

And there are a few favorable newbies. One-third of the eligible voters will be non-white and one in 10 will be Generation Z, according to the Pew Report.

"Boogaloo Bois"

Support our protesters but resist the Boogaloo Bois and the destruction they brought to our neighborhoods. Continue to give counsel to the young people (Black Lives Matter, et al) in their negotiations. This is a serious moment.

We can't end racism and we won't change police completely, but if those of us who have created change and have a voice connect with the younger people causing this global outcry, we will make a difference and move the needle towards justice.

George Floyd's neck under the white policeman's knee has gone GLOBAL! Like the man challenged: "Hey Chicago, you want some of this?"

SPACE TRADERS AND CORONA
CHAOS CRUSADERS

Derrick Bell in 1992 published "Face at the Bottom of the Well: The Permanence of Racism". One short story embedded in Bell's opus is a prescient allegorical tale titled *The Space Traders*. I've met Bell. We are both members of Alpha Phi Alpha Fraternity.

The Space Traders came from another planet on an aircraft carrier-sized ship that landed on waters off the eastern part of the United States. At that time America had an economy in shambles, toxic waterways teeming with dead fish, and an energy-raped environment. The Space Traders walked on the water from their ship to meet the U.S. representatives.

The Americans were relieved that the foreigners we are not a threat, but the aliens did have specific proposals. The Traders were willing to provide gold, safe renewable energy, and special chemicals to restore the environment to pristine condition.

In return for these much-needed items, the Traders wanted all the Black people in the U.S. to come back with them. (That is, every American citizen categorized as Black on a birth certificate or other official identification.)

The ship landed on January 1 and the Traders gave America until January 15th – MLK's birthday – to accept or reject the offer. While the decision was being made, the US tested the equipment and assayed the gold. All expectations were exceeded.

One meeting held by the President to evaluate the proposition assembled the all-white cabinet along with a Black non-cabinet member named Gleeson Golightly. He was an acceptable conservative (Think Supreme Court Justice Clarence Thomas or the Samuel L. Jackson "Django" character – Stephen.)

America wanted the deal, but worried about the optics. So the Traders amended their offer to exclude all Black people 70 years and older and those who were seriously ill or injured. Additionally, 1,000 otherwise eligible Blacks and their immediate families would be left behind as trustees of Black property and possessions, all of which was to be stored or held in escrow in case the Blacks were returned to this country.

Bell's conclusion is intentionally omitted, but the willingness of White America to go on its merry way without Black America is central to the tale.

In many ways and in real time, we are now living through a similar situation in America. According to Black scholar and author Ta-Nehisi Coates, Trump's legacy will be to expose the patina of inter-racial decency for what it is, and more worrisome, to reveal just how much a demagogue can get away with.

Consider our situation. The U.S. Supreme Court, newly packed with ultra conservatives, appears poised to undo 50 years of civil rights reforms. The Attorney General is exonerating Trump's friends despite the fact that they pleaded guilty.

Black voter suppression schemes are being launched by Republicans in preparation for Trump's re-election. Farmers are killing hogs, turning over crops, and crushing eggs while urban food pantry lines stretch for blocks.

Ahmaud Arbery – the Black Georgia jogger – is killed and videoed by three white men. Minneapolis' George Floyd joins Eric Garner in the Black "I can't breathe" death club at the hands of white police.

A Reality Stanger Than Fiction

With a nod to Derrick Bell's *Space Traders*, I submit that we are now being invaded by what I'll call the Corona Chaos Crusaders. Whereas the Space Traders walked on water, the Crusaders are invisible yet lethal virus molecules riding on coughs, sneezes and touches.

As of this writing, over 60,000 Black people have been slain by the Corona killers. You do not have to be a conspiracy theorist to see our national leadership's passivity toward prevention and cavalier response to mass fatalities.

This absence of leadership ought not be attributed to inefficiency alone. It would be quite simplistic to say this is a viral attack only against Black people, going unattended. This would be a mistake because scores of white people are dying, many of whom have gone uncounted.

Consider just two hot spots – nursing homes and prisons. At least 28,100 residents and workers have died from the coronavirus at nursing homes and other long-term care facilities for older adults in the U.S.

The virus has infected more than 153,000 at 7,700 facilities, according to *The New York Times* data base. Older adults often have pre-existing conditions and can spread the virus more easily inside congregated facilities where many people live in a confined environment and workers move from room to room.

One-third of U.S. corona deaths are linked to long-term care facilities. In 14 states the number of residents and workers who have died account for more than half of all deaths from the virus. In Illinois, it's 410 facilities, 11,437 cases, 1,563 deaths.

The Corona Chaos Crusader continues its laser-like attack on Black people. Nursing homes with a significant number of Blacks and Hispanics have been twice as likely to be hit by the virus as those where the population is overwhelmingly white.

In the suburbs of Baltimore, workers at one nursing home said that they were given rain ponchos to protect from the infection. So far, 27 employees at this facility, where most residents are African Americans, have tested positive for the coronavirus.

Separate, Not Equal

COVID-19 has been particularly virulent toward African Americans. Nursing homes where these groups make up a significant portion of residents – no matter their location, no matter their size, no matter their government rating – have been twice as likely to get hit by the coronavirus as those whose population is overwhelmingly white.

More than 60 percent of nursing homes where at least a quarter of the residents are Black have reported at least one coronavirus case. That is double the rate of homes where Black people make up less than five percent of the population. In Illinois facilities where patients are at least 75 percent Black or Hispanic, there have been 75 cases. Where minorities are less than five percent, only 24 cases.

The nation's nursing homes, like many of its schools, churches and neighborhoods, are largely segregated. And those that serve predominately Black and Latino residents tend to receive lower grades on government ratings. Those facilities also tend to house more residents, and to be located in urban areas, which are risk factors in the pandemic.

Eric Russell, who moved his mother to a different nursing home in the Chicago area after she tested positive for the virus, said the prevalence of cases in homes with more Black residents is alarming and needs to be more widely understood and examined by the authorities. As reported by the Chicago Sun-Times, at The Villa at Windsor Park on Chicago's South Side, at least 121 residents and employees have been infected and 24 people have died.

Small nursing homes which are disproportionately occupied by white residents tend to have fewer outbreaks than larger facilities and urban nursing homes have more outbreaks than suburban or rural.

The *Times* found that a racial disparity remained even after accounting for a variety of factors, including the size of a nursing home, the infection rate in the surrounding county, the population density of the neighborhood, and how many residents had Medicaid or Medicare.

Large homes with few Black and Latino residents were less likely to have outbreaks than large ones with more Black and Latino residents. A home in an urban area was less likely to get hit by the virus if it had a small Black and Latino population.

Robin Grant of National Consumer Voice for Quality Long Term Care, worries that: "The sheer numbers are horrifying. The underlying factors that have contributed are no surprise. They've been issues of concern for a long time."

Not until mid-April did the Federal Center for Medicare and Medicaid Services announce a reporting system to track COVID-19 in nursing homes and funnel data to the Centers for Disease Control and Prevention.

Dr. Phillip Stone states," Nursing homes, cruise ships, and prisons all share large numbers of people in extremely small spaces, so it's hard to do isolation." Black people are in the minority on cruise ships!

It has become tragically obvious that changes are needed in nursing homes, which should:

1. Expand rapid testing and contact tracing;
2. Establish a full-time position for contagion prevention and resource management;
3. Change design of living spaces;
4. Increase worker compensation; and
5. Change visitor policies to have a relative or close friend undergo regular testing and learn the purpose for and use of PPE, or personal protective equipment.

This close look at nursing homes is not just another case of outsized victimization of Blacks by the Chaos Crusader. Scant attention has been paid to the Black nursing home workers who catch the virus inside the facility from the elderly and go untested. They go out into the larger Black community and unintentionally infect family, friends, and neighbors spreading the virus exponentially.

As for prisons, both guards and inmates are at risk. Guards at Rikers Island in New York sued for protection. Inside Chicago's Cook County Jail, detained men staged a protest strike over the lack of safety precautions and placed hand-made signs in their windows reading, "Help us! Don't let us die!"

The Damage Done

Everywhere, Black America is under siege. News reports tell us that 40 percent of Black businesses are shut, with many likely to disappear altogether. As of April, the country had lost nearly 450,000 African American business owners as the pandemic intensified, from beauty salons and barber shops to taxi services and day care centers. Indeed, the childcare industry has collapsed, with a devastating effect on working families.

Black businesses have been devastated by the coronavirus pandemic.

White Supremacy was at play in the founding of America, was reinforced during African slavery, and is alive and well today. The Corona Chaos Crusader has attacked Blacks in an outsized way. It's as if corona is a flood and Blacks live in the basement and lower floors. Whites reside on the upper floors and penthouse – out of harm's way. White supremacy created this paradigm.

What to do? A quick list:

1. Volunteer with organizations out to correct these challenges;
2. Organize over social media;
3. Stay informed on the issues;
4. Contribute financial support;
5. Participate in virtual and webinar meetings;
6. Support Stacey Abrams' fight against Black Voter Suppression.

Ta-Nehisi Coates nails it when he writes: "The most powerful country in the world has handed over all its affairs – the prosperity of its entire economy, the security of its 300 million citizens, the purity of its water, the viability of its air, the safety of its food, the future of its vast system of education, the soundness of its highways, airways and railways, the apocalyptic potential of its nuclear arsenal – to a carnival barker who introduced the phase 'grab 'em by the pussy."

It is as if the white tribe united in demonstration to say, "If a Black man can be president, then any white man – no matter how fallen – can be president."

Enough of this. Derrick Bell, please send us the Space Traders!

THE FIRST DUNCE AND
THE LAST DANCE

This was the American landscape that lay open to the coronavirus.

In prosperous cities, an affluent class of globally connected desk workers were blithely dependent on a class of precarious and invisible service workers. In the countryside, an aging class of marginally employed or displaced ex-workers were fearful of, and in revolt against, the modern world.

On social media, mutual hatred and endless vituperation raged between the opposing camps. In an economy that boasted full employment, a large and widening gap separated those connected to global capital and those who were not.

In Washington, a government all but shorn of professionals was led by a con man and his intellectually bankrupt political party. Everywhere there grew a mood of cynical exhaustion with no vision of a shared identity or future.

This is the pre-COVID-19 state of the nation as described perfectly by staff writer George Packer in the June 2020 issue of *The Atlantic* Magazine.

By now we're generally aware that among the con man's many screw ups was the way he botched preparation for and response to the coronavirus attack.

In April 2018, he proposed cutting the budgets of the Centers for Disease Control (CDC) and other public health agencies. He disbanded the White House National Security Council's Directorate for Health and Biodefense, an office set up by President Barack Obama after the 2014-2016 Ebola outbreak to coordinate future responses to epidemics.

So, one after another, there has occurred a litany of screwups and lost opportunities. Intelligence briefings dating to early January about the initial outbreak in Wuhan, China went unread and unheeded. Little or no early effort was made to develop and deploy a test for the virus, or to produce and distribute sufficient personal protective equipment (PPE) for health care workers. Same with mechanical breathing ventilators for the stricken.

Instead, the con man referred to the fast-spreading pandemic as "a hoax" promoted by his enemies to make him look bad. Later, he encouraged the public to consider drinking or infusing chlorine bleach for a good "cleanse."

More recently, he's been on a campaign to "liberate" states from various stay-at-home and business shutdown protocols set up by several governors, contrary to recommendations by the scholarly Dr. Anthony Fauci, director of the National Institute for Allergies and Infectious Diseases.

COVID And The Black Incarcerated

Far less attention is being paid, however, to the way COVID-19 is exposing certain other "underlying conditions" that long have festered in Black America. Consider the number of inmates and prisoners in federal, state, and county jails.

The mass incarceration of Black people has been chronicled well by writers such as Ta-Nehisi Coates in *The Atlantic* and in books. The non-profit

Prison Policy Initiative had warned us that "it is a matter of time before a prison or jail starts to suffer serious consequences of having a lot of people packed together, supervised by people that view them as a serious threat rather than a population to be cared for."

Then there is the big overlap between those jailed and those who are simply homeless. The City of New York had the nation's only 24/7 subway system. It recently cut service between 1 and 5 a.m. for purposes of cleaning and disinfecting. Many homeless slept on those trains during overnight hours. Now, as trespassers, many are being herded to jail or crowded shelters.

The threat of coronavirus extends to prisoners, visitors, security staff, and custodial workers in jails. Some prisons are banning visits. The Washington Association of Sheriffs and Police Chiefs, according to German Lopez of VOX, has issued these guidelines for their state:

1. Release prisoners on their recognizance.
2. Establish a list for downsizing (especially for the non-violent).
3. Release older prisoners.
4. Release those with health conditions that make them virus vulnerable.
5. Encourage inmates to notify medical staff if they have symptoms.

The Cook County powers-that-be needed to make similar concessions to the new reality. Block Club Chicago's website has reported that more than 500 people currently incarcerated at the Cook County Jail have been infected with coronavirus. Of them, 264 detainees are currently sick, including 10 who are being treated at local hospitals. Another 255 detainees have recovered. Seven detainees have died due to complications related to COVID-19.

What to do? For visitations, jails and prisons could host meetings in non-contact rooms or move visits to video or phone calls. Medical services need to be more accessible, beginning with the initial screening and testing of inmates and then the subsequent isolation of the infected.

Consideration must be given to the release of aged Black ex-offenders and/or temporary furloughs of non-violent Black inmates. Many would be returning to neighborhoods on the South and West Sides, but will they be tested before release to assure that they are not bringing the virus home to friends and family? If they are released to a half-way house, what testing and medical coordination will take place?

It's easy to imagine that, just as the pandemic curve is flattening, returning ex-offenders will unintentionally re-introduce the coronavirus back into the Black neighborhoods. This is not a NIMBY (Not In My Backyard) shout. This is a heads-up to Black communities. We must insist that any early release of Blacks from prison and jails must be accompanied by testing, quarantine of the sick and virus-free housing. These necessities are loaded with caveats, to be sure.

Ta-Nehisi Coates reports that 600,000 inmates are released from America's prisons each year. He writes: "Just as ex-offenders had to learn to acculturate themselves in prison, they have to learn to re-acculturate themselves to the outside. But the attitude that helps one in prison is almost the opposite of the kind needed to make it on the outside."

Craig Haney, a professor at University of California at Santa Cruz who studies the cognitive and psychological effects or incarceration, has observed: "A tough veneer that precludes seeking help for personal problems, the generalized mistrust that comes from the fear of exploitation, and a tendency to strike out in response to minimal provocations are highly functional in many prison contexts, but problematic virtually everywhere else." If Haney is right, can you imagine an inmate going to a security guard and reporting coronavirus symptoms?

Advice On The Big Picture

Two organizations well-positioned to advise decision-makers are the Massachusetts-based Prison Policy Initiative (*prisonpolicy.org*) and Chicago's own Health & Medicine Policy Research Group.

Among Prison Policy Initiative's victories was its *Mass Incarceration: The Whole Pie*, an effort at "uncovering the big picture on mass incarceration." The report assembles data on everyone who is incarcerated or confined in different kinds of prisons, jails and other correctional and detention facilities in the United States. Their main graphic has become a widely used visual in the field.

The Health & Medicine Policy Research Group (*hmprg.org*) was founded by the iconic Dr. Quentin Young and is now headed by Margie Schaps and Dr. Claudia Fegan. It has issued a must-read, followed and supported report, *Health & Medicine's Vision and Priorities During the COVID-19 Crisis: Now More Important Than Ever.*

Among H&M's pioneering efforts is advancing the Chicago HEAL Initiative (Hospital Engagement, Action and Leadership); enhancing hospitals' role in violence prevention through workforce development; creating opportunities in the neighborhoods these hospitals serve; and healing trauma.

Keep in mind that our oversized representation among the incarcerated is hardly the only issue facing Black America during the COVID-19 crisis.

The National Newspaper Publishers Association's (NNPA) President Dr. Benjamin Chavis Jr. has issued this solemn national public warning and alert to nearly 50 million African Americans: "Black America is now in a state of emergency as a result of the disproportionately deadly impact of the coronavirus pandemic on our families and communities across the United States."

New York Times columnist Thomas Friedman adds: "At a time when we need high social trust in order to have a coordinated response at home, Trump's political strategy of dividing us and playing everything both ways – even telling people to rise up against their governors and to lock down according to his guidelines – is the opposite of the 'all in this together' approach we need to win this battle."

Pretty grim, right? Well, let me end this essay with a brightener.

Perhaps like you I've been mired lately in gloom-and-doom virus-speak. Then along comes an unusually happy Magical Media Moment! ESPN Films has hooked up with Netflix to produce *The Last Dance*, composed of five two-hour segments on Michael Jordan and the Chicago Bulls.

It is splendid! It documents the 1991-1998 quest of the Bulls' two "three-peats". My company had a skybox then at the United Center, so I know of a few things that were left out to protect the innocent! I'll report on that later, hopefully after The Dunce is gone … and we're all again able to Dance.

STAY SAFE, STAY HOME...
BUT STAY FOCUSED

Given the changes to our daily lives – churches closed, services on-line, working remotely – it's hard not to use an expletive when thinking about the current White House occupant. He could have prevented much of this by paying attention to contingency plans prepared by his predecessor and to warnings by his own scientific staff.

But he didn't, so we suffer. It is becoming apparent, however, that some of "we" are suffering more than others. Some recent examples:

- The Office of Federal Contract Compliance has issued a blanket exemption that waives all affirmative action obligations on supply, service, and construction contracts involved with coronavirus relief. This will have a damaging effect on Black businesses and Black jobs that could have flowed from the $2 trillion stimulus program recently enacted by Congress.
- The EPA has rolled back Obama-era vehicle emission standards, thereby raising limits on exhaust emissions for years to come and gutting one of the nation's biggest efforts against climate change.
- The Department of Agriculture is imposing draconian changes to the Food Stamp program that require greater evidence of a recipient's employment search in order to continue in this lifesaving program.

These attacks, falling largely on African Americans, are deserving of far greater attention and analysis. But they won't get it, because just now the coronavirus pandemic is posing the ultimate threat: a deadly offer that Black Americans cannot refuse…or ignore.

African Americans And Coronavirus

Ibram Kendi, writing for *The Atlantic*, asks why we don't know who those stricken by the coronavirus actually are. There is little publicly available data about the racial makeup of those Americans who have been tested, those who have tested positively, those who have been hospitalized, those who have recovered, or those who have died.

This information is hiding in plain sight, but the Centers for Disease Control and Prevention, the Johns Hopkins University data base, even *The New York Times*, along with state, city and private labs, are not releasing a racial breakdown.

One of the exceptions is the Illinois Department of Public Health, which found a pandemic within the pandemic. African Americans are significantly overrepresented in the infection rate for Illinois, while whites and Latinos are substantially underrepresented as of April 8.

Black people make up 14.6 percent of the state's population, yet 28 percent of confirmed cases of COVID-19. Whites comprise 76.9 percent of the Illinois population, yet only 39 percent of confirmed cases. Latinos' 17.4 percent, but just seven percent of cases.

To withhold this racial information is crazy. You can't win the battle if you don't know where to apply your resources. If the virus is disproportionately infecting and killing Black people, then what we have here is yet another manifestation of another, more familiar, pandemic – the age-old plague of racism.

Yet there appears to be little interest in this possibility among whites in media or in politics. Some may fear that if racial data on COVID-19 shows the virus is mainly harming Black people, white people would stop caring. Possible. Yet whichever race is the most infected, the entire population is surely affected.

By percentage, more Black people are dying from COVID-19 than any other group.

As of this writing more than 4,000 coronavirus patients have died during outbreaks in Chicago, Detroit, Milwaukee, New Orleans and New York. Guess where Blacks tend to live?

Kendi concludes: "Without racial data we could end up stranded in Trump's America years after the worst pandemic in American history, flooded out of truth, justice and fairness; homeless like the Black Mississippians in the 1927 river upheaval."

Peter Wehner nails it in *The Atlantic* article "The President is Trapped." Referring to the Covid19 pandemic, Wehner writes, "A former White House adviser who has worked on past pandemics told me, 'This fool will bring the death of thousands needlessly. We have mobilized as a country to shut things down for a time, despite the difficulty. We can work our way back to a semblance of normality if we hold out and let the health system make it through the worst of it.'

"He added, 'But now our own president is undoing all that work and preaching recklessness. Rather than lead us in taking on a difficult challenge, he is dragging us toward failure and suffering. Beyond belief.'"

There's something distinct about this moment compared to every other moment in the Trump presidency, that proves to be utterly disorienting and unsettling for the president. Hush money payments won't make

COVID-19 go away. He cannot DISTRACT people from the global pandemic. He can't because the next news cycle will also be about the pandemic. He can't easily create another narrative, because he is often sharing the stage with scientists who will not lie on his behalf.

An "Urban" Problem

As of March 27, the Wisconsin Department of Health Services reported that about half of the state's COVID-19 deaths and half its total cases were in Milwaukee, a city of 600,000 residents that is more than 1/3 Black. As of then, all eight people who died from the virus in Milwaukee County were Black and seven lived in the city.

ProPublica's Akilah Johnson and Talia Buford reported on April 3 under the headline: "Early Data Shows African Americans Have Contracted and Died of Coronavirus at an Alarming Rate."

Their reporting shows that the virus took root in Milwaukee's Black community and erupted. When the shelter in place order came, there was natural pushback among those who recalled other painful government restrictions like segregation, mass incarceration, or when Black people were discouraged from gathering or walking together.

In Milwaukee, simply being Black means your life expectancy is 14 years shorter on average than whites. As of this writing, African Americans made up almost half of Milwaukee County's 945 cases and 81 percent of its 27 deaths, even though the population is only 26 percent Black.

The state of Michigan is 14 percent Black, yet African Americans have made up 35 percent of the cases and 40 percent of the deaths. Detroit, which is majority Black, has emerged as a hot spot with a high virus death toll. Likewise, New Orleans has 40 percent of Louisiana deaths and Orleans Parish is, of course, majority Black.

The Bigger Picture

Yet, the federal Centers for Disease Control, while releasing location and age data, has been silent on race. So, why is it likely that a disproportionate number of those who will die are Black?

The reasons are the same reasons that African Americans have disproportionately high rates of maternal deaths, low levels of access to medical care, and higher rates of asthma. COVID-19 is just illustrating anew the deep disinvestment in our communities, plus the historical injustice and impact of residential segregation.

"This is the time to name racism as the cause of all of these things. The overrepresentation of Black people in poverty and white people in wealth is not just a happenstance…it is because we're not valued," Dr. Camara Jones, an epidemiologist and visiting fellow at Harvard University, told *ProPublica*.

"We declared racism as a public health issue," said Dr. Jeanette Kowalik, the city's African American health commissioner. "It frames not only how we do our work, but how transparent we are about how things are going. It impacts how we manage an outbreak."

ProPublica reported that in early March, Wisconsin officials were aware of just one case. State officials considered it low. A month later, 19 people had died of illness related to COVID-19 in Milwaukee County. All but four were Black. Records show that at least 11 of the deceased, 8 had hypertension and 15 had a mixture of chronic health conditions that included heart and lung disease.

Black people in Milwaukee are less likely than whites to own homes, therefore putting Blacks who can't pay rent at the mercy of landlords who can evict them during a job-killing economic crisis. Black people are more likely to be uninsured than their white counterparts.

In places like New York City, the virus' epicenter, Black people are among the only ones still riding the subway. Gordon Francis Goodwin says, "This is a matter of taking a look at how our history kept people from being fully included."

Fred Royal, NAACP leader, is hearing that people aren't necessarily being hospitalized, but are being sent home to "self-medicate." What is alarming about that is a number of those individuals were sent home with symptoms and died before the confirmation of tests came back.

A day later, the city's second case was someone who contracted the virus while in Atlanta. Within a span of a week, Milwaukee went from having one case to nearly 40. Most of the sick people were middle-aged African American men.

In another week, the city had over 350 cases and by April 3, there were 945 cases countywide. The bulk live in the city of Milwaukee where the population is 39 percent Black. People of all ages have contacted the virus and one half appears to be African Americans.

"What Black folks are accustomed to in Milwaukee, and anywhere in the country, really, is pain not being acknowledged and constant inequities that happen in health care delivery," added Dr. Kowalik.

She was born in the same neighborhood where fury and frustration sparked protests and riots in 2016 when police shot a 23-year-old Black man, Sylville Smith. It's the same neighborhood that has oversized rates of lead poisoning, infant mortality, and now COVID-19.

Despite the work being done in Milwaukee, Linda Sprague Martinez, a community health researcher at Boston University, worried to *ProPublica* that "government is not paying close enough attention to race and as the disease spreads, will do too little too late."

When the COVID19 passes and we settle losses, she said, "its impact is going to be tied to our history and legacy of racial inequities. It's going to be tied to the fact that we live in two very different worlds."

This take from Trump on the virus is very, very wrong.

Lessons To Be Learned

So we've considered the current state of U.S. leadership, so critical during an attack on our economy and our very lives. Our national CEO is like a drunk driver on a Saturday night demanding to drive himself home from the Loop.

Adamant that he can do it, he declines a cab, or a ride with us, or our offer to pay for the parking and pick up the car tomorrow. In this case, the only option is to take away the car keys or call the police to escort the guy home. If you are a Black person and don't know the police, the latter is not an option, however.

We've considered the high incidence of Black illness and death due to the coronavirus. It's noted that the virus makes those with pre-existing health issues most vulnerable. A further examination points out how Milwaukee has an outsized number of Blacks with COVID-19, while little is public on this in other states and cities.

The elephant in the room is that the CDC does not provide race/ethnic information on cases, conditions, causes and conclusions. We know that African Americans ae vulnerable, but don't know who and where they are.

Senator Elizabeth Warren and Representative Ayanna Pressley have sent a letter to Health and Human Services (HHS) Secretary Alex Azar calling out an apparent lack of information of racial data. Further, they urged HHS to monitor and address disparities in the national response to the coronavirus outbreak. Senator Kamala Harris, Illinois Representative Robin Kelly, and Senator Cory Booker have signed the letter in support.

As action items, we need to provide information to Rep. Robin Kelly and others in D.C. in support of educational, community health and medical professionals working to combat the silence on racial identification. We need to separate fact from fiction, to distinguish between medical remedy and racial harm in reaction to this latest attack on African Americans.

"We are all in this together," the slogan goes, but as usual, some of us are a lot more "in" than others. So, stay home…but stay focused.

BIDEN, BLACKS AND CORONA

Joe Biden was saved by Black voters in South Carolina.

Black voters resuscitated Joe Biden's campaign for the presidency. Is it not, then, high time to consider some quid pro quo?

That Blacks rescued Biden's sinking ship is indisputable. Exit polls show Biden got close to 69 percent of the African American vote in his big turnaround event – the South Carolina primary.

His Iowa caucuses and Nevada primary disappointments fast forgotten, Biden parlayed a resounding victory in S.C. into a Super Tuesday near sweep, racking up 70 percent of the Black vote in Virginia and Alabama and margins close to that in Texas, North Carolina, and Tennessee.

It's often argued, with justification, that Democrats take the Black vote for granted. But after a rescue mission like this, and with the Black vote looming central to Democratic chances come November, you don't need to be a Latin major to start thinking this-for-that.

How, and by what means, can the now-probable Democratic nominee repay Black voters for our overwhelming support? This exercise is not as simple as drafting a wish list. America's political, cultural and suddenly – biological – situation is shifting like few other times in our nation's history.

Polar Chill

Take the matter of polarization. Ezra Klein, an editor of the newsy website Vox, explains the ever-widening gap between the left and the right in his book "Why We're Polarized".

He cites many examples, but one especially resonates: "It has been found, for instance, that priming white college students to think about the concept of 'white privilege' leads many to express more racial resentment, not less, in subsequent surveys. Turns out the simplest way to activate someone directly is to threaten him or her, to tell them they don't deserve what they have, to make them consider that it might be taken away. The experience of losing status and being told your loss of status is part of society's march toward justice is in and of itself radicalizing."

When you're accustomed to privilege, Klein argues, equality feels like oppression. There's truth to this lens, but it cuts both ways. To the extent that it's true – that the loss of privilege feels like oppression – then that feeling needs to be taken into account if one's goal is to muster political support. If left to fester, this resentment can be weaponized by demagogues and reactionaries.

This is a problem for Democratic office seekers who need to promote diversity while achieving an electoral majority. Post-election, moreover, the pluralistic work of governing requires that the needs and concerns of many different groups be balanced against one another.

Klein points out that voters are more motivated by their antipathy for the other party than by affinity for their own. It has become a kind of self-reinforcing loop in which the public becomes even more polarized as the candidates, special interests, and even some media stoke the antipathy… further polarizing the public, and so on and so on.

Scholar Lilliana Mason posits in "Uncivil Agreement: How Politics Became Our Identity" that "the crisis emerges when partisan identities fall into alignment with other social identities, stoking our intolerance of each other to levels that are unsupported by our degree of political disagreement."

The problems of resentment and antipathy compound when we add demography. Race becomes more of an issue when many white voters look around and see more brown Hispanics mowing their lawns or more Blacks on TV.

Identity steps up as an issue when society's racial composition changes. Recall the white college students' resentment when tasked to think about white privilege.

Donald Trump exploited this polarization masterfully to become president. The Hillary Clinton campaign didn't help by spending insufficient time and money in Michigan, Wisconsin, and Pennsylvania, where blue-collar whites helped deliver those key electoral prizes by a miniscule 100,000 votes combined.

Trump's rise benefitted from a perfect storm of larger economic, social and demographic change and the profoundly disruptive effects of globalization and technology. Historian Richard Hofstadter once described the "paranoid style" of American politics. "The right feels dispossessed, that America has been largely taken away from them and their kind, though they are determined to try and repossess it."

More recently, historian Joe Meacham states, "Extreme racism, nativism and isolationism tend to spike in periods of economic and social stress, periods like our own, when change of every sort is blowing across the globe."

Retreat From Reality

Then there's the plight of the young millennials without advanced educations or the ability to code software in the new, digital workplace. Many realized that they were looking at jobs in the gig economy, driving for Uber or delivering carry-out for Grub Hub, perhaps buried under years of tuition debt. Workers in the manufacturing sector found themselves downsized or out of work.

Meantime, too many kids became addicted to videos games, binge-watching "streamed" entertainments and other escapes from lived reality. Escape into compelling fictional worlds is one way many are coping with political outrage and fatigue.

Trump appeals to a different type of nostalgia – to an era when white men were in charge and women, African Americans, Hispanics and immigrants, knew their place. Many Trump supporters inhabit the echo chambers of right-wing media.

No surprise then that the president's hard core of supporters stubbornly respect the lies and conspiracy theories that cycle through his Twitter feed, or believe the rants of Russian trolls on Facebook, or white nationalists and random crackpots on Breitbart.

Michiko Kakutani is spot-on with her book "The Death of Truth", a catalogue of the lies and half- truths that have dominated the Trump administration from the get-go. She writes:

"This is why Republicans and Democrats; conservatives and liberals increasingly have trouble even agreeing on shared facts or (even) developing that which has contributed to trust between different groups.

"Rather, what resulted was a fueled incivility and sped up nichification of culture that began years ago with the advent of cable TV and the Internet. Facebook, Twitter, and Instagram- ("influencers") replaced experts, scientists and scholars. Memes and misinformation started to displace facts and in an era of data overload and short attention spans, it's not the most reliable trustworthy material that goes viral, it's the loudest voices, the angriest and most outrageous posts that get clicked and shared."

"When politicians constantly lie, overwhelming and exhausting us while insinuating that everyone is dishonest and corrupt, the danger is that we grow so weary and cynical that we withdraw from civic engagement and that's bad.

"Truth is a cornerstone of our democracy. We cannot control whether our public servants lie to us. But we can control and hold them accountable for these lies or whether in a state of exhaustion or to protect our own political objectives, we look the other way and normalize our indifference to the truth."

Joe Biden, should he win the 2020 presidential election, will have huge number of fixes to make on the screw-ups made by his predecessor, Donald Trump. Chief among them will be restoring foreign relations and internal civility.

Staring him in the face, demanding immediate attention, will be:

- Response to, and a plan for, defeating the COVID-19. pandemic, which Trump mishandled from the beginning.
- Economic recovery from COVID-19.
- Rescue of the Justice Department and the restoration of confidence in the FBI.
- Re-establishing TRUTH as the Presidential messaging imperative.

- Appointment of Cabinet secretaries who will advance rather than destroy agency goals.
- Repairing global partner relationships torn asunder by Trump.
- Establishing a national reconciliation plan based on leading by example.

These are his general imperatives. What about his quid pro quo? What about the actions he will owe Black America after our rescue of his sinking primary election ship?

The Pro Quo

Here's my partial list of Black Citizens Goals. Biden will have to "walk and chew gum at the same time":

- Appoint a Secretary of Labor who will be mandated to establish a construction, technology and service training program for Black men who are parole-eligible or recently released from the mass incarceration of recent years.
- Select a Secretary of Education who will increase the reading level of Black elementary school children so that they can enter high school with chances for advancement.
- Create a national charter school initiative that will mirror Chicago's Urban Prep (full disclosure: My son Tim King is founding CEO) in efforts to prepare Black young men for college.
- Appoint an Administrator of the Small Business Administration to aggressively direct loans, grants and technical assistance programs to stimulate the growth and development of Black businesses.
- Select a Secretary of Housing and Urban Development who will combat the disinvestment and abandonment on the South and West Sides of Chicago and other urban areas. This can be a Demonstration Plan for major cities.

These are not the only ways a President Biden must begin to repair the neglect foisted upon Black America, but it's a start. Remember Ray Benson's lyric: *"You got to dance with who brung you. Swing with who swung you"*

Remember, also, South Carolina.

MOURNING MINDFUL
MEDIA DURING 'OF COLOR'
HISTORY MONTH

An Irish classmate of mine at De LaSalle High School once told me that his dad read the newspaper from back-to-front. The old man flipped from the sports section to the obituaries to the political headlines, ever alert to any items related to his family or to their jobs.

Reliable local journalism: This is – or regrettably was – an essential nutrient for both our family and the neighborhood grapevines.

It's all well and good to know about the latest blowup in the Middle East or how the big presidential impeachment vote went down. But when the mayor has a falling-out with your ward committeeman, or when CPS withdraws charter school funding from next year's budget, well, that's a 4-11 alarm bell.

But like there are "food deserts" on the South and West sides, where when a grocery chain closes, aldermen go in search of a replacement to avoid Blacks having to catch the bus for a loaf of bread, we find ourselves often in a "media wilderness", where the trio of relevant writing, proofreading and fact checking by an editor, and a publisher on hand to insure civic benefit, is absent.

So although I'm not always in agreement with *The Chicago Tribune*'s editorial page – or its approach to covering the African-American community – I shudder to think what's ahead now that a cost-cutting

New York hedge fund has purchased a big stake in the holding company that controls our city's oldest and largest newspaper.

An Urgent Threat

Elsewhere, these cost-cutters have slashed local news gathering in favor of less expensive wire service reports from D.C., Paris or Beijing. Why pay skilled reporters and editors to dig into thorny issues at City Hall, or review an opening at the Lyric, never mind cover prep sports, when pages can be filled more economically with wire stories about Congress, about diet dinner recipes, and gossip about the Oscars?

In a recent and gutsy op-ed published in *The New York Times*, *Tribune* investigative reporters David Jackson and Gary Marx warned that their newspaper "faces an urgent threat." That is, if Alden Global Capital does in Chicago what it has already done to newsrooms in Denver and other cities where it has pounced.

"Alden has imposed draconian staff cuts that decimated *The Denver Post* and other once-proud newspapers that have been vital to their communities and to American democracy," wrote Jackson and Marx in their Op-Ed. "Those newsrooms, which put a spotlight on local political corruption, have served as forums for community voices and have driven the coverage of regional television, radio and online outlets."

Granted, this situation is not new amongst newspapers and other print media nationwide. A capital-intensive business model that begins with chopping down Canadian trees and ends with door-to-door physical delivery is no match for the Internet, where entry costs are minimal and virtually anyone can play at being a reporter/editor/publisher.

So now we have a Web-based media jungle that has bombarded us with disinformation, misinformation, and outright lies, not to mention politicians - no names, please- who thrive in just such an environment.

It's a situation that has driven many, including this writer, to turn increasingly to *The New York Times, The Washington Post* and *The New Yorker* Magazine-publications that adhere to time-honored standards of truth and tell-both-sides fairness.

Not that I don't still have bones to pick with our "legacy" print media. But if publications like *The Chicago Tribune* are to somehow rebound, they'll need to do a better job speaking to the informational needs and habits of Blacks, a logical urban constituency. But, I'd argue that our print journalism has rapidly lost ground in its coverage of and about Black people, and issues that are of concern to us.

Insulting "Of Color" Usage

One issue that has beleaguered and baffled me is the media's frequent use of the term "of color" when referring to Blacks, or "African-American" when referring to Black people.

Consider our journey from negro (small n) to Negro, thence to "colored", thence to Black in the 1960/'70s when "Black is Beautiful" rang true. This regression to "of color" – an expression reminiscent of "colored" – strikes me as offensive, maybe even intentionally so.

A recent *New York Times* page 2 article headlined "Political Parties and the Black Vote" used the term "of color" over 12 times in referring to Blacks. Try to imagine routinely referring to whites as people "not of color"!

Even Casey Cep, writing in *The New Yorker* about the struggle to identify and preserve landmarks of Black history and culture, succumbs to the "of color" slur. Ms. Cep follows the work of Brent Leggs, director of the African American Cultural Heritage Action Fund, which is part of the National Trust for Historic Preservation.

Preservationist Leggs is working with activists, archeologists, and historians to preserve and promote the Fort Monroe site in Hampton Beach, Virginia. This is an army base on the spot where African slaves first arrived in America in 1619. Later it became known as Freedom Fortress, after 500,000 slaves emancipated themselves during the Civil War.

Another Leggs project is The Hill, an historically Black neighborhood in the town of Eaton on Maryland's Eastern shore. Since its founding in the '60s, the NHPA has identified nearly two million locations worthy of preservation and has engaged millions of Americans in the work.

It has helped to generate an estimated two million jobs and more than a hundred billion dollars in private investment. However, racial bias written into the selection criteria means the lion's share of these benefits has gone to mostly white (people "not of color"?) Americans.

Modest buildings like slave cabins and tenement houses were long excluded from consideration. Meanwhile, historically Black neighborhoods were actively erased, often intentionally, by insurance-motivated arson, or in later decades by highway construction, gentrification and urban renewal. Connecting the dots between burning down slave cabins to Negro Removal (urban renewal), Cep has done a major civic informational service.

But she disappoints when she writes the following: "While state and federal institutions were largely neglecting these areas, communities of color began protecting them on their own." How can a writer who knows better, writing about slave cabins and Black neighborhood destruction, start talking about communities "of color"?

The late, great playwright August Wilson said it best in his seminal book "The Ground on Which I Stand".

"We are not ashamed and do not need you to be ashamed for us. Nor do we need the recognition of our Blackness to be couched in abstract phrases like 'artists of color'. Who are you talking about? A Japanese artist? An Eskimo? A Filipino? A Mexican? A Cambodian? A Nigerian? An African American?

"Are we to suppose that if you put a white person on one side of the scale and the rest of humanity lumped together as nondescript "people of color" on the other side, that it would balance out? That whites carry that much spiritual weight? We reject that. We are unique and we are specific."

Finding Solace And Joy

The "of color" horse may be too far out the barn now, but we can lock the door more securely. Media-wise, we find ourselves between two boulders and a hard place. One boulder being social media – Facebook, Instagram, etc. – whose output does not have the journalistic cred to insure that what the reader gets is not garbage.

The other fast-moving boulder is the rapidly declining print newspaper. The hard place is the advertising- and subscription-supported *New York Times* et. al., who may mean well, but continue to sling the degrading "of color" term…among other slights.

Still, it is imperative that we support and appreciate a well-written piece of literature – be it a print newspaper explainer, an online magazine article, or a book – and perhaps more importantly, that we transfer our delight in these things to a next generation too easily dazzled by the snap, crackle and pop of Internet ephemera and outright lies.

For those who have learned to be critical but not cynical about the written word, I say, come on in, the water's fine.

And then, once you hit a vein of literary gold, relay your findings to, say, a Hermene Hartman of *N'DIGO* publications or a Melody Spann-Cooper of WVON radio. They might host a forum among radio disc jockeys, writers, TV hosts, students and seniors to discuss the use of terms like "of color."

Is this an improvement from where we've come from, when we were commonly and openly called the N-word? Moreover, how can we let our dissatisfaction be known about the shallowness of today's print media and the unfiltered disinformation flooding our cell phones?

Where do we go for relief from our technology addiction and somehow find solace and joy in the written word and subsequent conversation it invokes?

Black people need to stay woke, sure, but we won't remain there unless we come up with our own latter-day version of those reliable but vanishing newspapers, the ones best read back-to-front.

THE FIRST AND THE WORST ON THE HIGH COURT

The current theatre of the absurd, with its cast of characters ranging from an unfit President of the United States to his cadre of clownish enablers, distracts us from the truly seismic shifts taking place in America.

Among these shifts are political tribalization, technological upheaval, calamitous climate change, unprecedented demographic shifts, and the persistent and pernicious racism visited upon Blacks.

Long after the current White House occupant is gone, this nation's federal courts will be making decisions and rendering judgements that will make or break the hopes and aspirations of our current and future generations. And no institution will have more impact than the Supreme Court of the United States (SCOTUS.)

I'm writing here about two Black Supreme Court Justices, both of whom I've met and spoken to – one with admiration, the other with bafflement.

Thurgood Marshall

The first, Thurgood Marshall, brought with him when he joined the High Court in 1967, both the practical experience and sympathetic wisdom gained after founding the NAACP Legal Defense and Education Fund.

Author Wil Haygood, in his book "Showdown: Thurgood Marshall and the Supreme Court Nomination That Changed America" (2015), gives an excellent account of how President Lyndon Baines Johnson worked to get the first African American Supreme Court Justice confirmed by the Senate.

Marshall was a member of my fraternity, Alpha Phi Alpha. As an undergraduate, I had the opportunity to meet with him and with Congressman Adam Clayton Powell.

When I blurted out what my University of Chicago education was going to do for me, etc. etc., Powell said, "Don't tell me how many degrees and diplomas you'll get; tell me how many pickets you have carried in the heat of the day."

If memory serves, Marshall joined in the knock-out with: "Damn right. We have to use our education and privilege to the benefit of other Black people."

Thurgood Marshall made good on this attitude in the Court's 1978 *Bakke* case, wherein a white plaintiff challenged the University of California's consideration of race in admissions to its medical school. It angered Justice Marshall when federal court rulings overturned remedies such as affirmative action.

"Face the fact that there are groups in every community which are daily paying the cost of the history of American injustice," Haygood quotes Marshall from a 1986 speech. "The argument against affirmative action is…an argument in favor of leaving that cost to lie where it falls."

Later, in the 1989 *J.A. Croson* decision, the High Court ruled against Richmond, Virginia's 30 percent minority business requirement, claiming it did not meet the "strict scrutiny" required by the court on racial matters. Marshall gave a vigorous, cogent dissent.

Clarence Thomas

Upon his death in 1991, Marshall's seat was filled by Clarence Thomas. No matter how he faltered in his Senate confirmation hearings, I had a hopeful notion that a Black man would adjust when he assumed the position of Justice on the Supreme Court and become a champion for Black people, as was his predecessor.

How wrong I was! My wife Loann said he would never change. Congressman Parren Mitchell even stated, "The man is evil."

Now comes author Corey Robin with a new book titled "The Enigma of Clarence Thomas", which allows us to learn more about this curious, quiet, often silent Justice and how he became that way.

The depth of Robin's investigative research is admirable and includes copious notes for those who want to figure out more about this puzzling Thurgood Marshall substitute.

Reviewing this book in *The New York Times*, Harvard Professor Orlando Patterson writes, "One of the most puzzling and disturbing aspects of popular extremism and racist revanchism is the fact that a Black man – Clarence Thomas, President Trump's favorite Supreme Court Justice … whose rise from the depths of Jim Crow to one of the highest and most powerful positions in the nation – (could) so relentlessly turn against the Civil Rights Movement and liberal state that made his ascent possible.

"How could a cruelly mocked victim of racism and intra-racial color prejudice come to hold all victims in contempt? Why would someone from the impoverished inner city become the leading defender of the carceral state and American plutocracy?

"How could a Black man who claims to loathe the memory of Jim Crow assail all integration policy and defend states' rights and racially targeted gerrymandering, all while living happily with a white wife?"

These are among the very questions I had expected Robin to answer, but he did state that he was writing about a mysterious, puzzling, hard-to-figure-out person.

A Personal Encounter

I once met Justice Thomas in Chicago. After his remarks to the Union League Club, there was a Q-and-A session. I asked, loudly, how can you, a beneficiary of Yale University's affirmative action admissions program, now rule against affirmative action?

Thomas asked if we could speak afterwards, which we did. He told me that he felt affirmative action demeaned Black people. I said, I'm co-founder of a construction business that benefits from affirmative action and am able to hire Black sub-contractors and Black employees. He said, "That's different." At that point, I saw the uselessness in continuing any conversation.

Yet, perhaps stranger still, as a college student Thomas was a proponent of Malcolm X and considered himself a Black Nationalist.

To that, Robin reports: "Black nationalism is selective. Still, many elements of the program he embraced in the 1960s and '70s – the celebration of Black self-sufficiency, the scathing attack on integration, the support of racial separatism and Black institutions, the emphasis on Black manhood as the pathway to Black freedom, the reverence for Black self-defense – remain vital parts of his jurisprudence today."

To my eyes, these virtues must be hiding in plain sight. I don't see it in his rulings on the High Court. In the 1995, *Adarand Constructors v. Pena case*,

Thomas voted with the majority in claiming that this case did not meet the strict scrutiny requirement. The loser here was a minority construction contractor.

The most damaging case in which Thomas supported the Court's conservative majority was 2013's *Shelby County v. Holder*. This decision fractured the 1965 Voting Rights Act that addressed racial discrimination in voting in certain parts of the country.

Five years after the *Shelby County* ruling, nearly 1,000 polling places had been closed throughout the United States, practically all in African American counties.

Thomas Unchained

Author Robin's scholarly research did not answer Professor Patterson's questions about Clarence Thomas...or mine. Sharing my bafflement with a trusted friend, he referred me to Quentin Tarantino's movie *Django Unchained*.

He likened Clarence Thomas to the character in the movie played by Samuel L. Jackson called Stephen. He was what was known as a "House Negro."

Two years before the Civil War, Django, a slave, finds himself on a mission to capture vicious outlaws. After they accomplish this, his white master, a Mr. Shultz, frees Django. Their travels then take them to a plantation where Django's long-lost wife is still a slave.

World Press Review called Samuel L. Jackson's interpretation of Stephen the greatest character of all time. This Uncle Tom is a Black man who will do anything to stay in good standing with the white man, including betraying his own people.

Stephen is a slave on a large plantation in Chickasaw County, Mississippi. The plantation owner leaves operations to Stephen, who pays the bills, calls the shots, and orders the punishment for runaway slaves.

Jackson plays Stephen as a three-faced card: forceful with his underlings; deferential when he's with his white visitors; a knowledgeable confidant with his white boss.

Stephen is a slave-driving race traitor to some. The first time he sees Django ride up to the door, he becomes rankled as to who this Black man is, riding a horse instead of walking.

The sight of an empowered Black freeman is offensive to his sense of order and position on the plantation. Stephen makes it his business to injure Django, in the interest of protecting his perceived power amongst the slaves.

It gives me no joy and injures my pride to liken the sole Black U.S. Supreme Court Justice to a fictional character who would sell out another Black person in exchange for some perceived favorable position.

The real danger in this parallel is that the Supreme Court will be ruling long after the current White House madness is over.

Justice Thomas will remain as a senior justice and will have tremendous influence, especially given the young age and rightist ideology of recent appointees.

So, What's To Be Done?

For starters, all truth-seeking students, scholars, activists, business organizations, fraternities and sororities need to read the books referenced above and discuss action plans, the most urgent of which is to get out the Black vote in the coming elections.

Recall that only 100,000 votes – **combined**! – across Wisconsin, Pennsylvania, and Michigan delivered the 2016 election to Donald Trump.

Voters in safely "blue" states like Illinois, meanwhile, need to organize bus trips next autumn to Milwaukee, Detroit, Pittsburgh, and wherever local African Americans need help tipping the scales toward ending this near-second Civil War mentality and anti-Black hostility.

Conference calls, webinars and all forms of social media need to be used to fight Black voter suppression and get out the vote.

Our people need to be educated on the issues and the local and national Democratic Party campaign coffers need to spend money in the Black community to support these efforts.

Much damage has been done. Yet now – **right now!** – is the time to begin playing the long game, to begin making sure that the next president, the next Congress, and the next SCOTUS, begin to right recent wrongs and move this country back onto the path to racial fairness.

"JUST MERCY"–A POIGNANT FILM ON BLACK INCARCERATION

It was slavery that gave America an abiding fear of Black people and a taste for violent punishment – a twisted inheritance that continues to taint our criminal justice system to this day. So **Bryan Stevenson** asserts in *The New York Times 1619 Project*.

Stevenson, founder of the ***Equal Justice Initiative*** (EJI), is that unique blend of intellectual, activist, lawyer, advocate and organizer. Unlike many thought leaders who analyze and write, Stevenson acts...and encourages others to join in finding solutions.

He wrote the 2014 best seller **"Just Mercy: A Story of Justice and Redemption"**, and more recently has collaborated on a cable TV docudrama titled *"True Justice."*

On Christmas Day of this year, a film version of his book **Just Mercy** opens nationwide. It shadows the world-renowned civil rights defense attorney as he recounts his experiences and details the case of a condemned death row prisoner whom he fought to free.

Stevenson's is one of 30-plus contributions to this outstanding work of analytic journalism contained in "The 1619 Project". It may even be the most important.

In his 1619 article Stevenson states, "Central to understanding this practice of mass incarceration and excessive punishment is the legacy of slavery."

He points out that Black children as young as 13 have been given life sentences for non- homicide offenses, and relates anecdotes such as that of the Black man lynched in South Carolina for successfully negotiating a better price for his cotton than a competing white man.

Stevenson asserts that three Reconstruction Era cornerstones are under attack right now in these United States: the 13th Amendment that abolished slavery; the 14th that guarantees equal protection under law regardless of race; and the 15th that assures the right to vote regardless of race.

No wonder that **Michelle Alexander,** author of the modern classic "The New Jim Crow", praises that "Bryan Stevenson is one of my personal heroes, perhaps the most inspiring and influential crusader for justice alive today. Just Mercy is extraordinary. The stories told within the pages hold the potential to transform what we think we mean when we talk about justice."

Consider how Stevenson tackles the treatment of Black youth – he writes about the 1944 execution in South Carolina of 14-year-old George Stinney Jr. The young Black boy was accused and convicted of murdering two white girls, ages seven and 11. He was executed by electric chair and became the youngest American ever sentenced to death and summarily executed.

Stinney's conviction was vacated in 2014 when a court ruled that he had not received a fair trial. Stevenson's writings show how the incident reflects racial politics in the South, not just the way children accused of crimes were generally treated.

It is an example of how policies and norms once developed to control and punish the Black population have filtered their way into today's criminal justice system. By the late 1980s and early '90s, persistent fear of Black crime fueled mass incarceration, including the mass jailing of children.

Staggering Imprisonment Numbers...

By 2010, Florida had sentenced more than a hundred children to life imprisonment without parole, several of whom were 13 at the time of the crime. All of the youngest 13- and 14- year-olds were Black or Latino. Florida had the largest population in the world of children condemned to die in prison for non-homicides.

Hundreds of thousands of Black men are incarcerated presently in the United States and many more are on probation or parole. Stevenson agrees with Michelle Alexander's comment that nothing short of a major social movement can successfully dismantle this new version of the old caste system.

Closer to home, **Dr. Paul Street** of the **Chicago Urban League's Dept. of Research and Planning** has found that the total population of Black males in Chicago with a felony record (including both current and ex-felons) is equivalent to 50 percent of the adult Black male population and an astonishing 80 percent of the adult Black male workforce in the Chicago area.

This finding reflects the increase in the number and race of those sent to prison for drug crimes. From the Chicago region alone, the number of those annually sent to prison for drug crimes increased from 469 in 1985 to 8,755 in 2005.

Stevenson's *Just Mercy* sandwiches the case of Walter McMillan, the death row prisoner he sought to free, between statistical proofs about the jailing of 13- and 14-year old boys – along with the bewildering number of Black men in the criminal justice system who suffer from mental deficiencies.

Currently, over 50 percent of Black prison and jail inmates have a diagnosed mental illness, a rate nearly five times greater than that of the general adult population. Nearly one in five prison and jail inmates has a serious mental illness.

There are more than three times the number of seriously mentally ill individuals in jail or prison than in hospitals, and in some states the number is 10 times greater, reports Stevenson.

Walter McMillan was a Black Alabama man accused of killing a white woman. It was clear that he had not been at the scene of the crime from the testimony of several of those with him at the time of the offense.

Yet the criminal justice cabal ensnared him into six years on death row. The corruption, lies, and money changes between and among Alabama police, prosecutors, and witnesses that Stevenson details is astounding. And all aimed at killing an innocent Black man. But after appeal, McMillan was freed.

So there has been a steady, well-researched drumbeat over the last decade nailing the problem: Michele Alexander's *New Jim Crow* in 2010, *Just Mercy* in 2014, *True Justice* in 2017.

Impact Of The Movie...

However, the new film version of *Just Mercy*, due to the broader reach of video, may finally move the needle of public opinion even among whites.

In August, my wife, son and I attended the sold-out world premiere of *Just Mercy* at the *Toronto International Film Festival*. It is an inspirational, well done film.

Jamie Foxx as *Walter McMillan* and **Michael B. Jordan** as *Bryan Stevenson* are faithful to the words, spirit, and passion of the book. The agony and hopelessness of Walter McMillan is given a face and a voice by Jamie Foxx. There's no way to understand what McMillan went through absent Foxx's representation.

Following the film's screening, the cast, producers, director and Stevenson came on stage for a discussion. After the routine congratulatory comments and queries, one Black female actor voiced an unexpected, but wholly sincere appreciation.

She said what an honor it was to be in the film, how the experience informed and inspired her, and importantly, how it challenged her to give purpose to the solutions Stevenson sought.

Delightfully surprising to this writer was the way Foxx and Jordan used their celebrity platform to support Stevenson's mission. Rappers and sports heroes, please take note.

In a separate two-hour event, Jordan and Foxx were clearly moved when explaining how they had to abandon their own personas and climb "into the skin" of their respective characters.

Jamie Foxx, coming from Terrell, Texas in the 1960s, said he could totally identify with the treatment of Walter McMillan. Both actors stated that their hope was to inspire younger people into action.

Bryan Stevenson repeated on stage what he says in the book. If I may paraphrase: With more than two million incarcerated people in the U.S., an additional 6 million people on probation or parole, there are endless opportunities for you to do something about criminal justice policy or help the incarcerated or formerly incarcerated.

If you have interest in working with or supporting volunteer programs that serve incarcerated people, organizations that provide re-entry assistance to the formerly incarcerated or organizations, please contact the **Equal Justice initiative** in Montgomery, Alabama. The website is *www.EJI.org*. Or, email them at *Contact_Us@eji.org*.

Here's my own short list of action items:

- Read the book *Just Mercy*; I guarantee it'll inform and move you to action.
- View the new film version that debuted in June on HBO cable TV.
- See the film in person and among friends when it reaches Chicago in December.
- Go to the EJI web site (above) to see how you can support their efforts.
- Contribute to a conversation that being against crime doesn't mean victimizing Black people with mass incarceration, jailing 13-year-olds, and imprisoning the mentally ill.

Personally, I'm working with Stevenson's representatives and other Black businesses leaders to bring him to Chicago in the interest of speaking and possibly establishing an EJI chapter here.

AT LAST: THE HIDEOUS TRUTH ABOUT SLAVERY

After my third visit to the slavery exhibit at the National Museum of African American History and Culture in D.C. recently, I was reminded of the horrendous brutality visited upon Africans by the then All-American institution of slavery.

I've read many books, seen the movies and attended lectures by, and studied with, African scholars. However, the Museum's visual, written, and three-dimensional depictions resonated with me differently this time. I was touched, angry and upset.

From its outset, the Museum has given urgent voice and painful face to the 12.5 million Africans sent across the Atlantic, not to mention the 1.8 million who died in transit and were discarded overboard like waste.

What I wasn't prepared for was the economic impact that slavery had on the emergence, survival and expansion of this nation. The Museum has upped the ante! By displaying the enormous role played by the cotton, rice and sugar industries, we begin to appreciate the fundamental role Black slavery played in the birth and development of these United States.

As a construction contractor, my company routinely estimated 50 percent of any project to be the cost of labor. Thus, a $10 million project would be budgeted with $5 million in worker pay. The balance would be equipment, overhead and profit.

But what if labor was free? That would enrich my company by $5 million on that job alone. Multiply that by numerous projects over a period of decades and you see enormous wealth creation for me, my partners, and generations that follow. Slavery provided free labor across multiple industries in the U.S. for over 200 years.

Following this last Museum visit, I joined my wife and two friends on a trip to George Washington's estate at Mount Vernon. The walls there are inscribed with quotes such as, "I cannot tell a lie," and, " I believe in America's Constitution."

Not only did these declarations not ring true, they offended me. George Washington became a slaveholder at age 11 after inheriting slaves from a relative. He embraced this travesty as a boy, ending up with over 300 slaves at Mount Vernon by the time of his death.

Midway through this tour of lies, my mind simply quit. How could the President this place was celebrating, with its founding Declaration of "All men are created equal," enslave millions of Africans and treat them as less than human?

It wouldn't compute. Did I miss the Kool Aid or the "Aha!" moment? The truth of the African History Museum simply didn't square with the Mount Vernon tableau, showing, for instance, a happy and contented "enslaved servant" working in Washington's wine press. I was betwixt and between.

Telling Unvarnished Truth

Then to the rescue came The New York Times with its 1619 Project. It's an 18-sheet special section and 100-page special magazine published Sunday, August 19, 2019.

The 1619 Project recognizes the 400th anniversary of 20-odd slaves transported to the Virginia Coast in August 1619 – the first contingent of what would become a veritable flood of transformative free labor.

The 18-pager cover has historian John Hope Franklin's quote, "We've got to tell the unvarnished truth." After all, 400 years after enslaved Africans were first brought to Virginia, most Americans still don't know the full story of slavery.

The 100-page magazine states: "In August of 1619, a ship appeared on the horizon near Port Comfort, a coastal port in the British Colony of Virginia. It carried more than 20 enslaved Africans, who were sold to the colonists.

"America was not yet America, but this was the moment it began. No aspect of the country would be found untouched by the 250 years of slavery that followed. On the 400th anniversary of this fateful moment, it is finally time to tell our story truthfully."

At a time when print news media is drastically losing readers, advertisers and in-house writers, *The New York Times* has created a journalistic masterpiece.

With literary contributions from over 29 noted writers and financial supporters that include Wilson Chandler, John Legend, and the NAACP Legal Defense and Educational Fund, this unearthing of forgotten truths is deserving of a Pulitzer Prize and other awards.

Why don't more Americans know about slavery, or simply dismiss it as a dated entry on an historic timeline?

Nikita Stewart suggests some answers on the first section of the 18-pager headlined, "Why we can't teach it?" She cites *The Geographical Reader For*

The Dixie Children by North Carolina's Marinda Branson Moore, which was published in 1863, the same year as the Emancipation Proclamation during the Civil War.

Excerpts from the book include these:

Q: Which race is most civilized? A. The Caucasian.

Q. Is the African savage in this country? A. No, they are docile and religious here.

Q. How are they in Africa, where they first came from? A. They were very ignorant, cruel, and wretched.

In 2017, the Southern Poverty Law Center (SPLC) reviewed 12 popular U.S. history books and surveyed more than 1,700 social studies teachers and 1,000 high school seniors to understand how American Slavery is taught and what is learned.

It turns out that there is widespread ignorance among students. In most cases, slavery was viewed as a point in a historical continuum, with 92 percent of the students indicating they did not know that slavery was the central cause of the Civil War.

Shortly after the Civil War, white southerners and their sympathizers embraced "The Lost Cause" narrative, ignoring slavery's role and casting the battle as a fight between the South and the North over "States' Rights".

The study further found that 80 percent of the country's 3.7 million teachers are white. So many educators who grew up believing the Civil War was about Southern states' right-to-govern are among those that select text books.

SPLC's Maureen Costello observes: "These decisions are being made by people who learned about slavery in a different way in a different time."

Elementary school children learn about the nation's founders, but do not learn that many of them owned slaves. They are revered as heroes...without the evil habit.

Hasan Kwame Jeffries, writing in the SPLC study concludes that "we are committing educational malpractice."

A Difference In Realities

The late Thomas Bailey of Stanford, whose American history textbook was popular across the country, was influenced by the so-called "Dunning School" of thought, which held that southern whites were more realistic about the prospects of Blacks becoming full citizens with voting and other rights.

They argued that the Reconstruction program imposed on the vanquished South by idealistic northerners was detrimental to whites and not all that helpful to freed slaves.

This idea, along with "the Lost Cause" notion, led to imposition and strengthening of Jim Crow laws, most of which were not undone until the 1960s. One could argue that these same racist attitudes continue to underlie white prejudice to this day.

Costello cites misleading language in books. For instance, Thomas Jefferson's relationship with Sally Hemings is described as "intimacy", and white masters are said to all-too frequently force their "attentions" on female slaves. Is this not a too-delicate way of describing rape?

This kind of sugar-coating history is crucial to understanding the difference in perspectives between Black and white Americans. Blacks have either heard about it in family talk, or intellectually investigated it, or something in between.

For those of us who benefitted from high school and college, our Black fraternities and sororities did much to communicate the Black experience across generations. White folks, without access to truth-telling history, without family discussions, within segregated schools and neighborhoods, are too often bereft of racial understanding and empathy.

This gulf explains why some things that are so obvious to Blacks can be deemed inconsequential by white friends. Our relationships and frames of reference are grounded in different informational realities.

Bridging this chasm about how slavery is taught, understood and analyzed is the first mission of "The 1619 Project". This is as it should be, for you cannot fathom the financial impact of slavery on Wall Street, of the Cotton Recession, of Black mass incarceration, or even America's dietary addiction to sugar without understanding Black slavery itself.

A great place to start is to teach "The 1619 Project" in schools. Teachers can find curriculums, guides, and activities for students developed at the Pulitzer Center, at *Pulitzercenter.org/1619*. Pulitzer resources can connect students with journalists who are featured in "The 1619 Project" issue.

Hampton University commemorated that first landing of the 20-odd slaves at Old Fort Comfort (now mostly known as Fort Monroe) and their research shows these Africans came from Angola and were traded to the white settlers there for food and supplies. The Hampton Branch of the NAACP hosted a prayer vigil at the 1619 marker on the Fort Monroe waterfront.

Hampton U. faithfully gives its students the idea that "a mind is a terrible thing to waste." Now The New York Times 1619 Project has given us an outstanding work of journalism, full of book references and scholarly research, that give this inquiring mind the impetus and ammo to write more about "these truths" so long unspoken.

DEMOCRATS' DILEMMA

Blues legend Bobby Bland often played a tune called *Keep it a Secret*. It has to do with a married man and his outside lady. It seems that the Democratic Party is developing a similar relationship with Black people.

I'm not talking about "people of color." I am referring to African Americans whose ancestors were U.S. slaves. Like a kept mistress, too often we don't get summoned 'til the need arises. That is, if we get summoned at all.

Consider Hillary Clinton's tragic 2016 campaign. She lost Michigan, Wisconsin and Pennsylvania by less than 100,000 votes combined. Of course, she did. She barely campaigned there, perhaps assuming Black folks don't need to be asked. An investment of time and funding in Detroit, Milwaukee and Philadelphia likely would have tipped all three states – and their pivotal electoral votes – in her favor.

Do not, however, expect things to be much different the next time around. It appears that the new crop of Democratic presidential candidates also has a "thing" about talking directly to Black folks about the things that matter.

Perhaps they have one eye on recent Appellate and Supreme Court decisions that frown on the classification of citizens by race. Or more likely, they're worried about how promises made specifically to Black voters will play among White "swing" voters.

As Bobby "Blue" Bland put it: "I 'd like to tell the world how I feel about you, but right now we just can't tell the truth." So, the candidates are afraid to identify any of their policy proposals as aimed at helping African Americans. Not when an aging White electorate might be alienated by what many derisively refer to as "identity" politics.

So, several candidates are taking a more "generic" approach to urban policy. Emily Badger in *The New York Times* notes the tortured complexity of the language being used about Black people.

Elizabeth Warren, for instance, wants to offer down payment assistance to home buyers in formerly "red lined" neighborhoods where banks and brokers once denied access to mortgages. Then there's Cory Booker, who would like to create "baby bonds" that would be worth more to children in poor families, helping them one day to buy houses or other assets.

These candidates know the courts wouldn't uphold Black baby bonds or housing programs explicitly for African Americans, even though such programs might aim to remedy historic wrongs visited mainly and directly on Blacks. So, eligibility for such programs must hinge on "household wealth," even though African-Americans, though fully 13 percent of our nation's population, hold but 2.8 percent of its wealth.

And it's not just politicians talking around race. Universities and other research institutions appear to be skirting the mention of Black people and coming up with socio-demographic euphemisms such as "Misery Index." The game is to distinguish between classes without specifying race or ethnicity.

The College Board that runs the SAT exam has gone to "race neutral" alternatives to affirmative action, according to *New York Times* education writers Anemona Hartocollis and Amy Harmon. School districts everywhere have been following suit.

Until a decade ago Chicago, with its long history of segregation, considered race when determining admission to the most competitive high schools. But in 2009, after a federal judge ended the school board's desegregation consent decree with the Department of Justice, the admissions process was effectively de-raced.

Selective high schools in Chicago now admit 30 percent of their students based on grades and test scores but use socio-economic factors for the rest. These consist of median family income, single-parent households, parents' education level, percent of owner-occupied homes, whether English is not the at-home language and achievement scores of neighborhood schools in the same census track. One can only imagine how all these factors might intermingle on an MS Excel spreadsheet!

No Help From The Media

In better times one could depend on tell-it-like-it-is journalism to speak frankly about historic injury to Blacks and ways society could provide recompense. But these are not better times for American journalism, especially the interpretive print journalism on which so many older voters rely.

Jill Abrahamson lays it out in her book "Merchants of Truth: The Business of Journalism and the Fight for Facts". All across America newspaper quality isn't surviving the deep staff cuts caused by vanishing advertising and circulation revenues. The newspaper industry shed $1.3 billion worth of editing and reporting jobs in the past decade. These positions have shriveled by 60 percent since 2000.

The kind of investigative stories that took months to report and still more time to edit are now a rarity. The trend is toward shorter, quick-hit Internet eye-candy that prompt maximum "clicks" or "likes" or "tweets" or "page views." "Time of engagement" is also measured, but advertisers aren't that interested in longer attention spans.

There is a deeper and more troubling phenom in this print medium downward spiral. That is the dependency the Black voter had in the newspaper as being factual, well investigated and "you could take it to the bank". That level of trust has vanished.

Consider the Chicago newspapers. Nothing illustrates the sorry state of the print media mess than some of the things at *The Chicago Tribune*. Once a repository of accuracy, precision and fact, it appears to have lost its way. Since the departure of that Editor Supreme, Marcia Lythcott in 2018, one is truly saddened by some of the paper's output.

A case in point is the story by one Chezare Warren titled, "Urban Prep put its reputation ahead of results." Urban Prep (full disclosure, its founder Tim King is my son) is a charter school whose students are African American high schoolers.

In 10 years, it has had over 1,700 Black boys admitted to colleges, close to $100 million in scholarships, in excess of 10,000 college admissions, with 20 of its graduates returning to one of the school's three campuses to teach.

During the Lythcott era at the *Tribune*, these feats were reported on and celebrated. What is most distressing about the *Tribune* and Warren is the fact that in 2017, he published a book titled "Urban Preparation", in which he states, "Teaching at the nation's first all-boys public charter high school represented an opportunity to help build a school that would be(come) a national model for how to best educate young Black men and boys who attend urban schools…teaching at the school is still one of my proudest professional accomplishments."

My disappointment with this is two-fold; the first is the author's conflicting statements and the second is that the *Tribune* published it. The fairness, fact checking and editing for accuracy vanished. To counter the Warren comments, Urban Prep graduates had to go to *The Chicago Reporter* publication and say that "Mr. Warren betrayed our trust."

Why this example is in a political analysis rests on the fact that if you can't trust the newspaper for accuracy, you must depend more on face-to-face conversation and that need appears throughout this essay.

Meanwhile, non-partiality – think Walter Cronkite — has gone out of style and is fast being replaced by polarizing cable TV news shows and shock-jock radio commentators with political axes to grind. So, while news has become ubiquitous in the digital age, it's harder to get trustworthy information underwritten by a financial model that can support such an effort.

So, what does all this mean for Black voter turnout in the 2020 primary and general elections? Will the seeming ban on racial frankness, coupled with the cacophony of shallow, hyper-partisan media, combine to keep Black voters on the couch and Donald Trump in the White House?

The Black Census Project

To the possible rescue comes Alicia Garza and the The Black Census Project with results of a private survey of 31,000 African Americans whose collected gripes and glories should be required reading for the candidates.

Garza started the Project in 2018 and has surveyed Blacks in all 50 states. Partnering with grassroots organizations and fielding 100 trained staff, their findings as reported in *The New York Times* are eye-opening:

— African American voters feel candidates talk at, but not to, Black people;

— The most common response was that no politician or pollster has even asked what their lives were like and how they viewed their life chances;

— In California, left-leaning groups in 2016 raised $200 million. In the last election cycle, they raised $30 million, but spent only $50,000 on Black engagement;

— Campaigns that fail to understand or try to remedy the ways that structural racism damages Black people's lives are missing a bet. Without this analysis, their solutions will always miss the mark when it comes to Black votes.

But even when candidates follow Garza's spot-on survey findings, both the language and the messenger must be believable, and ready to make face-to-face contact. That's the lesson from last year and Stacey Abrams' nearly successful run for the Georgia governorship, along with Doug Jones' Alabama Senate victory.

Democrat Stacey Abrams ran against GOP Secretary of State Brian Kemp after becoming the first Black woman to win a major party's nomination for Governor in American history. The 1,923,685 votes she received exceeded Barack Obama's 2012 Georgia total.

In 2018, she captured more African American votes than the total of all Georgia Democratic votes in 2014. She later told me that the scandal-plagued, Black-voter-suppressed election was rigged in that her opponent was "contestant, referee and scorekeeper"!

Democrat Doug Jones won over Roy Moore in Alabama's 2016 Senate race due to a massive turnout by African Americans. He's the first Democrat elected to the Senate from Alabama in 25 years.

In Georgia and in Alabama, it was the Black vote that made history. Sure, they used phone banks, radio and social media. But these teched-up maneuvers were eclipsed by the effectiveness of swarming Black areas with organized get-out-the-vote canvassing and good ole door knockin'. So was arranging transportation to and from voting booths.

The ACLU, NAACP, Black churches, African American fraternities, and sororities, in addition to HBCUs, worked non-stop in the Alabama race. Early fundraising was key. In Alabama, the Senate Majority PAC raised in excess of $6 million, which helped fund the ground game. Other PACs donated over $4 million in order to get to rural and hard to reach areas.

In Georgia, Stacey Abrams' campaign received $4 million from the Democratic Governors Association. In addition to getting corporate support, Abrams put individuals on "payment plans."

Alicia Garza's survey clearly states how Black voters feel about candidates, about candidates' attitudes toward them. The Abrams and Jones races made clear that, in order to win, there needs to be a laser-like focus on the African American voter. And not just media buys, but press-the- flesh personal outreach.

Using the lessons from Garza, Abrams and Jones, the Democratic Dilemma can become a Democratic Direction toward victory. Be not afraid to talk candidly about race, past wrongs, and future remedies. Listen, too. It is said that the definition of insanity is doing the same thing over again… and expecting a different result.

ZORA AND LANGSTON

After weeks of watching, listening and reading about Donald Trump's travails, I was beginning to identify with Canada Bill Jones, the famed riverboat gambler who memorably uttered: "I know the game is rigged, but it's the only game in town." Yes, I'd been spinning in the non-stop vortex of chaotic Trump stuff.

Does this sound familiar? First it was necessary for the Democrats to win the 2018 mid- terms; then we had to wait for impeachment until the Mueller report came out; then ponder if a Special Prosecutor could indict a sitting president; or whether it's up to Congress to impeach; and now if the White House can invoke "executive privilege" to keep the nasty stuff under wraps; and how the Roberts' Supreme Court – now with "only a beer" Brett Kavanaugh as a justice – might rule if asked. What to do? How to escape the Trump whirlpool?

Like a drowning man thrown a lifeline, I grabbed onto a new book by **Yuval Taylor** titled "Zora and Langston: A Story of Friendship and Betrayal".

A work both beautiful and true, Taylor's carefully researched account of the Harlem Renaissance and two of that Black cultural watershed's leading lights provided the perfect antidote to my overdose of Trump Trauma.

(*Nota bene*: To achieve this desired effect, the book should be accompanied by a personal pledge to turn off *CNN*, only glance at headlines of newspapers, and ignore all forms of political punditry for one glorious week.)

"Zora and Langston" author **Yuval Taylor** is the former senior editor at **Chicago Review Press**. Co-author of "Darkest America: Black Minstrelsy from Slavery to Hip Hop" and "Faking It: The Quest for Authenticity in Popular Music", Taylor has also edited three volumes of African-American slave narratives. He lives in Chicago.

Zora Neal Hurston and **Langston Hughes** were strategic leaders of the *Harlem Renaissance*. Much has been written about them and the work of that movement's luminaries has been widely studied and published.

The Harlem Renaissance...

The **Harlem Renaissance** was, of course, a confluence of Black intellectual, creative, literary, political, and musical creativity. It began with Black geniuses living and working in Harlem in New York City during the 1920s. They were even lovingly referred to as the *"Niggerati"* by Harlem Renaissance charter member **Wallace Thurman**.

Many Harlem Renaissance members were Afro-centric in their approach.

Consider **Langston Hughes'** 1925 poem, "The Weary Blues." In the book, Taylor quotes Hughes: "The blues was one of the few unchallenged modes of African-American expression. Spirituals were, in part, derived from Methodist hymns; ragtime owed a great deal to European pianism; jazz came to some extent out of the military band. But the blues owed nothing to white culture."

August Wilson picked up the Langston Hughes theme in his 1996 documentary, "The Ground on Which I Stand." He takes issue with the term "of color" when referring to African Americans, as do I.

Wilson says, "We are not ashamed and we do not need you to be ashamed for us. Nor do we need the recognition of our Blackness to be couched in the abstract phrases like 'artists of color.'' Who are you talking about? An Eskimo? A Filipino? A Mexican? A Cambodian? A Nigerian? Are we to suppose that one white person balances out the rest of humanity lumped together as a nondescript 'people of color?' We are unique and we are special."

The Feud...

As to the "betrayal" referred to in the title of Taylor's book: Henry Louis Gates stated that the fissure that took place in January/February 1931 between Hurston and Hughes "was the most notorious literary quarrel in African-American cultural history."

"Zora and Langston" had agreed to collaborate on a theatrical play – *Mule and Man* – with both attempting to shield the effort from the "pre-approval control" demanded by their funding patron Charlotte Osgood Mason.

In October 1930, Zora copyrighted the play under the title *De Turkey and De Law* in her name alone. After copyrighting it, Zora continued to work on the play, excising as best she could whatever she considered Langston's contributions.

Hughes heard about this and asked of a colleague, "Is there something about the very word 'theatre' that turns people into thieves?"

On January 19, 1931, without consulting Zora, Langston used his version of the play, which he called *Mule Bone: A Comedy Of Negro Life*. He gave Zora credit for her contributions and listed her name on the title page. And he got the play copyrighted despite the fact that the entire play had been copyrighted previously by Zora alone.

The quarrel ended up involving literary agents, lawyers, theatre impresarios, and many attempts at reconciliation. No matter which side you agree with in the custody battle over their theatrical offspring, Hurston appears to have had some character flaws.

Casey Cep, in her New Yorker review of "Baracoon," written by **Zora Neale Hurston**, points out that she made another slip. Cudjo, the former slave and the book's main subject, was said to be the last living survivor. Hurston found out that there was a former slave woman, Allie Beren, still alive and ignored this, continuing to refer to the Cudjo as the last and only.

After other acts of self-sabotage, Hurston died in 1960. **Alice Walker** went looking for Zora's unmarked grave and when she found it in 1973, she paid for a gravestone. And, to our great benefit, Walker resurrected Hurston's work for posterity, publishing in MS magazine her article, "In Search of Zora Neale Hurston".

Here are a few other take-aways provided by author Yuval Taylor in the book:

- Wealthy white patron-of-the-arts **Charlotte Osgood Mason**, who insisted that she be referred to as *"The Godmother,"* subsidized Hurston, Hughes and several other Black artists, spreading around some $75,000 – or about $750,000 in today's coin.
- Harlem Renaissance members included such geniuses as **James Weldon Johnson, Dr. WEB Du Bois, Langston Hughes, Alain Locke, Jean Toomer, Claude McKay, Jessie Fauset, Countee Cullen, Zora Neale Hurston**, and **Aaron Douglas**.
- They helped one another. For example, **Alain Locke** introduced Hughes to Charlotte Osgood Mason; Hughes in turn introduced Hurston to Mason – Hughes and Hurston ended up receiving stipends of $200 a month, equivalent to about $2,000 today.

Harlem Renaissance Legacy...

The Harlem Renaissance laid the groundwork for many things, including most collegiate African-American Studies programs.

In addition to the art and stylish protest, the Harlem Renaissance movement set in motion enduring processes that continue to benefit Blacks – and the larger society – to this day.

For instance, **WEB Du Bois** founded the **NAACP**, the Black organizational powerbase that most recently assisted **Democrat Doug Jones** in his struggle to become the U.S. Senator from Alabama.

Countee Cullen was the middle school teacher of author James Baldwin, who in turn cast an outsized imprint on current Black thought leader **Ta-Nehisi Coates.**

Langston Hughes wrote for the *Chicago Defender* for 20 years, influencing Black housing and employment issues. He also introduced **Ralph Ellison**, the author of the classic "Invisible Man", to **Richard Wright**, who gave Ellison his first published book review opportunity.

Pulitzer Prize-winning playwright August Wilson was once being steered into becoming a lawyer. But reading Langston Hughes and Ralph Ellison set his mind on fire – or so he told me not too long ago over dinner – and led him to becoming a writer. One can hear Hughes' rhythms in Wilson's play *Joe Turner's Come and Gone.*

Consider Pulitzer Prize recipient **Jackie Sibblies Drury**, her achievement in "Fairview," a comedy turned confrontation that challenges the white gaze through which Black art is often filtered. The play exudes the art of August Wilson with its mystic power. So, make it Hughes to Wilson to Drury – tic, tac, toe.

Then there's *The Fire This Time*. **Michael Paulson** and **Nicole Herrington** further illustrate in *The New York Times* the connecting link between the Harlem Renaissance and today's Black playwrights.

Now comes the immense value, practical utility and just plain delight of Yuval Taylor's new book "Zora and Langston". More than ever, I think, it's critical for Black people to get woke to the importance of these cultural icons.

To that end, here are some other sources of inspiration:

- The **Vivian Harsh Society Research Collection**, located in the Carter Woodson Library at 95th and South Halsted Streets, has Langston Hughes papers available for study.
- August Wilson's play *"Joe Turner's Come and Gone"* remains inspirational, with its echoes of Ralph Ellison and Langston Hughes.
- The **Smithsonian Folkways Recordings CD**, *"Every Tone A Testimony"* includes Claude McCay's recitation of *"If We Must Die"* and *"The Negro Speaks Of Rivers"* recited by Langston Hughes. I guarantee you won't feel the same after hearing those.
- The **DuSable Museum** has an unforgettable Harlem Renaissance collection.
- In print or online, one can read the plays of August Wilson and connect the dots to Langston Hughes' poetry.

But first, check out Yuval Taylor's "Zora and Langston". Hold on tight, because it's strong enough to pull y'all safe from the Trump vortex!

WHEN WHITES MAKE THE CASE FOR REPARATIONS...

Columnist David Brooks has joined Paul of Tarsus, Augustine of Hippo and C.S. Lewis of Belfast in making one of the most profound conversions in history.

Brooks is a widely recognized author and journalist, a *New York Times* *Op-Ed* regular and public television commentator, generally regarded as a moderate Republican/Conservative.

But this past March, in a column headlined "The Case for Reparations," he sided with Ta-Nehisi Coates, the eminent Black author and intellectual thoughtleader, in supporting long-overdue reparations for African Americans whose ancestors were injured by U.S.-authorized slavery.

Talk about a turnaround! Brooks' about-face constitutes an astounding transformation, and perhaps more importantly, a signal that white America is grudgingly coming to grips with the legitimacy of an issue – reparations – it had heretofore dismissed as unrealistic, if not ridiculous.

Just a few years ago, in a 2013 essay, this same Brooks railed against race-based affirmative action, claiming it wrongfully discriminated against Asian Americans, reinforced crude racial categorizations, and even hurt its intended beneficiaries by overmatching them into colleges and jobs for which they were not prepared.

So what happened? What triggered this "Aha!" moment, this epiphany, this "Come to Jesus" conversion? Turns out there were at least two bolts of lightning.

One was Brooks' re-reading of Ta-Nehisi Coates' seminal 2014 article in *The Atlantic* Magazine, which Brooks initially disagreed with, that systematically makes a solid case for reparations. The other prompt, more of a gut-punch than a reasoned argument, was talking with an elderly Black woman in South Carolina, who told him that her kids were facing far greater challenges now than any she met growing up in Jim Crow 1953.

Now, the woke Brooks likens Black slavery to sin, quotes Scripture, and beckons others to mend their ways vis-à-vis racial justice. He observes that "the racial divide doesn't feel like other divides. It is more central to the American Experience…born out of sin."

Sin, writes Brooks, "is anything that assaults the moral order. Slavery doesn't merely cause pain and suffering to the slave. It is a corruption that infects the whole society. It is a collaborative debt that will have to be paid."

I know Ta-Nehisi Coates and have had numerous meetings and conversations with him. For Brooks to express solidarity with Coates' carefully argued positions is like Darth Vader leaving the Dark Side to join Luke Skywalker.

Coates opens his *Atlantic* manifesto with this clarion call: "American prosperity was built on two-and-a-half centuries of slavery, a deep wound that has never been healed or fully atoned for…and that has been deepened by years of discrimination, segregation, and racist housing policies that persist to this day. Until America reckons with the moral debt it has accrued and the practical damage it has done to generations of Black Americans, it will fail to live up to its own ideals."

Reparations And Affirmative Action

Coates' call for reparations has special meaning for me because I have a keen interest in its smaller cousin – affirmative action, particularly as it applies in the construction industry.

Affirmative action was first invoked in 1961 when President John F. Kennedy issued an executive order stating that federal contractors should not discriminate against racial minorities. That was a start, but it was President Lyndon Johnson's Executive Order 11246 that became the lynchpin of Black advancement.

LBJ's order essentially says that it is not enough to just stop discriminating against African Americans, you have to take steps – AFFIRMATIVE ACTION – to correct the effects of past discrimination.

"You do not take a person who for years has been hobbled by chains and liberate him, bring him up to the starting line of a race and then say, 'You are free to compete with all the others' and still justly believe that you have been completely fair," Johnson declared.

Since then, race-conscious affirmative action programs for education, employment and construction contracting have been enormously beneficial to millions of African Americans. Yet attacks on these programs have been both caustic and consistent for the past 50 years.

It's not hard to understand that if you create systematic Black Injury, some healing balm is not only right, but necessary. Consider, however, some of the benighted pushback lately being sounded against Coates' timeless argument and Brooks' new-found enlightenment.

We can't truly cross the divide unless there is a society-wide and soul-deep acceptance of the sinfulness that has perpetuated that divide.

For this generation, reparation of any minority would not heal, but rather exacerbate feelings of resentment and distrust between racial groups. Should I pay reparations for what slave states did in 1850, even though all my grandparents came to the United States in the 20th century?, the argument might go.

In answer, I say that becoming an American citizen entails both gaining the benefits and taking on the liabilities created by those who came before.

The concept of reparations for African Americans has been around for years. Former Michigan Congressman John Conyers introduced HR 40 to the 115th Congress of 2017. This bill establishes the Commission to Study and Develop Proposals for the African-American Reparations Act. Congressman Sheila Jackson Lee took over the sponsorship of the bill after Conyers retired and it has yet to see the light of day.

The Case Of Renty The Slave

Yet the reparations issue continues to make news; witness the recent case of Harvard University's disputed rights to daguerreotype photos of a slave named Renty.

Pictures of Renty and his daughter Delia were taken after they were stripped naked against their will in 1850 as part of a racial study by Harvard biologist Louis Agassiz, whose theories on racial difference – that Blacks are inferior –were used to support slavery in the United States. The pictures are thought to be among the earliest photos of American slaves in existence.

The Lanier family of Connecticut claims to be the descendants of Renty and is thus entitled to these haunting, perverted pictures, which have been kept in a controlled atmospheric, light- sensitive encasement by Harvard. The family has retained noted attorney Benjamin Crump to advance their case.

Their lawsuit asserts that "the images are the spoils of theft" because as slaves, Renty and Delia were unable to give consent. It says that the university is illegally profiting from the images by using them for "advertising and commercial purposes such as using Renty's image on the cover of a $40 anthropology book."

To some this may seem a small matter, but it raises the over-arching question of what descendants of slaves are entitled to. Monetary reparations? Or some other compensation? Ta- Nehisi Coates weighed in on the Renty / Harvard case on the side of the Laniers.

Coates says, "That photograph is like a hostage photograph. This is an enslaved Black man with no choice being forced to participate in white supremacist propaganda – that's what the photograph was taken for."

Remember that Harvard is but one of many colleges that benefited from Black slavery; colleges now facing choices about what must be done to compensate victims' descendants. In a previous *N'DIGO* article, I outlined the case of ante-bellum Georgetown University selling a number of Black slaves when the school was near financial collapse. Georgetown atoned, in part, by granting those slaves' descendants preferred admission enrollment.

David Brooks' 180-degree journey from hostility toward affirmative action to support for reparations raises immeasurable questions. What prompted it? What happened in the intervening years to create this new position?

The Chicago Humanities Festival is bringing Brooks to Chicago on May 4, which is also Kentucky Derby Day. The CHF tickets are on the way, but as a thoroughbred fan, I was concerned about a conflict.

A friend bailed me out and will place my selected wager. If my horse wins, and if I get an upfront seat for Brooks, and if I can ask my two-part question about his dynamic conversion...well, that will be a sho'nuff TRIFECTA!

NO TRUMP...AND IT'S NOT WHIST!

Yoni Appelbaum's cover story in the March issue of *The Atlantic* fosters the impeachment of Donald Trump, the media complicity in his election, where Black people ought to direct their attention/activism, and finally, some lessons learned and action items.

Someone once wrote that Donald Trump doesn't *hate* journalists; he *uses* them. Staying on script, almost like Pavlov's dogs, the newsies did it again! In the midst of Trump's campaign captain Paul Manafort getting more jail time; his personal lawyer, Michael Cohen, sentenced to prison; and defeats in the mid-term elections, he appears against the ropes.

Then Trump gets Pelosi-punched and he's unable to get funding for his wall (a project Mexico was to pay for). Then almost predictably comes classic Trump trickery – he declares a national emergency based on an imaginary invasion.

This is textbook distraction. After losing a bruising battle, just create a national constitutional crisis and deflect all manner of media attention toward that illusion. Comparing Trump to Houdini and Mandrake the Magician is fun, with apologies to Mandrake and Houdini.

The Magician-in-Chief

I am less interested in arguments that Trump is unfit for office, that he obstructed justice, he disrespects women, he violates presidential norms, his campaign was corrupt, that he is a nativist, and that he is a racist. All but an ostrich would know of his character flaws well before the 2016 election.

Holocaust survivors say, "Never Again" and Republicans borrowed this notion in dealing with Barack Obama. Perish the thought of another Black chief executive. There would be no Trump presidency were there not an Obama two-term White House.

Thus, Black voter suppression; Virginia "blackface"; Iowa's Steve King; and the constant animus toward Blacks from Trump's so-called "base" dedicated to dehumanizing, disrespecting, and demeaning African Americans.

While this clanking multiverse continues, there is a quiet surgical-like incision slashing Black gains through executive orders and agency policy shifts.

These are seismic moves that eliminate or alter the regulations and policies benefiting African Americans that have been achieved through decades of activism, hard work, and sometimes the loss of life of progressive people on behalf of Black advancement.

Here are some points from the Lawyers Committee for Civil Rights and the Leadership Council on Civil and Human Rights outlining some of these Black attack moves:

1. The Consumer Financial Protection Bureau wants to gut rules that protect against predatory payday loans, where Black women are the most victimized and whose communities are inundated with these loan shark outfits.
2. The Department of Education rescinded guidelines related to Title 9 and schools' obligations regarding sexual violence and educational opportunity.

3. The Federal Communications Commission cut their Lifeline program that was dedicated to providing phone and internet service to Black and other low income people in rural and deprived areas. It also eliminated ownership opportunities for Blacks and other minorities in broadcast media.

4. The Justice Department demanded of 44 states intrusive sensitive personal data about all of their registered voters.

5. The Department of Justice (DOJ) re-directed resources toward investigations over affirmative action plans deemed to discriminate against white applicants, citing reverse discrimination.

6. The DOJ issued resolutions against fair pay and safe workplaces, which requires federal oversight.

7. The DOJ filed a statement of interest opposing a consent decree negotiated by Chicago Mayor Rahm Emanuel and Illinois Attorney General Lisa Madigan to overhaul the Chicago Police Department. (Think Laquan McDonald.)

8. The DOJ ended its agreement to monitor the Juvenile Court of Tennessee, which addressed actions against Black youth, unsafe conditions, and no due process at hearings.

9. The Department of Labor's Office of Federal Contract Compliance was merged into the Equal Employment Opportunity Commission.

Taking the above into consideration, let's review Yoni Appelbaum's impeachment argument.

On its face, the hot mess that is the Trump administration has been a major setback to the hopes of African Americans, of immigrants, of all who value truth, science, and equal opportunity under the law.

But this dismal and perilous moment is also an opportunity, for we have been able to stare directly into the abyss...without as yet taking the plunge into totalitarian fascism. This moment will not, however, last. Something must be done and done quickly. But what?

One option – impeachment of Trump by the new Democratic House majority – is laid out in convincing detail by senior editor Yoni Appelbaum in his cover story for the March issue of *The Atlantic* magazine.

Granted, some will argue that with the next presidential election just 20 months away, impeachment proceedings would be more of a distraction than a practical tactic – or worse, an exercise in futility, what with spineless Republicans still in charge of the Senate, where impeachment charges are adjudicated.

Appelbaum, however, reminds that impeachment is a process, not an outcome. Indeed, it is the only process for removing a president outlined by the Constitution and, in this case, a process that would yield several benefits during the fraught months leading up to November 2020.

He explains that once the process begins, the president loses control of the public conversation and his devilish ability to change the subject; it paralyzes a president's ability to advance more undemocratic elements of his agenda; it serves as a rules-based tool of public discovery and discernment; and it dampens the potential for explosive political violence.

So yes, there is a great deal of logic behind Michigan Congresswoman Rashida Tlaib's seemingly impulsive exclamation that, "We're gonna impeach the (mf)."

Lessons From 1868…

African Americans need to take Appelbaum seriously because the last time impeachment proceedings actually came close to removing a president – the

1868 Senate trial of President Andrew Johnson – the issues of racial hatred, mob violence and presidential unfitness were eerily similar to today's situation.

No president in history more resembles the 45th than the 17th. Like Trump, Johnson was egotistical to the point of mental disease and had become both the tool of nefarious intrigues (think Russia) and the hero of maniacal sycophants (Charlottesville torch-bearers?)

Back then Congressional Republicans had approved the 14th Amendment extending the rights of citizenship to all Americans, and voted to enlarge the role of the Freedman's Bureaus and passed the first civil rights bill.

But Johnson and his supporters found intolerable the extension of citizenship beyond the province of white men and subsequently vetoed the civil rights bill and the Freedman's Bureau legislation.

Then and now, the question facing Congress and the public was: What to do with a president whose every utterance and act undermines the Constitution he is sworn to uphold?

The situation had grown critical in places like New Orleans, where efforts to enfranchise Black voters sparked a riot with mobs led by police, firemen, armed youths, and Confederate veterans who shot, stabbed and mutilated dozens, including Black veterans of the Union Army.

Johnson chose not to suppress the violence, using fear of disorder to build a constituency more loyal to him – the Charlottesville "very fine people on both sides" reasoning of its day.

Fast forward now to white nativists in MAGA caps on torchlight parade; to brown children wrenched from mothers' arms at the border; to Black citizens turned away from polling places due to bogus technicalities or outright ruse.

Yet we've also seen what works, and what doesn't, in the struggle against a pernicious form of populism based on paranoia, resentment and hucksterism. We are woke now to the tactics of the tweet storm, of the phony narrative, of the stage-managed rallies before crowds of chanting fanatics.

Even the mainstream media, which started out covering Trump as an entertaining bonanza of higher ratings and wider circulation, has slowly come to its senses with serious fact-checking and healthy skepticism.

Beyond Impeachment

The task now is to get busy on strategies and tactics aimed at making sure the electoral disaster of 2016 is not repeated in 2020. Applebaum's points are well taken, but in 1868, the Senate ultimately failed to convict Johnson of "high crimes and misdemeanors," although the "process" did indeed kill his chances for re-nomination by the then-segregationist Democrats.

Ultimately it was the voters of 1868 who enabled Ulysses S. Grant to restore the party of the martyred Abe Lincoln to the presidency…and that may be the biggest lesson of all. Impeachment may prove a useful preliminary tactic, but what are we, the aggrieved, prepared to do about 2020?

Here we have good tactical examples a lot more contemporary than 1868. One is the 2017 upset defeat in Alabama of retrograde Judge Ray Moore in a special Senate election thanks to a hastily organized progressive coalition led by Black Alabama organizations, the ACLU, Lawyers Committee for Civil Rights, and Alpha Phi Alpha Fraternity and other Black Greek organizations.

By 2017, Republicans had won every U.S. Senate election over the past 25 years, a key tactic being the artful suppression of the Black vote. Moore was an alleged pedophile, but had Trump's endorsement and was poised to win.

A coalition of Black groups, especially Black women, helped Democrat Doug Jones (above) defeat Republican Judge Roy Moore (below) in the 2017 election for an Alabama U.S. Senate seat.

Yet, Black Alabama set a resistance effort in motion. The state NAACP, working with local churches, the National Pan-Hellenic Council (Black fraternities and sororities), the ACLU, and Planned Parenthood held a series of rallies about what was at stake.

Legal Services Alabama and the local ACLU led a "restoration program" to get ex-offenders voting rights. Taking down Roy Moore required not just TV ads, but unprecedented levels of person-to-person outreach.

According to author Carol Anderson, there were 1.3 million phone calls, 220,000 post cards, and social media videos that garnered 1.4 million Facebook hits. But more importantly, very few of the 650,000 African Americans across every county in Alabama went untouched as organizers swarmed communities and knocked on doors.

And, mind you, many were paid organizers. Not only is nothing wrong with that, but funding ground troops is a necessity. The Senate majority poured over $6 million into Alabama, much of it going to door-knockers, envelope stuffers, and drivers to shuttle isolated voters on election day to the polls. One driver remembered providing round-trips to pecan pickers so they, too, wouldn't miss a day's pay.

Still, Moore led 49 percent to 43 percent among likely voters just weeks before the December 12th special election. But the Democrat Doug Jones kept going to Black churches, barbecues and fish fries. He spoke about health care and jobs.

He also reminded African-American voters that he was the prosecutor who had successfully gone after the Klansmen that planted the bomb in Birmingham's 16th Street Baptist Church that killed four little Black girls.

Meanwhile, the Lawyers Committee for Civil Rights and the National Bar Association had their attorneys on the ground to assist with information about voting rights. On election day, the voters of Alabama's black belt counties, though weighed down by everything red state Alabama could throw at them, delivered an average 73.4 percent plurality for Doug Jones amid turnouts that averaged much higher than the state average.

The new Congress responded to Alabama's and other states' Black voter suppression with HR-1. See the Brennan Center for Justice for the litany of Black voter purges; the demand for exact matches between driver's license and utility bills; Kendall County, Illinois, where erroneous information was circulated prior to voting day.

This first legislation signals a response to the attack on African-American political power and should be embraced and understood by all. Under the legislation, voter registration would be made easier. Citizens could register online or get registered automatically, via driver's license or other government sources.

For federal elections, states would have to provide same-day registration and at least 15 days of early voting. Election Day would be a federal holiday. The bill would crack down on efforts to take voters off the rolls or prevent them from casting ballots. Felons could regain voting rights after finishing their sentences.

Federal elections would require paper ballots to prevent computer tampering. State chief election officials couldn't get involved in federal elections. The bill would attempt to revive core anti- discrimination provisions of the Voting Rights Act of 1965 that were effectively shut down by the Supreme Court six years ago.

Some Action Items

1. Congressmen Danny Davis and Bobby Rush and Congresswoman Robin Kelly should hold Informational Hearings on HR 1 and encourage voters to get involved.
2. Strategic alliances should be established with ACLU, Brennan Center, and Lawyers Committee for Civil Rights.
3. West Side Justice Center should be supported to lead in one of the above.
4. Black fraternities and sororities should establish voter education/get out the vote teams with their chapters in Wisconsin, Michigan and Pennsylvania (Clinton lost all three states in 2016 by less than 100,000 votes combined).

One of the most serious efforts to rob African Americans of the franchise surfaces once again in the attempt to diminish the Office of Federal Contract Compliance by snatching it out of its cabinet-level position at the Department of Labor.

This merger attempt is not new. It was first attempted by the Richard Nixon administration at the behest of labor unions. In 1971, OFCC Director John Wilks encouraged Rev. C.T. Vivian and myself to go to Washington and educate elected officials on how harmful this would be to our fight for Black worker integration and Black contractor advancement.

Senators Harrison Williams of New Jersey and Birch Bayh of Indiana were responsive and the merge effort was defeated. This is a serious lesson learned.

"Fake News" Redefined

Central to what happens in 2020 will be media coverage and interpretation of what's actually happening, not just on the various campaign trails, but back in the halls of government where high-level appointees are being replaced, policies changed, and regulations either re-written or discarded. On this score, our media, even respected mainstream media, have been an abysmal failure during Trump's first two years in office.

Ralph Alec Mackenzie, author of a seminal book on time management called "The Time Trap" cites distraction as the enemy of effectiveness. One need not be a rocket scientist to see that the media has been a critical partner in aiding Trump's fine art of distraction. As the late blues icon Muddy Waters would say, "He's been playing us like a $10 guitar."

As former CBS newsman Dan Rather puts it, "What we did last time was emphasize the sound and fury because Trump provided both in lavish measure. When you cover this as spectacle, what's lost is context, perspective and depth. And when you cover this as spectacle, he's the star."

Frank Bruni in *The New York Times* calls the media "Trump's accomplice," but goes on to offer more mea culpas than a Latin language Catholic mass. It has been credibly reported that when Trump first declared in 2015, the number of stories about Trump in the nation's most influential newspapers and principal newscasts significantly exceeded his support as reflected in the polls. His outlandish behavior was simply good copy and even better TV.

But what's being covered? The smoke or the fire? Bruni admits "Trump now has an actual record in office" and journalists need "to discuss that with as much oxygen as we do his Twitter feed."

Instead of covering Trump tweets upfront as "breaking news," why not cover them in the last five minutes after sports, weather and man-bites-dog? The president doesn't hate journalists; he uses them.

But it's Jill Lepore of *The New Yorker* who says it best. Sure a select few newspapers and the cable news networks are thriving because of the so-called "Trump bump" in public interest. But the coverage, like the Red vs. Blue divide in public opinion, is getting more argumentative and less fact-based.

"Sometimes what doesn't kill you doesn't make you stronger; it makes everyone sick," says Lepore. "The more adversarial the press, the more loyal Trump's followers, the more broken American public life. The more desperately the press chases readers, the more our press resembles our politics."

The big take away here is to get out of the object posture and get into the subject position. That can only be done by becoming informed – separate the fact from fiction, realize that you cannot depend on what's published being in your best interest; form strategic alliances, embrace lessons learned and fight like hell.

ANOTHER ATTACK ON AFFIRMATIVE ACTION

At Harvard, affirmative action opponents are trying to pit Asian Americans against African Americans.

A group representing Asian-American students has filed a federal lawsuit against Harvard University, claiming that the school's admission process that considers an applicant's racial background illegally discriminates against Asian Americans.

Is this an anti-discrimination plea or a cynical attack on affirmative action?

That might sound high-minded to some. But when the Trump Justice Department this past summer filed a "statement of interest" supporting the plaintiff's complaint, those of us who've been following the struggle to save affirmative action had an "aha!" moment.

The Harvard lawsuit, now going to trial, was prepared and filed by longtime opponents of affirmative action. It's a poorly disguised Trojan horse – a cynical use of Asian Americans to slam the door on African Americans.

According to Harvard, the recently admitted class of 2021 is approximately 50 percent white, 15 percent African American, 22 percent Asian American, 11 percent Hispanic, and two percent Native American/Pacific Islander.

Harvard concedes that race is among the factors used to achieve a mix of backgrounds needed to enrich the college experience of all.

To maintain that mix, Harvard may turn away a number of Asian Americans who have superior test scores and high school GPAs. Yet several who have been admitted plan to testify that this practice ought not to be used as a weapon against assisting Black youths struggling to overcome centuries of vicious discrimination.

Chinese-American Sally Chen doubtless knows her family has never been traumatized like that of Laquan MacDonald, the Black teen who was killed by 16 shots fired by white policeman Jason Van Dyke in Chicago.

Jang Lee, a Korean American, hasn't seen friends butchered, as was Trayvon Martin, a Black youth killed by self-appointed neighborhood vigilante George Zimmerman in Florida.

The ancestors, family and friends of Thang Dick from Vietnam were never massacred in the USA, as were the pastor and eight Black worshippers at an AME prayer meeting in Charlottesville, South Carolina by white racist Dylann Roof.

So if their percentage of their Harvard class is well beyond their percentage in the U.S. population, and if they've not had the violence visited upon them that African Americans have, what exactly is the Asian-American beef?

Known as the "Students for Fair Admission", the plaintiffs argue that the consideration of race in the admission process simply violates the Constitution's Equal Protection Clause.

The Culprit Behind The Scenes

Looming large in the Harvard case is one Edward Blum, a non-lawyer but ardent conservative strategist behind dozens of lawsuits against both affirmative action and civil rights protections.

Several years ago, Blum engineered the *Abigail Fisher v. University of Texas lawsuit that challenged an admissions process there that favored African Americans and Latinos. According to the ACLU Justice Program, Blum also was behind the Shelby v. Holder* case that gutted portions of the Voting Rights Act.

Emory University African-American Studies Professor Carol Anderson, author of "White Rage", has written a new book called: "One Person, No Vote: How Voter Suppression is Destroying Our Democracy".

In it, she says of the Shelby ruling… "this decision effectively allowed districts with a demonstrated history of racial discrimination to change voting requirements without approval from the Department of Justice."

In addition, the ACLU asserts that Blum's go-to tactic is to orchestrate divisiveness among Blacks and other minorities.

But the elimination of affirmative action will not, ultimately, inure to the benefit of Asian Americans or any other group supposedly put at a disadvantage by these necessary compensations.

The World War II internment of Japanese Americans, the lynching of African Americans, the snatching of Native American land, are all historic efforts in protecting white privilege and power. The unceasing attack on Blacks is the most egregious.

Our fellow white citizens cannot, with plausibility, claim that today's racist resurgence is the doing of a small cadre of fanatics. Witness the passage by referendum of Proposition 209 in California in 1996.

It attacked affirmative action and the use of race in California colleges' and universities' admissions practices. The result was that Black student enrollment at the University of California Berkeley and at UCLA subsequently plummeted by 50 percent.

Some History

Affirmative action as we know it was initiated by Executive Order #10925 by President John F. Kennedy in 1961. It required government contractors to take "affirmative action" to achieve non- discrimination.

Lyndon Johnson in 1965, with Executive Order #11246, dramatically advanced the cause, triggering an unprecedented level of Black advancement in education, business and employment.

In a June 4, 1965 speech to Howard University, LBJ declared: "You do not take a person, who for years has been hobbled by chains, and liberate him, bring him up to the starting line and say, 'You are free to compete with all others' and still justly believe that you have been completely fair. Thus, it is not enough just to open the gate of opportunity. All our citizens must have the ability to walk through these gates."

Today's opposition to affirmative action conveniently forgets this history, this truth, this realization that white privilege not only exists, but is having a frightening resurgence.

Harvard's own Professor Khalil Gibran Muhammad reminds us, "It is impossible to comprehend American history without understanding slavery's role in every aspect of its early development." And author Sven

Beckert ("Empire of Cotton") points out, "Slave plantations, not railroads, were in fact America's first big business."

Does it not follow that if African slaves contributed greatly to the success of American enterprise, even while suffering racial violence for two centuries, that today's affirmative action is justified in correcting that unfortunate legacy?

This, I believe. That is why in 1969 I helped form a coalition of leaders who shut down over $80 million in Chicago construction projects. Back then, there were hardly any Blacks in the trade unions and no Black contractors on those projects.

Using Executive Order #11246 requiring minority participation in HUD-funded projects, as well as other affirmative action rules, we elevated the issue nationally. We caused passage of Minority Business Utilization laws and Black hiring policies that remain in place today.

Racist Upheaval And The White House

But for how long? That's why focusing on the Harvard lawsuit and its bogus claims of discrimination against Asians asks all the wrong questions.

It's a deflection Blum and his ilk want us to take. The real issue is the blatant venom being renewed against African Americans at a time when so many of us thought we were beyond this.

This aggression comes from all sides. FBI data show hate crimes rose the day after Donald Trump was elected. According to The Washington Post, there were more hate crimes reported on November 9, 2016 than any other date that year.

The proximity of these racist upheavals to the current White House occupant appears to be a kind of "permission" to behave in this way. The incendiary rants and tweets from D.C. give license to synagogue massacres, shootings, and other evil acts.

Since that 2016 presidential election, there's been a veritable parade of hate-inspired plans and attacks against minorities.

Recently, Shane Robert Smith, a white man, was sentenced to more than three years in prison after pleading guilty to forming an armed-to-the-teeth group out to kill Blacks and Jews. Apparently, a like-minded bigot has now achieved that twisted goal at a Pittsburgh synagogue. Also, recently, a white man killed two Blacks in a Kentucky Kroger store and parking lot, shouting, "Whites don't kill whites!"

Yet even these nut cases have their defenders, albeit indirectly, among those who plead that these are tough times for the white people who voted for Enabler-in-Chief Donald Trump. They talk of white disenchantment with the economy and of joblessness, of opioid addiction and of automation.

They explain that many white people feel threatened with becoming a minority in future generations. But to blame this upsurge of racism on automation or the rapid pace of societal change is ludicrous.

There's an elephant in the room. How do you eat an elephant? One bite at a time. The elephant (political symbolism intended) is too big to confront all at once.

The mid-term elections of November 6 are a start. Beyond that, we need to understand what's happening and explain it to others. We need to fund and organize a voter education program going into 2020.

We need to convene a leadership forum involving veteran allies such as the Southern Poverty Law Center and the ACLU, along with local leaders such as State's Attorney Kim Foxx and The West Side Justice Center, to assess our current situation and suggest action.

Socially engaged writer Lisa Ko nailed it in The New York Times when she wrote: "Asian Americans have benefited from affirmative action. We continue to be used as a 'strategic tool' by white conservatives who are opposed to it. The anti-affirmative action lawsuit against Harvard is a result of a campaign by conservative strategist Edward Blum."

That's common ground for Blacks, Asians, Hispanics, and others. You don't need to be a Harvard PhD to realize that being used as a Trojan horse is an insult…if not a white-collar hate crime.

WHITE SPACE?

There are some scholars whose prescience defies belief and imagination. **Elijah Anderson**, the Yale University sociologist, is such a scholar.

In 2015, he wrote a paper titled "**The White Space**." The piece continues to draw knowing smiles of recognition from Blacks like myself who traverse that "Space" almost every day. But lately it also provides essential background to a flurry of infuriating news stories about race.

A boiled-down abstract of Anderson's paper explains:
"Since the end of the Civil Rights Movement, large numbers of Black people have made their way into settings previously occupied only by whites, though their reception has been mixed. Overwhelmingly white neighborhoods, schools, workplaces, restaurants, and other public spaces remain.

"Blacks perceive such settings as 'the white space,' which they often consider to be informally 'off limits' for people like them. Meanwhile, despite the growth of an enormous Black middle class, many whites assume that the natural 'Black space' is that destitute and fearsome locality so commonly featured in the media – the iconic ghetto. White people typically avoid Black space, but Black people are required to navigate white space as a condition of their existence."

Anderson's full paper is well worth reading, but here's one passage that all but sings the truth:

"For Black people, white spaces vary in kind, but their most visible feature is their overwhelming presence of white people and their absence of Black people. When the anonymous Black person enters the white space, others there immediately try to make sense of him or her – to figure out who that is or to gain a sense of the nature of the person's business and whether they need to be concerned…especially in the case of a young Black male, not because of his merit as a person, but because of the color of his skin and what Black skin has come to mean, as others in the white space associate it with the ghetto."

(Anderson's full paper can be found at https://sociology.yale.edu/sites/ default/files/pages_from_sre-11_rev5_printer_files.pdf.)

Ya' Can't do that in White Space!

If all this sounds depressingly familiar, it may be because the news has been loaded lately with "white space" violations. Some of the lowlights include:

- In York, Pennsylvania, at the Grandview Golf Club, police were called to the scene by white golfers who complained that three Black women were playing too slow;
- In Rialto, California, three Black Airbnb guests were leaving with their bags when a white neighbor called the police, prompting an overhead helicopter to respond to the "robbery;"
- In Oakland, a Black man brought a grill to cook out in a park only to have a white woman call the police reporting that charcoal grilling was not allowed in that part of the park. Police wisely let the grilling continue;

- At Yale University, a white student called campus police on a female graduate student napping on a couch in a dorm common room;
- At an Alabama Hobby Lobby, a white employee called police to report that a Black man was committing a crime. He had come there, receipt in hand, to return an item;
- At an LA Fitness gym in Secaucus, New Jersey, two Black men had the police called on them even though one was a member and the other had a guest pass. That day they happened to be the only Black people in the gym;
- In Memphis, a white woman called police on a Black man walking around the property. He was a prospective buyer inspecting the building;
- At a Nordstrom Rack in St. Louis, a white employee called the police on three Black men for theft. They were shopping for prom clothes;
- In Philadelphia, a white Starbucks employee called police on two Black men minutes after they arrived to prepare for a business meeting.

There are many more such examples. All these incidents should have provoked widespread indignation, but only the last one got the nationwide publicity it deserved, perhaps because it was Starbucks, or because a bystander captured the arrest of the Black men on a soon-to-go-viral video, or because the entire Starbucks chain subsequently shut down for a few hours to educate staff on the proper way to treat guests.

What's a Black person – or for that matter, an embarrassed white person – to make of all of this?

Emily Bazelon of The New York Times Magazine recently speculated that as white America becomes increasingly uneasy about the growing non-white populations around them, many are pushing back by, for instance, calling the cops when their self- perceived white space is somehow violated. Or worse.

Bazelon noted a white Starbucks customer "observing the maltreatment of the Blacks" tweeted, "All the other white people are wondering why it's never happened to us when we do the same thing."

The Root website gives the answer that some whites "exist in a state of racial obliviousness, from intentionally clueless to intentionally condescending."

Bazelon observed, "A majority of white Americans currently believe that their own race is discriminated against. News accounts fill with white resentment and torchlit white power marches. White Americans who 'seem lost' are searching for something important: how to see ourselves without turning awful in the process."

But while white folks are "searching," Black people are being embarrassed, traumatized, threatened, and abused. It is not enough for Nordstrom, Grandview Golf Club or Starbucks to apologize.

This brings to mind Ta-Nehisi Coates' comment, during a recent Chicago visit, that if someone beats you with a 2-by-4 for 20 minutes and finds you are the wrong person, stops the beating and apologizes…you are still injured!

Counter Measures…

So, what's to be done? How about these measures for starters?

1. In Illinois, urge victims of "**call the police on Black People**" to contact the **Illinois Human Rights Commission (www.Illinois. gov/hrc)**, or t**he City of Chicago Commission on Human Rights (312/744-4111)**, or the **Cook County Commission on Human Rights (www.cookcountyil.gov)**. State's Attorney Kim Foxx is updating her office's Hate Crimes Task Force to address some of this.

2. Insist on adequate compensation for insulting and demeaning discrimination. It is not enough for Starbucks merely to apologize and have a day of "training" for staff. There are precedents for fast food chains doing damage to Black people.

In 1994, Denny's agreed to pay $54 million to settle lawsuits filed on behalf of thousands of Black customers who had been refused service or forced to wait longer or pay more than white customers. In 2004, Cracker Barrel settled a racial discrimination suit for $8.7 million after segregating Black clients into the smoking section and denying them service.

1. Rather than cash settlements, offenders should contribute to systemic improvements to the community they've denigrated. How about funding a Starbucks "star" program at Urban Prep Academies here in Chicago (full disclosure: my son Tim King is Urban Prep's Founder/CEO).

2. Tailor these compensatory programs to include part-time paid internships and pre-employment training to include client communication, customer satisfaction, customer courtesy, and product promotion. The goal is to build confidence in communicating with the public.

3. Fund a "college scholar coach" who would mentor and counsel young Black men about entering and remaining on college campuses.

4. Negotiate to establish two Black-owned Starbucks franchises here in Chicago through the Business Leadership Counsel. Starbucks doesn't use the franchise model in the U.S., but they do in Europe, and a pilot program here would go far both to redress past wrongs and tap respectfully into the Black marketplace. If that's not doable, how about franchises for the company's Seattle's Best Coffee subsidiary?

All the above do not come close to what Denny's and Cracker Barrel cases cost their defendants, but it's a difference in degree, not a difference in kind.

What's more, the Lawyers Committee for Civil Rights Under Law, the West Side Justice Center, and the Cook County Bar Association should all examine the "white space" issue and consider establishing a hot line for innocent victims who have had the police called on them by white people.

Melody Spann-Cooper at WVON 1690-AM radio has a call-in number **(773/591-1690)** for this purpose. The specter of a class action lawsuit might accelerate a behavioral change by these franchises.

Three years ago, Yale's Elijah Anderson more-or-less predicted what's been happening with alarming frequency. His warning: "Today, the iconic ghetto and its relation to the white space form the basis of a potent and provocative new form of racism."

We ignore this at our own peril.

"BARRACOON" IS WAKEUP READING!

Christina Sharpe, professor of English at Tufts University, urges Black people to come to grips with our situation through the practice of "self and communal care" beginning with reading, study and collaboration. She terms this "wake work."

A good way to begin is by reading an 87-year-old, yet newly published book, **"Barracoon: The Story of the Last Black Cargo," by the late Zora Neale Hurston.**

The author, who passed in 1960, did her fieldwork in the late 1920s by repeatedly visiting and interviewing an octogenarian ex-slave believed to be the last surviving veteran of the infamous "Middle Passage" from West Africa.

For decades, Hurston's in-his-own-words manuscript of **Cudjo Lewis'** experience lay unpublished on the library shelves of Howard University. Seems there was no popular market for the memories of an elderly Alabama Negro who spoke in the vernacular of the rural South.

Now, thanks to the brilliant editing of **Deborah Plant**, a Zora Neale Hurston scholar, we have an eminently readable first-person account of the trans-Atlantic ordeal that faithfully preserves not just the language, but the basic humanity of a genuine survivor.

Hurston's writing is iconic. What she does with lyrical language – both hers and that of her subject Mr. Lewis – is akin to what her **Harlem Renaissance** peers **Duke Ellington** did with piano notes and painter **Jacob Lawrence** with canvas and oils.

But First Some Background...

The **African Diaspora** in the Americas represents the largest forced migration in the history of the world. According to historian **Paul Lovejoy**, between the years 1450 and 1900, more than 12.8 million Africans were enslaved. Other scholars put that number closer to 60 million when considering those thrown overboard, forgotten and uncounted.

Britain abolished the African slave trade in 1807 and the United States in 1808. However, an Alabama shipbuilder and slaveholder named Timothy Meaher built the ship Clotilda in 1860 and, in violation of the law, navigated to the west coast of Africa in search of people to enslave.

Oluale Kossola, whose slave name became **Cudjo Lewis**, was among 116 Africans abducted, sold to Meaher, and loaded aboard the Clotilda for the trip to America.

At the age 67, Cudjo Lewis told author Hurston about that trip aboard the slave ship and, almost as harrowing, the experience of being Black in the Deep South following the Civil War.

The Middle Passage And More...

In succession in the book Barracoon, we learn about:

- Lewis growing up in his African village until the age of 18;
- His capture and survival in a "barracoon" – which was a holding pen for slaves awaiting shipment; and also where the derogatory term "coons" comes from.

- Passage across the Atlantic Ocean from Africa to America;
- Life as an Alabama slave;
- Post-bellum "freedom" and Lewis' confusion about what to do and where;
- Informal agreements among many Africans to live together, despite tensions among different tribes-of-origin;
- Refusal by his former slaveholder Meaher to provide Lewis with even a small plot of land;
- Creation of an African town;
- Loneliness, marriage, family, and the death of loved ones;
- Encounters with Alabama's Jim Crow laws.
- Every chapter of Lewis's story is suffused with the power of a first-person re-telling and, importantly, the humanity of his speech.
- For instance, Lewis goes to Meaher and asks for some land for his people after freedom. They don't have money to go back to Africa or the resources to buy land.
- He hopes Meaher can give them a small parcel based on their years of unpaid servitude. From Hurston's writing in the book:

   "Capn Tim, you brought us from our country where we had lan. You made us slave (5 years and 6 months). Now dey make us free but we ain got no country and we ain got no lan! Why doan you give us a piece dis lan so we can buildee ourself a house? Capn jump on his feet an say, 'Fool, do you think I goin give you property on top of property?'"

- Thoughtful Black readers will find in this exchange certain similarities to modern-day discussions about government benefits, affirmative action and reparations. Lewis was exploited by Meaher for over five years with no pay and the added trauma of being seen as and treated as less than human. At freedom, he seeks some land on which to farm and live.

- But the slaveholder is baffled. Why should he give property (land) to his former property? Lewis, though freed, remains sub-human and deserving of nothing for his past treatment, according to Capn Tim.

Present-Day Denial...

It wasn't until a hundred years after this exchange that President Lyndon Johnson acknowledged that a national program of affirmative action was needed to redress the damages of slavery and subsequent Jim Crow discrimination.

LBJ's assertion is still being challenged in the courts and at the polls. We know well of this struggle. Former Congressman John Conyers attempted for decades to hold hearings on reparations for the descendants of Black slaves. Never happened.

To illustrate the denial depth of the slaveholder plunder and abuse, today, as they open a new Thomas Jefferson facility in Monticello, there are still some white Jefferson descendants who refuse to acknowledge kinship with the offspring of Sally Hemings, Jefferson's slave mistress. With DNA proof, there is double kinship between them: Jefferson's father-in-law John Wayles fathered Sally Hemings by his slave mistress Betty Hemings.

In the book, Barracoon editor Deborah Plant provides an invaluable glossary, along with helpful notes and an afterword that offers context and clarity on critical elements of Hurston's opus.

Along with the authentic first-person narrative of Cudjo Lewis, Plant's editing achieves what may be the most concise, important, informative book on the subject of African slavery yet published.

Plant writes of Hurston's achievement: "In her endeavor to collect, preserve, and celebrate Black folk's genius, she was realizing her dream of presenting to the world, 'the greatest cultural wealth on the continent' while contradicting scientific racism…the body of lore Hurston gathered was an argument against such notions of cultural inferiority and white supremacy."

Inspired To Action…

This reader/reviewer is inspired to do several things after reading this book:

1. Donate 25 books, 25 e-books and 25 audio versions of Barracoon to Chicago's Urban Prep Academy, where my son Tim is founder/CEO and wants to revive a Real Men Read program.
2. Urge all public and private high schools to make this book required reading.
3. Ask Goodman Theater Director Chuck Smith to coordinate a reading of the Cudjo Lewis narrative onstage.
4. Approach WVON radio about airing serial installments of the audio book.
5. Suggest that Northwestern and Roosevelt universities build courses around, or integrate into existing curricula, Hurston's masterpiece.
6. Approach Professor Waldo Johnson at the University of Chicago about hosting a Barracoon Blast at the college that would be co-sponsored by Black businesses.

The rediscovery of Zora Neale Hurston's chronicle of the ordeal of Cudjo Lewis – an ordeal that remains an unhealed wound on a body politic that would sooner forget – is a literary event of the first magnitude.

Black youth talk of being "woke." Let Barracoon be for us a wake work watershed.

TIME FOR A NEW VOTER
EDUCATION PROJECT

Terrence Crutcher, Philando Castile, Samuel DuBose ....

The list of Black people killed by police in the past continues to grow, while too many of us with the most to lose continue to be distracted by the circus in the nation's capital promoted round-the-clock in the media.

Of the many processes associated with the human mind – decision-making, memory, etc. – attention is surely the most crucial because it is tied so clearly to perception. Attention is the process of selectively concentrating on a discrete aspect of information. And the enemy of attention is – you guessed it – distraction.

Distraction? Recently we've been hit with a deluge of distraction. Some lowlights:

- Facebook founder Mark Zuckerberg goes to Congress to say everything's going to be okay with online personal information, even though we're also informed that he once called his customers "dumb f–ks" for trusting him with details that can be profitably sold to commercial marketers and political mindbenders.
- Fired FBI director James Comey is touring the nation to tout a new book in which he calls the current White House Occupant (WHO) "morally unfit" to hold that office.

- Special Counsel Robert Mueller is creeping ever closer to the WHO, not just for possible collusion with Russian election-stealers, but for allegedly hushing a porn star with a $130,000 payment using legally restricted campaign funds.
- The alleged arranger of said payment, Fixer-to-the-Chief Michael Cohen, recently received a lesson on "lawyer-client privilege" when federal prosecutors reminded him there's no such thing when criminal fraud is suspected.
- House Speaker Paul Ryan, having secured his rich-get-richer tax "reform", decides to quit while he's ahead, not run for re-election, and let someone else deal with the WHO.

Meanwhile, barely noticed against this barrage of hot news, the assault on Black people continues unabated. Never mind that for all the Black blood spilled, only one officer among our nation's shoot-first police departments is likely facing prison time.

Akai Gurley, Laquan McDonald, Keith Lamont Scott ...

According to The Washington Post, there were 223 Black people killed by U.S. police and law enforcement officials during 2017. Yet most of the lethal shooters have either been wholly exonerated or given administrative hand-slaps.

One would think, given the severity of the situation, that Black Americans everywhere would be mounting a united get-out-the-vote campaign not just to support Black candidates, but all office-seekers of good intent who want to end the injustices that surround us.

But one would be wrong in that thinking. It is estimated that fewer than 29 percent of Black registered voters in the State of Illinois opted to exercise their precious franchise in the primary last March 20th. And that's just 29 percent of those who bothered to register in the first place. Roughly half of eligible Black voters aren't registered at all!

Paul O'Neal, Alton B. Sterling, Christian Taylor ...

Despite this sorry turnout, we can be thankful that State Sen. Kwame Raoul prevailed in his multi-candidate race to be the Democratic nominee to replace the retiring Lisa Madigan as Illinois Attorney General.

Clearly the state A.G. has great influence in dealing with police violence against Black people. Lisa Madigan has given her successor a big headstart by calling for a federal investigation of the Chicago Police Department's use of lethal force, and by insisting that all tapes and transcripts be made public in the 16-shot slaying of Laquan McDonald. Compare that to the recent whitewash by the Louisiana A.G. following the Baton Rouge police shooting of Alton Sterling.

But unless I'm missing something, there seems to be no great stirring in the Black community to ensure that Senator Raoul is elected in November to become just the fourth African-American state attorney general in the U.S.

We have the unprecedented potential of Kwame Raoul as our state's top legal officer, combining with Cook County State's Attorney Kim Foxx as a dynamic duo in the pursuit of unbiased law enforcement.

There are no Black people in Cook County or Illinois whose lives are not touched directly or indirectly by the policies and methods of these two offices, especially now, with Jefferson Beauregard Sessions III at the helm of the U.S. Justice Department.

Sessions has stated that police morale and safety are his most important concerns and he promises to reverse the Obama-era policy of the Justice Dept. getting involved in law enforcement cases at the local level.

Yet Black elected officials whom I've talked with say too many of our people simply aren't connecting the dots. They do not connect our inability to elect public officials sympathetic with our concerns to the injustices we face daily regarding public safety, educational resources and business opportunities.

Sandra Bland, Freddie Gray, Walter Scott …

So what's to be done?

It is time, I believe, to resurrect the old-fashioned Voter Education Project. Beginning in 1962, major foundations raised and distributed funds to Civil Rights groups in the South until 1968 for voter education and registration.

Back then, Black voters across the South faced violence and death threats for daring to vote. Along with education and registration, the VEP curriculum included tactics to avoid injury in pursuit of the right to vote.

But white violence wasn't the only obstacle. Black indifference also played a part – the obtuse notion that voting was "white folks' business" and that no election could or would improve their life chances.

Today, 50 years later, even after a Black Chicago mayor and a Black Chicagoan became president, there remains among voting-eligible Blacks a disturbing amount of apathy, a belief that it's all corrupt, that my vote doesn't count, that my needs won't be addressed – all wrapped in a lack of knowledge about the political system.

Do not dare tell me that low-income Blacks are lazy. Early every Friday morning, I witness over 200 shivering in the cold and rain outside my St. Ailbe Parish food pantry on the South Side, pull-wagons and shopping carts at the ready, waiting to get donated produce, canned goods and other staples.

Why do they do that? Because they trust they'll get something for their efforts. Come Election Day, though, not so much.

Combine this skepticism with intentional Black voter suppression, racial gerrymandering, and other nefarious tactics taking place in states across the nation, and it's no wonder that northern industrial states rich in potential Black votes – Wisconsin, Michigan, Ohio, Pennsylvania, etc. – factored mightily into the narrow electoral victory of the WHO.

Borrowing from the Voter Education Project of memory, I hereby urge creation of a new coalition of foundations (think the Chicago Community Trust, the Joyce Foundation, the Field, the Polk Bros. the MacArthur) to step up to the plate.

A good first step would be to engage local universities – think Professors Erik Gellman and Al Bennett at Roosevelt University along with Waldo Johnson at the University of Chicago, guided by a Black Advisory Group led by the Rev. Johnny Miller of the JLM Center, along with leaders of the West Side Justice Center and others – to engage in a non-partisan and IRS-compliant effort to identify problems and devise solutions.

Problems and solutions such as:

1. Finding out why so few Blacks vote.
2. Educating the uniformed as to how voting affects policies that impact their lives.
3. Facilitating voter registration.
4. Convening non-partisan educational meetings on the South and West sides and suburbs where there are many Black residents.
5. Facilitating early voting and Election Day get-out-the-vote efforts.
6. Investigating and reporting cases of unlawful partisan steering.

7. Establishing a social media model for voter education and registration, thereby motivating Millennials who are so quick to join noisy, albeit warranted, protests, yet so slow to work the more powerful levers of political action. Kids, there is no point- and-click voting app.

Tamir Rice, Eric Garner, Michael Brown...

It's a long list and getting longer. For those who are educated, well-read, in business and issue-informed, the value of the vote is obvious. This is not so for too many others.

In addition to voluble protest, there must be a sustained political pressure leading to policy and process reforms. Voter Education Projects have worked in the past. It's time to make them work again.

GOVERNOR'S RACE CANDIDATES MUST ADDRESS BLACK CONCERNS

The elections of 2018 are significant in many ways. Nationally, the congressional races will be a referendum on the chaotic first year of what's-his-name, while in Illinois, voters will decide whether to blame an incumbent Republican governor or Chicago Democrats who run the legislature for our state's financial mess.

All but lost in the upcoming carnival of mud-slinging and rhetorical noise is that 2018 is also the 50th anniversary of the assassination of the Rev. Dr. Martin Luther King.

The slaying of Dr. King and the racial rupture that followed continues to drive and divide our politics as much as any issue, foreign or domestic. Racial rupture? After King's murder, riots broke out in over a hundred cities, people died, arrests were made, and federal troops brought in.

Whites generally viewed the rioters as arsonists and looters, not frustrated fellow Americans pushed past the breaking point. Too many saw this spasm not in a social justice context, but as a dangerous breakdown of civil society.

Richard Nixon's presidential campaign of that year took full advantage, appealing directly to a "silent majority," many of whose members still view even peaceful protests by Blacks as "acting out."

Cultural critic Louis Menand reminds us in a recent issue of The New Yorker that it was 1968 when America's historic divide between right and left began widening into today's seemingly unbridgeable chasm. Yet the fault line was already there, waiting to be exploited.

Describing a 2014 study by political scientists Doug McAdam and Karina Kloos, Menand observes, "Since 1960 our politics has been driven by two movements: the civil rights movement and what they call a 'countermovement,' which could be broadly described as anti-integrationist."

So who are the anti-integrationists? Menand includes outright racists, but also many white Americans who acknowledge the principle of racial equality, but in practice resent involuntary race mixing such as affirmative action quotas.

Menand especially commends the conclusion reached by McAdam and Kloos, that "The collapse of the postwar consensus was not because of Vietnam; it had everything to do with race."

The solid core of Nixon's Silent Majority still exists as the so-called "Trump base." Here in Illinois, it is making itself heard in the Republican primary for governor, where the incumbent is be challenged not from his party's center, but from the far right.

Read About Plantation Politics. Click Here!

And what of the Democrats? Has any gubernatorial candidate actually earned the backing of African American voters in the March primary? Or even in the general election?

It's stunning that three of the early frontrunners are multi-millionaires – two of them billionaires. According to press reports, JB Pritzker, the Democrats' early favorite, comes in at $3.4 billion; incumbent Republican

Bruce Rauner a tad below $1 billion; and Democrat Christopher Kennedy in excess of $40 million.

So, what have they been doing with all their money? For African Americans, that's a fair question.

Have they, for instance, entrusted some of their millions to Illinois Black businesses such as Loop Capital? Have they availed themselves of Black-owned accountancies such those run by Lester McKeever and Odell Hicks? Which Black contractors have rehabbed the Kennedy-managed Merchandise Mart or are building those skyscrapers rising at adjacent Wolf Point?

Have any of their billions been directed as charitable contributions to schools such as Urban Prep Academies, where young Black men are being readied for college? (Full disclosure: Urban Prep's CEO Tim King is my son.)

This isn't to say such hirings and contributions haven't been made…just that Black voters need to know if they have or have not. After all, Black participation in the March primary and November general elections are absolutely key to the outcome.

Doubt it? Consider the recent Alabama U.S. Senate race. In spite of attempts at voter suppression, Black voters made a winner of a Democrat who once prosecuted the Ku Klux Klan over a Republican who was alleged to be a sexual predator.

It should be noted that the winning Doug Jones campaign hired Black consultants, campaigned with or dispatched Black surrogates, and spent nearly a third of its budget on measures to boost Black turnout.

It also circulated race-specific messaging, including a tableau of a young white girl being victimized by an older white man with the caption, "If he'd been Black, he would have been lynched." (Crude, sure, but with Alabama's racist history, it resonated.)

Taking The Black Vote For Granted

Kashana Cauley, a New York Times Op-Ed contributor, nailed it in a recent column headlined, "Black Voters to Democrats: You're Welcome." She points out that most Blacks think they're taken for granted by the Democratic Party.

Cauley wrote, "We are drowning in reports on how Democrats can win the white working class. But Blacks are the ones who have a much more robust history of turning out to vote and winning elections for Democrats. Nor does the Democratic Party spend enough money addressing the concerns of Black voters. It does not routinely condemn racial inequality out of fear of turning off white voters, nor does it make specific appeals to Black voters on issues like jobs and education." (As my Bahamian relatives would say, "They wanna go to heaven but don't want dead.")

Yet when Blacks do vote, they vote heavily Democratic. Why? Bowdoin College Professor Chryl Laird offers in VOX.com that specific social dynamics explain why. If a politician wants greater support of Blacks, her best bet is getting social processes within the community working in her favor. This is such a profound statement its worthy of repeating.

Laird's research goes on to note that Black voter response is greater when offered by a Black presenter, less when offered by a white presenter, and least when offered online.

Take a look at the 2008 Obama presidential campaign. I was on the National Finance Committee, which teleconferenced every Friday morning.

Mantra Number 1 was to maximize turnout of the base. Number 2 was to do nothing to have him come off as an "Angry Black Man." Black support for Obama was obvious, but turnout was at record levels because the campaign valued it, put money into it and worked at it!

Likewise, Doug Jones succeeds in Alabama by pouring resources into Black turnout, which ended up being the key to his more than 20,000 votes win. Compare that to Hillary Clinton's 2016 effort, wherein she tried to balance a white working- class message with an assortment of feminist and LGBTQ pitches.

In the end, her campaign's "take 'em for granted" approach to the Black community helps explain why she lost Michigan by 10,704 votes, Pennsylvania by 44,000 and Wisconsin by 22,748.

Had the Clinton campaign addressed Black concerns, delivered by credible Black surrogates with a process adequately funded, the entire United States, not just Blacks, wouldn't be quaking over what gaucherie what's-his-name will commit next.

The Power in the Black Vote

Adopt This Black Strategy

So, with all of this experience to draw from, what should a successful candidate for Illinois governor do in 2018? Here's my Top 10 list:

1. Focus on Black turnout by engaging Black media consultants such as Hermene Hartman of N'DIGO and Melody Spann-Cooper of WVON. The candidates need to understand the reach and respect these women enjoy in the Black community.

2. Agree on a Black-themed message and engage credible Black messengers – those who understand the subtle differences between various communities.

3. Provide support, within federal tax rules, to Black grassroots organizations that have genuine connections to – and the respect of – Black voters

4. Visit uplifting efforts such as Urban Prep Academy, in person, and let your visit inspire a commitment to the education of these young Black men using both public and private resources.

5. Meet with Dr. Gary Slutkin of Cure Violence and commit to support this innovative public health approach to the South and West side homicide epidemic.

6. Meet with State's Attorney Kim Foxx and agree to a workforce development strategy for preparing and placing Black ex-offenders.

7. Meet with Frank Clark, Jim Reynolds and leaders of the Business Leadership Council to develop a state office for Black business utilization. (Not just direct state spending, but also state-subsidized projects.) This office should be staffed and run by an experienced advocate for capacity building among Black businesses.

8. Establish a state "Prompt Payment Policy" so that contractors are paid in a timely manner. Absent this, establish a state guaranteed, low-interest line of credit for contractors awaiting unpaid receivables.

9. Meet with innovative workforce development pioneers such as the Rev. Johnny Miller (a CTA board member and leader of the West Side JMA Center) to recalibrate and redouble state efforts to boost Black employment levels.

10. Meet with other innovators such as Rev. Kevin Ford of St. Paul COGIC, whose Project Pride is the leader in getting Blacks into construction unions. Other Black organizations such as

CrossRoads, West Side Justice Center and Black Lives Matter also are deserving of support.

Admittedly these actions aren't your typical billionaire's recipe for success. But to ignore legitimate Black expectations for improved economic support is surely a recipe for political failure. That's the lesson, 50 years in the learning.

TA-NEHISI COATES ILLUMINATES THE BLACK EXPERIENCE

Too rarely does a curious businessman such as myself have the good fortune to encounter a truly deep thinker, someone whose writing and speaking shines an unblinking light on the dark history of the Black experience in America.

For me of late, that special person has been Ta-Nehisi Coates, national correspondent for The Atlantic Magazine. No one better connects the dots that lead from slavery's Middle Passage to Jim Crow to today's Trumpian version of benign neglect.

His work shows a kinship in thinking with James Baldwin ("The Fire Next Time") and Derrick Bell ("Faces at the Bottom of the Well: The Permanence of Racism") Yet Coates' true genius is best illustrated by what he does not write or say: What exactly is to be done about all this? These decisions – these plans of action – he leaves squarely to us. So we are challenged, not consoled.

My awakening to Ta-Nehisi Coates began with his June 2014 article in The Atlantic titled, "The Case for Reparations." It's a well-researched and coolly argued case for nationwide recompense, not just for slavery and Jim Crow, but for the pervasive and malevolent treatment of Black people to this day.

His writing in that piece set my mind afire with its poetry, passion and power. Instead of dry legalisms or examples of cruelty too easily dismissed as anecdotal, he traces the evolution of white-sponsored predation and plunder that has created a still untreated wound that Coates terms "Black Injury."

In a recent review of a Coates' book in The New York Times, cultural historian Kevin Young cites his 2014 article as Coates' calling card – a remarkable pocket history of the financial toll of white supremacy, from Southern disenfranchisement to Northern (need we say Chicago?) urban renewal land grabs and mortgage/insurance redlining.

His article traces how Black people were viewed as a spreading contagion, how FHA- insured loans benefited white sellers but greased the skids under entire neighborhoods, how the unavailability of standard loans and homeowner insurance became an accepted practice across the entire real estate industry.

This targeting of Black neighborhoods surely continues – simply witness the outsized number of foreclosures caused by the recent epidemic of sub-prime mortgage lending. As one major bank ex-employee explained: "Wells Fargo had an emerging markets unit that specifically targeted Black churches because it figured church leaders had a lot of influence and could convince congregants to take out sub-prime loans."

The Roosevelt University Lecture...

Inspired by the sweep of Coates' indictment, I approached Roosevelt University Professor Erik Gellman about bringing Coates to Chicago for an October 2014 lecture.

Prior to this "sold out" free event, Prof. Gellman and I met with Coates and eight students and guests. It turned out that his soft-spoken demeanor is 180-degrees from the anger and frustration of his written words. His lecture at Roosevelt was so over capacity that security guards posted at both the college's Michigan and Wabash Avenue entrances had to turn away many hopeful audience members.

Coates gave a splendid accounting of his logic, research and conclusions. But he then surprised nearly everyone by what he would not say. During the post-speech Q-and-A, he was asked by a well-respected Black advocate: "What should we do?"

His response was that he was a writer, not an activist. When his questioner demanded at least "a suggestion," Coates suggested we might lobby for passage of a bill sponsored annually by the former U.S. Rep. John Conyers of Detroit that would create a commission to study "Reparations Proposals for African Americans."

After the lecture, my wife and I, along with a Roosevelt benefactor and Gellman, enjoyed a private dinner with Mr. Coates. The man has – what? – a baffling brilliance.

During the dinner conversation, he challenged me personally about my own thinking and activism on behalf of more Black participation in Chicago's building trades and contracting.

How he knew of my past I know not, but allow me to paraphrase his challenge:

"You've been fighting for years for Blacks in construction, based on President Lyndon Johnson's references to slavery. Now 40 years later, the courts have ruled such a remedy off limits because it is 'reverse discrimination.'"

His cryptic but accurate summation of affirmative action had me and other guests asking for more, so we inquired about his concept of Black Injury.

Coates replied: "Imagine you were beating a thief with a 2-by-4 across his head and body for over 20 minutes, then someone came along and told you this was the wrong man. You would stop beating and apologize. However, even though you stopped the beating, the man is still bruised and injured."

Chicago Humanities Festival

Fast forward to October of 2017, by which time Ta-Nehisi Coates had won both the Polk and Stowe Awards for his Atlantic magazine work, a National Book Award for his tome, "Between the World and Me," and a MacArthur Foundation "Genius" grant. This time he was back in Chicago for a speech to the Chicago Humanities Festival and another "sold out" audience at Rockefeller Chapel on the campus of the University of Chicago.

The line of ticketed guests – many clutching his latest book, "We Were Eight Years in Power," a collection of essays Coates wrote for The Atlantic while Barack Obama was POTUS – snaked all the way along Woodlawn Avenue to 59th Street. All told, some 1,500 people wanted to hear Humanities Medalist Krista Tippett interview Coates about issues hardly anyone seems to be talking about in this, the white nationalist Age of Trump.

No Offer Of Solutions . . .

In the course of their dialogue, Tippett asked, "I am a white person. What do you want me to do?" To the surprise of none of us who heard him at Roosevelt University, Coates punted – not once, but again and again, like the Chicago Bears.

"I read Ta-Nehisi Coates' fascinating article," complained an Atlantic reader. "I found it convincing. I am white. Now what? My question for Mr. Coates is this: If you were writing to someone you no longer needed to convince, if the arguments were all done with, what would you have him do?"

Again I paraphrase Coates' thoughtful, if maddening, response:

"The title 'public intellectual' has been attached to me and I saw that what came with it was not just the air of the dilettante, but the air of a solutionist. The Black public intellectual need not be wise, but he better have answers.

"I felt the expectation that if I was writing or talking about problems, I should be able to identify an immediately actionable way out – preferably one that could garner a 60-vote majority in the Senate.

"There was a kind of insanity to this – like telling doctors to only diagnose that which they could immediately and effortlessly cure…to interpret them in some way that promised redemption. But this is not work for writers and scholars, who thrive in privacy and study, but for performance-prophets who live for the roar of the crowd."

Another occasion for evasion at this event, raised by Tippit and by the audience, had to do with hope. Should we be hopeful, or does hope get in the way of angry insistence?

Coates emphatically sidestepped that one, too, though a close reading of Eight Years In Power is revelatory. "In all of American life, there is a bias toward a happy ending," Coates writes, "toward the notion that human resilience and intellect will be a match for any problem.

"This holds especially true for the problem of white supremacy. For white people who have not quite taken on the full load of ancestral debt, but can sense its weight, there is a longing for some magic that might make the burden of slavery and all that followed magically vanish.

"For Blacks born under the burden, there is a need to believe that a better day is on the horizon, that their lives...are not forever condemned to carry that weight, which white people can only but sense. I felt this need whenever I spoke to audiences about my writing since, invariably, I would be asked what I could say that would give the audience hope. I never knew how to answer the question."

Columnist Salim Muwakkil has sagely observed that Ta-Nehisi Coates has taken on the role of our nation's most prominent skeptic of racial progress. The year-ago presidential election only validates that skepticism, Muwakkil writes in In These Times, arguing that "the backlash to Obama's presidency and the reactionary election of Trump (are) all part of this nation's routine racial choreography: one step toward racial progress, two steps back."

Suggestions for "What Now?"...

So we are left to develop our own answers to the "what now?" question that Coates refuses, on principal, to address. For starters, I turned to my Roosevelt University friend Professor Erik Gellman, associate director at the school's St. Clair Drake Center for African and African-American Studies. His ideas include:

- Start by understanding your own white privilege, then identify institutions that perpetuate it and work to democratize them. This process can be overwhelming, so perhaps choose an institution you know best as a starting point – that could be one's workplace, school, neighborhood or group.
- Do not be shy to speak out against assumptions, statements, and policies made by whites against other groups, especially when people of color and those other groups are not present.

- Support and join local groups that seek transformation, such as Cure Violence and the West Side Justice Center.
- Identify community groups that empower people rather than pity them. Donate your money and time, but do so with no strings attached. Do not fall into the philanthropic trap that your funding necessitates your advice or leadership. Prompted by Gellman's advice, I'd add the following to the "what now?" question:
- Investigate and financially support educational efforts such as Urban Prep Academy (in full disclosure, the school's president is my son Tim King). This charter school serving Black young men has for the past six years sent 100 percent of its graduates to college, several of whom have come back to teach and mentor at Urban Prep.

  More specifically, help Urban Prep with its "10-for-10" campaign to raise $10 million each of the next 10 years to support, expand, replicate and advance the best practices developed at this culture changing high school.

  Statistics show that the costs of gun violence –including ambulance, medical autopsy, hospital acute trauma, rehabilitation, police overtime, etc. – totals $100,000 or more per incident. This makes the 10 for 10 for Urban Prep a bargain.

- Encourage and support those who advertise in N'DIGO, on WVON radio and in other media that support and defend Black cultural life. Read N'DIGO's weekly print newspaper and online website and stay tuned to WVON on radio or cellphone to be informed.

  There are no substitutes for media mavens such as Hermene Hartman and Melody Spann-Cooper, who cover issues of importance to Black Chicago. They give voice to those ignored by other print, radio and TV outlets, countering the suppressed, ignored, and unpublished news about Black people, issues and events.

Think that's too harsh an assessment? Check out the new and semi-apologetic book "UNSEEN: Unpublished Black History From The New York Times Photo Archives." It features hundreds of stunning never-before-published images from Black history languishing in that vaunted paper's vaults and tells the stories behind them. As Maya Angelou famously said, "There is no greater agony than bearing an untold story inside you."

- Contact Jim Reynolds, John Rogers, or Karen Riley of the Business Leadership Council (BLC) to understand the mission, vision and values of our organization. Seek to do business with BLC members. This group of Black businesses and professionals not only advocates for businesses and embraces emerging businesses, but also creates and develops Black employment.

Ta-Nehisi Coates is an intellectual rising star who must be read by those who seek a better life. And not just Blacks, but by an entire nation suffering from willful ignorance or outright denial. The "what now?" question he purposefully leaves for us is surely the unavoidable challenge of our time.

FOXX NEWS SHOULD
TRUMP TRUMP

Let's stop wasting our valuable time following the Comey Comedy, the Donald Drama, and the Carson Cartoons. These Parodies-on-the-Potomac will grind on and on without our precious attention.

President Barack Obama, in an interview with *The New Yorker's* David Remnick, nailed it when he said, "The capacity to disseminate misinformation in a wildly negative light without any rebuttal…has accelerated in ways much more polarizing to the electorate and makes it very difficult to have a conversation."

In other words, in the new media ecosystem, everything is true and nothing is true. So I'd advise my fellow African Americans, and especially Black Chicagoans, to stay focused on things that matter – and will continue to matter – long after the Trump fiasco plays itself out.

Like these things:

- African-American males are six times more likely to be incarcerated than white males and 2.5 times more likely than Hispanic males. If this trend continues, one of every three Black American males born today can expect to go to prison in his lifetime, according to the DC Sentencing Project in 2013.

- 25 percent of Black male prison inmates are emotionally traumatized or mentally challenged, according to Bryan Stevenson's Equal Justice Initiative.

It has become so expensive to maintain the million Black men in America's criminal justice system that two of the nation's foremost ideological combatants, the Koch Brothers and Senator Cory Booker of New Jersey, agree that a reduction of Black prison inmates needs to be achieved.

The New State's Attorney

Locally, consider the once-in-a-lifetime opportunity we now have to address these issues with the election of Kim Foxx as Cook County State's Attorney.

Sure we've had Harold and Barack, but never a Black officeholder – not to mention one who grew up in the CHA projects – with this level of leverage to begin solving an immediate and crucial problem.

After all, our State's Attorney controls the second largest prosecutor's office in the United States. Her office directs approximately 900 attorneys among its more than 1,600 employees and they handle all misdemeanor and felony crimes in our state's largest county.

"We've never had a Black officeholder – State's Attorney Kim Foxx – with this level of leverage to begin solving an immediate and crucial problem."

In light of the unprecedented powers now held by Kim Foxx, I was motivated to pick up John Pfaff's book "LOCKED IN: The True Causes of Mass Incarceration —And How to Achieve Real Reform." Pfaff argues the most effective way to reduce Black incarceration is to reduce admission to prison in the first place.

To do that, we must change the practices that have led prosecutors to file felony charges against so many. Pfaff posits that prosecutors have more power than ever because, in general, state legislators have enacted laws affording prosecutors a wider range of options.

The criminal justice trifecta has three horses: police, prosecutors and judges. This is the axis upon which all spins – who's arrested, who goes to prison and for how long, and who gets let go.

Within this trio – think of a drummer backed by piano and guitar – the most powerful is the prosecutor. The police, theoretically at least, operate in public and have constitutional and judicial oversight. Judges must explain their decisions in writing and are subject to appeal. Legislators must answer to voters at election time.

But prosecutors act behind a relative veil of secrecy, as described recently by David Cole in *The New York Review of Books*. Prosecutors, moreover, have the power to agree to drop charges if the arrestee agrees to counseling, behavior changes, mediation, etc., all likely monitored by reporting periodically to the court.

Consider just the veil of secrecy. We know almost nothing about how they decide whether to charge a defendant. There is no requirement that state's attorneys offer any explanation for their decisions.

Too often this has led to race-based abuse, a prime example being the 1969 home invasion and killing of Black Panthers Fred Hampton and Mark Clark orchestrated by Cook County State's Attorney Ed Hanrahan.

Compare that travesty to how a compassionate Kim Foxx might establish alternative sentencing for young defendants. She could, for instance, take advantage of pre- apprenticeship programs for construction jobs on County projects.

And if violent behavior is indeed a public health challenge comparable to alcoholism, a theory that Chicago Dr. Gary Slutkin advances, Foxx could widen the menu to include compassionate, consistent and interventional counseling.

Think about this again. A Black female, having grown up in Chicago's public housing, now has the power to decide who gets charged, with what, and who goes to jail…or gets diverted toward a more positive outcome.

How We Can Help Foxx

Realizing this, here are some things Black Chicago needs to keep in mind:

1. Understand what the State's Attorney can do.
2. Lay out a set of expectations for that office.
3. Volunteer for citizen advisory councils to that office (I was on one back in the day).
4. Support Ms. Foxx electorally, organizationally, and financially.
5. Recognize that other interest groups, including some whose pursuits don't match ours, will also be jockeying for position.
6. Hold her accountable for responding to Black community concerns.

We also should take a lesson from, of all places, Oklahoma. In November 2016, folks there voted overwhelmingly for Trump, yet simultaneously approved a ballot initiative to reduce many drug and property crimes from felonies to misdemeanors, and to invest the savings in rehabilitation programs for convicted criminals. (This wasn't about Black people; it was about dollars.)

With what other Cook County State's Attorney could you even have had a conversation about this in the past? Yet, it's a great idea – to shift convict maintenance costs to external prison counseling and guidance.

Of course, the devil is in the details. If Cook County saves $20,000 by keeping a Black man out of prison for one year, what portion of that savings could go directly to his or her rehabilitation? Or as importantly, to the protection of the community to which he will return?

There are many ways these savings could be applied. Illinois already offers a five percent income tax credit – not to exceed $600 per eligible employee – to encourage contractors to hire ex-offenders.

Cook County, at the urging of Commissioner Richard Boykin, is experimenting with a "bid credit" giving employers of ex-cons an edge when seeking competitively bid contracts. And the savings could subsidize pre-apprenticeship programs to which offenders would be assigned as an alternative to jail.

I am involved with the Drake Center at Roosevelt University, where planning is underway for a September 2017 conversation between State's Attorney Foxx and the aforementioned Dr. Gary Slutkin, who founded CeaseFire Illinois, also known as Cure Violence.

A University of Illinois epidemiologist, Dr. Slutkin is an advocate for recognizing the homicide epidemic among young Black men as a public health issue that cannot be addressed by external force.

His staff runs a cell phone hotline with four Black community trauma centers that, when a shooting takes place, steps in to cool the inevitable fever for retaliation.

There are many other opportunities to engage the State's Attorney and to establish and maintain ongoing dialogue toward change.

The Historic Black Colleges remind us that a mind is a terrible thing to waste. I agree. But so are rare opportunities such as the election of Kim Foxx. So let CNN worry about President Humpty Dumpty and his Wall. We've got more immediate fish to fry.

MAKING IT RIGHT FOR
HENRIETTA LACKS

Just when White America thought it was safe to come out its defensive crouch against charges of historic racism, here comes Oprah Winfrey starring in a film version of Rebecca Skloot's book, "The Immortal Life of Henrietta Lacks."

Lacks was a poor southern Black woman who suffered from cervical cancer. Before she passed and without her knowledge her cells were extracted and scientifically cultured to become the first strain of human tissue to become, well, immortal.

Known as HeLa, the cells remain alive today, nearly seven decades after her death. During that time, according to Skloot, these same HeLa cells have been instrumental in the development by medical science of multimillion-dollar industries ranging from biological materials to in vitro fertilization, to cloning, to gene mapping and even to the polio vaccine which by itself made its investors billions of dollars.

So here's another example of what author Ta-Nehisi Coates has called "Black Injury," an unspeakable injustice that ranks right up there with the Tuskegee "Bad Blood" experiment, wherein Black men were infected with syphilis.

Johns Hopkins Hospital in Baltimore compounded the original offense by subsequently using material drawn from Ms. Lacks' husband and children in its HeLa research without their informed consent.

Today, many of Lacks' descendants live in or near poverty, some without education, employment and, most ironically, healthcare.

Here's a case of an uninformed Black family that was violated, with the violation resulting in huge scientific and business profits for the larger White society. Yet the descendants of this Black woman are without decent lives or life prospects.

Two themes recur both in the book and the film:

1. The Lacks family has justifiably distrusted White people seeking information, access and/or cooperation in pursuing the story of Henrietta and her immortal cells; and
2. There's an expectation and determination by the family to benefit somehow from the profits made from Henrietta's ill-gotten cells.

Speaking to point No. 2 above, The New York Times quotes Winfrey: "I get really upset when I hear people complain (namely some members of the Lacks family) that Rebecca or I or HBO haven't done anything. When one of the sons started a Henrietta Lacks Healing Center, I did make a six-figure donation to it. And we offered them to be consultants on the film, but a small portion of the family didn't want to be a part of it. So, I don't know what they wanted other than the $10 million they wrote me asking for."

But what about Johns Hopkins Medical Center? Their spokesman recently stated: "Johns Hopkins part in the Mrs. Lacks story is complex and, in several respects, regrettable and yet it has helped us to deepen our understanding of informed consent."

This is tantamount to saying it's regrettable that Laquan McDonald got shot and killed, but the upside is that police reform is taking place in Chicago. Laquan McDonald is still dead! Let Henrietta's gift be immortal not the injustice of what happened to her and her family. **Make It Right** Johns Hopkins and others who profited from the HeLa cells would do well to look down Interstate 95 at an attempt at reparations developed by Georgetown University.

Recent scholarship unearthed the fact that, in 1838, the good Jesuits of Georgetown University sold some 272 African slaves to plantations in the Deep South. The sale netted in today's dollars $3.3 million and supposedly saved the institution from going under.

In response to this discovery and to faculty and student reaction the university took the following steps:

1. Issued a formal apology.
2. Established a working group to consider how it should address this history.
3. Renamed two buildings previously named for the Jesuits involved in the sale, one for one of the sold slaves and the other for an educator of Black girls.
4. Launched research into the descendants of the sold slaves with the idea of engaging with them and soliciting their recommendations.
5. Announced preferential admission, with possible financial aid, for the slave descendants.
6. Created an institute for the study of slavery.

Taking a cue from the Hoya playbook, Johns Hopkins ought to convene a working group composed of Lacks family representatives; Merck Pharmaceutical (their Sigma Aldrich unit still sells millions of HeLa cells); Washington University of St. Louis, whose Ethics Professor Rebecca

Dresser has weighed in fairly on the Lacks interests; Lawyers Committee for Civil Rights Under Law; the ACLU; and The National Institute of Health

Some recommendations which Johns Hopkins should pursue, on behalf of the Lacks family might include:

1. Free medical care to Lacks descendants.
2. Employment counseling and preferential hiring by Johns Hopkins and other companies that have profited from Lacks sales.
3. Financial grants, accompanied by financial counseling provided by the likes of Amazon (another cell seller).
4. Scholarships for Lacks descendants to colleges and universities engaged in research associated with Henrietta's cells.
5. An institute to determine what profits HeLa cells have generated, leading to an apportionment of same to Black charitable organizations selected by the Lacks family.

For those who fear that this may be an underhanded attempt at dreaded reparations – it's not. It is a variation on the corrective action taken by Georgetown. In the absence of this, what?

Let Henrietta's gift be immortal not the injustice of what happened to her and her family.

WHITE ANGER'S
COWARDLY REVENGE

"That the electorate has, in its plurality, decided to live in Trump's world of vanity, hate, arrogance, untruth, and recklessness, his disdain for democratic norms, is a fact that will lead, inevitably, to all manner of national decline and suffering." — David Remnick, The New Yorker, Nov. 9, 2016

The recent Presidential election was a lot more about race than economics. It was yet another time when Black achievement and Black advancement unleashed a flood of white resentment.

Carol Anderson, in her book, "White Rage: The Unspoken Truth of our Racial Divide," says "the trigger for white rage, inevitability is Black advancement. It is not the mere presence of Black people that is the problem, rather it is Blackness with ambition, with drive, with purpose,, with aspirations and with demands for full and equal citizenship. It is Blackness that refuses to accept subjugation, to give up. A formidable array of policy assaults and legal contortions has consistently punished Black resilience.

The History

Let us recount White Anger's shameful past:

1. **Reconstruction** – After the Civil War, white Southerners resorted to Black Codes, Jim Crow, lynching and all manner of violence against Black former slaves, claiming they were needed to avoid lawlessness and vagrancy.

2. **Brown v Board of Education** – Faced with SCOTUS-ordered integration, Southern governors redirected public education dollars to white private schools and reduced funds to public schools attended by Black students.

3. **The Voting Rights Act of 1966** – A half century after acknowledging federal oversight was required to ensure Blacks were able to vote in Southern states, the high court gutted the Act in 2013. Chief Justice Roberts disingenuously explained it was a new day in the South "largely because of the Voting Rights Act, voting tests were abolished, disparities in voter registration and turnout were erased and African Americans attained political office in record numbers." Result — subtler forms of Black voter suppression quickly ensued.

4. **The fate of Affirmative Action** – In 1965 President Lyndon Johnson stated that, in order to redress the vestiges of slavery and racial discrimination, affirmative action in federal hiring and contracting was necessary. Ever since there has been an assault on these policies. With Blacks taking precious slots in medical, law and other prestigious schools, complaints of "reverse discrimination" have swelled to the point that the Supreme Court is deliberating whether "race" can be considered in college admissions. Now, with Trump poised to nominate the ninth and tie-breaking justice, the fate of affirmative action appears sealed.

The Obama Bash

No instance of Black achievement has so energized white resentment as the 2008 election of Barack Obama as President of the United States.

It is safe to say that, without Barack Obama, the very idea of a President Donald Trump would have been laughed at by a vast majority of the voting public. But Obama, who never had any political, financial, sexual or social scandal, nonetheless was so vilified and disrespected, so insulted by calls to "take our country back," that the preposterous became reality.

This vilification and disrespect of our first Black president has been constant, yet it helps to recall some lowlights. From the get-go in 2008, with citizen Trump leading the "birther" cry, right-wingers began charging that Obama was not born in the U.S. and therefore ineligible for the office. In 2009, during his address to a joint session of congress, a South Carolina congressman yelled at the President "You lie!"

Later the Speaker of the House invited the Israeli prime minster to address the Congress without clearing it with the White House. For his part, the Republican Senate Majority Leader, Mitch McConnell, stated without equivocation that his main goal was to deprive Obama of a 2nd term.

The Media

At no point during this string of insults did the mainstream media – a supposedly leftist force in American life according to conservative rhetoric – call out Obama's detractors for their obviously racist behavior. Had racism become, as the pop-psych expression has it, "normalized?" Had Jim Crow been let out of the closet? That question is answered now by the seemingly impossible ascendance of Donald J. Trump, a billionaire real estate mogul with a flair for publicity and zero governmental experience. It has been estimated that television, radio and social media provided his campaign with over $2 billion worth in free coverage. This is known in the political trade as "earned media" … as if the candidate's racist, xenophobic rants deserved something other than condemnation. In one case a Sunday TV talk show broke all precedents and allowed Trump to be interviewed via telephone rather than require him, to come to the studio. The CEO of CBS stated it best when he quipped that the Trump campaign roadshow "may be not be good for America but it's damn good for CBS"

The FBI

The Justice Department has long-standing guidelines against public comment by prosecutors concerning ongoing investigations. There is even a policy, for instance, of avoiding the filing of completed indictments against candidates for political office within 60 days of an election. Yet in his letter to Congress on October 28, 2016 regarding the FBI's supposedly closed investigation of Hillary Clinton's emails, agency Director James Comey's action moved the needle of public opinion away from Clinton and toward the previously unthinkable. His public reversal less than a week before the election served only to remind voters that she might have done something wrong.

The Polls

For the first time in over 20 years, most polling data proved off by over 4%, not just for the presidential race, but for many House, Senate and state elections. Statisticians will parse the numbers, but given the highly-charged racial and gender subtext of the campaigns, one can reasonably assume much of this error was due to interviewees not telling the truth about whom they supported. Yet these same polls had enormous impact on candidates' decisions on resource allocation and ground game emphasis. Leading the polls by 2% in Wisconsin, for instance, Hillary Clinton skipped personal appearances there … and ended up losing the state by just 30,000 votes.

The Angry White Guy

Several mainstream analysts, trying to assess the motives of Trump supporters, have cited statistics showing a decline in quality-of-life among blue-collar whites. And indeed there's been a slight and as-yet-unexplained decline in his life expectancy, a rise in drug and alcohol abuse as well as suicide, and perhaps non-coincidentally a 30- year stagnation in real wages.

No doubt many blame their troubles on what they themselves see in everyday life – increasing numbers of immigrants from Asia and Central America, with more apparently on the way from the war-torn Middle East. Highly publicized incidents of domestic terrorism – think San Bernardino and the Orlando nightclub – feed his sense of unease-turning-to-outrage. Like Howard Beale in the movie "Network," he's mad as hell and not going to take it any longer.

This analysis goes on to argue that Trump listened to this AWG as no other candidate has … and offered blessed relief. I can understand this, though as a Black American whose people have endured far worse for far longer, I do not totally sympathize with Mr. AWG. What I do not understand is why AWG sees Donald Trump – an alleged tax-avoiding billionaire with a litigious history of stiffing local contractors and buying foreign supplies – is suddenly viewed as the agent of AWG's salvation. Might it be that race, not economics, is the more plausible explanation for what happened Nov. 8?

The Way Forward

It's been said that winners write history, so as Trump's noisy self-congratulation unfolds in Washington I would urge fellow scribes to review and remind about the achievements of Barack Obama. While the mainstream media continues to parrot Trump's denigration of his predecessor, let us set the record straight.

We must review, for instance, the impact that Obama's choice of Eric Holder as Attorney General and consider how significant that was in responding to police misconduct toward Blacks in places Ferguson, Baltimore and Tamir Rice's Cleveland. We must record the genuine relief and hope given to Black people with pre- existing health issues ... now able to get insurance. We must not forget the pride and self- affirmation we saw in young Black boys who in 2008 saw someone like themselves become President of these United States.

"All politics is local," the late Speaker of the House Tip O'Neil once reminded. This will be another focus for me. For the first time Chicago and Cook County will have an African American directing traffic at the intersection of police and prison. Incoming States Attorney Kim Foxx will need support, direction, and advice. Let us, for a time, tend our own garden rather than be distracted by vaudeville on the Potomac.

The last word

Still, one cannot help but be profoundly disappointed by what happened Nov. 8.

Disappointed not just in the result, but in fellow Americans who allowed fear and resentment to guide their vote. In the end it is their loss, not ours.

Toni Morrison said it best: *"In order to limit the possibility of this untenable change and restore whiteness to its former status as a marker for national identity, a number of white Americans are sacrificing themselves. They have begun to do things that they clearly don't want to really be doing, and to do so they are 1) abandoning their sense of human dignity and 2) risking the appearance of cowardice."*

"SWEET SPIRIT" – NATIONAL MUSEUM OF AFRICAN AMERICAN HISTORY AND CULTURE OPENING

The refrain of an old Gospel hymn, *"There's a sweet, sweet spirit in this place,"* are the words that come to mind as my wife and I visited the opening of the National Museum of African American History and Culture in Washington D.C. as it opened on September 24, 2016. Some 9,000 attended but the experience was delightfully intimate — courtesy, fraternity, hospitality and cordiality abounded.

The building was designed by a team led by Ghanaian architect **David Adjaye.** A dramatic, glassy lattice opens up the 400,000 square-foot building to sunlight even though 60% of the structure is below grade level. Some say the multilevel lattice is reminiscent of a West African crown — starting smaller at the base and expanding upward.

Many celebrities spoke. In addition to **President Barack Obama, Patti La Belle** got a big whoop when she closed her rendition of "A change is gonna come" by adding "with Hillary Clinton." My attention was seized by two speakers in particular. First, there was **John Lewis**, the timeless Georgia Congressman, who at age 76 lived to see the beatings, baton smashes, dog bites and racist rants encountered as a youngster – all now memorialized in this building – a building located a few feet away from where he marched with the Rev. Dr.Martin Luther King Jr. Congressman Lewis spoke without notes and with glistening eyes full of passion.

Then there was U.S. Supreme Court Chief Justice **John Roberts.** He commented that the Court considered Plessy v Ferguson and got it wrong; considered the Dred Scott case and got it wrong; and later considered the Brown v. Board of Education and got it right. Pointing to the Museum, he said that you can find out about the issues and deliberations surrounding those landmark decisions in this building. I wanted to ask him, however, how he could rule that the country has moved so far beyond its racist past that the voting rights Act could be selectively set aside; and that it was ok for Indiana to demand photo ID from voters, knowing full well this will have a winnowing effect on minority voters.

As invited guests, we were allowed to go into the museum ahead of the thousands lined up to enter. My attention was drawn to slavery exhibits. I believe Black Slavery and the attendant white supremacy are seeds of bitter fruit harvested now in the misery and disadvantage of so many African Americans. For instance, there is a statue of Thomas Jefferson, who owned 609 slaves. Behind him was a course of bricks, staggered for effect, with the names of each of his slaves etched thereon. There were slave collars that bound one slave to the other and small foot shackles for children. The Thomas Jefferson exhibit was also an eye-catcher, especially the preserved draft of his Declaration of Independence wherein the slave holding President stated that all men were created equal. It's clear that he didn't think Black people were human or equal, though he managed to father a child with the Black slave Sally Hemings.

Economics of the Slave Trade Exhibited

A splendid multi-media exhibit explained the economics of the sugar trade — how it enriched Europe and the United States and the important part it played in the evolution of the U.S. as a world power. It pointed out how enslaved Africans working in America and throughout the Caribbean Diaspora provided free labor essential to this Euro-American trade cycle. Then came the Cotton Station. The exhibit explained that the combination of lands expropriated from Native Americans and African slave labor created fabulous wealth for its owners. As early as 1807 a Mississippi cotton plantation was said to return 22.5% annually to its investors. Notes by Harvard historian Sven Beckert, author of "Empire of Cotton," state that European weavers of American cotton grew concerned about "the increasing uncertainty of this continuance of the system of slavery" and that "the blood-stained produce constituted a suicidal dependence on the crime of American Slavery." Yet it continued, and this exhibit shows in the harshest visual terms how the U.S. economy was nurtured by free slave labor and European moral indifference.

Reparations

My National Museum of African American History and Culture experience, though all too brief, sharpened my view that this country needs to conduct a serious discussion of "reparations".

To those that say "I didn't own and my family didn't own slaves" -this museum screams that the power, perceived freedoms, financial stability and economic basis of the U.S. was built on the backs of enslaved Blacks. All Americans, including those living today, have benefited from that Original Sin.

Georgetown University, not part of the National Museum of African American History and Culture, is coming to grips with this notion of atonement and reparation. In 1839 the Jesuits of Georgetown were on the brink of financial ruin. Their solution was to sell 272 of their Black slaves to southern plantations, the profits from which kept the school afloat. Students protested recently following the unearthing of this sordid history, prompting additional research and much soul searching. Now the President of Georgetown has recognized this disgraceful act, apologized, renamed buildings previously named for Jesuits complicit with slave profiteering and guaranteed preferential admissions to the descendants of the 272 slave families. This is a huge precedent, and one that needs repeating nationwide. (It should be noted, moreover, that Georgetown already had a policy of not admitting students without providing financial assistance to those in need.)

The National Museum of African American History and Culture, with its thousands of objects and displays, does not overtly state a demand for reparations. But its contents should stimulate the conversation.

President Obama remarked at this Dedication:

"And yes a clear-eyed view of history can make us uncomfortable, but it is precisely because of that discomfort that we can learn and grow and harness our collective power to make this nation more perfect."

BLACK INJURY

In spite of the nagging pain, Black America can find some comfort in that the current run of unjustified police killings of African Americans is occurring at a time when deep thinking journalists and scholars are placing these travesties in their wider context.

Two that stand out are Ta-Nehisi Coates of *The Atlantic* magazine and Bryan Stevenson of the NYU School of Law.

As a Black Businessman deeply concerned with these matters, I have arranged to meet several times with Coates, both privately and publicly, and find his analysis complete and his conclusions beyond challenge. When I asked him to distill his indictment into its simplest form, he said: "Plundering Black people in such a way as to wound us and create permanent black injury."

Black Injury????

Black injury. We hear a lot about White Privilege. But what exactly is **Black Injury**? It's right in front of you. Just look around. When public policy combines with racial animus, the victim goes on being harmed even though overt oppression and aggression may have ceased. Take, for instance, the red-lining of US government- backed home loans in decades past, not just here in Chicago but elsewhere across the U.S. When banks and other lenders refused to issue mortgages and home improvement loans in neighborhoods deemed un-creditworthy, thousands of Black homebuyers in places like Chicago's racially-changing West Side were forced to buy "on contract." This greatly interrupted the accumulation of Black wealth and economic stability, for most buyers never really owned those homes, even after making down payments and expensive repairs.

So for Coates, the continued economic depression and joblessness on Chicago's West Side is no surprise. Even after the redlining technically stopped, the damage had become endemic. In the simplest analogy: If I beat you across the arms and legs with a 2-by-4, then stop and apologize, you are still injured after I say "sorry."

Yet Coates doesn't take the bait when asked what Black people should now do. He sticks by his position of analyst, leaving action to others.

Bryan Stevenson, who I've also talked to, is both a brilliant writer and activist. In his book, "Just Mercy," he advocates for Black Juveniles not being incarcerated with adults. His Equal Justice Initiative in Montgomery, Alabama, provides legal representation for many Blacks unable to obtain such services Stevenson writes convincingly that America's prisons have become warehouses for the mentally ill. Largely fueled by the "War on Drugs" and excessive sentencing, the mass incarceration of hundreds of thousands of Black poor and mentally ill has had a devastating effect on the communities from which they have been removed ... and to which they will return.

Mental Illness in the Black Community

Stevenson and other mental health advocates argued for the transfer of the non-violent mentally ill to community support centers ... yet such facilities are few and far between. In 1955 there was one psychiatric bed for every 300 Americans. By 2005 it was one bed for every 3,000.

It is this inability of low income Black people to receive treatment or necessary medicine that dramatically increases the likelihood of a police encounter that too often results in jail or prison time. By default the cell has become most states' strategy for dealing with drug use and dependency. We're seeing a flood of mentally ill Blacks consigned to prison for minor offenses and drug crimes …. or simply for "behavior" their community is unwilling to tolerate.

Today over 50 percent of Black jail and prison inmates have a diagnosed mental illness. Nearly one in five have what's rated a "serious" mental condition. There are more than three times the seriously mentally ill behind bars than in hospitals. There they are often abused and preyed upon. Stevenson has also successfully litigated against Black children being sent to adult prison. He argues their often shocking and senseless crimes can't be evaluated honestly without first understanding the lives these teens had been forced to endure.

In banning the death penalty for juveniles, the U.S. Supreme Court has more-or- less acknowledged the relevance of brain science in assessing juvenile crime and culpability, finding that many youngsters are impaired with immature judgment and an undeveloped capacity for self-regulation and responsibility. Our nation's historic dismissal of this truth surely has led to more Black Injury.

Lately I've been speaking and writing on these matters, especially with reference to the impending release of large numbers of early-parolees and the impact they will have on the Black communities to which they will return.

Again we are fortunate to have thinkers and researchers capable of providing both context and data points. One such is Matthew Epperson of the University of Chicago, a scholar who connects the dots. Twenty years ago, as a social worker at Cook County Jail, he noticed how frequently the police were called upon to deal with Black folks with mental illness. These encounters, especially involving the poor and homeless, too often ended in violence and death.

Consider the Christmas weekend killing of Quintonio LeGrier. He was wielding a baseball bat and loudly demanding entry to his father's West Side apartment. Without investigating the causes or reasons for the call, he and an innocent Black neighbor were shot and killed by police newly arrived on the scene. LeGrier had a mental condition. Of course he did. According to The Washington Post, of 1,000 people (mostly Black) who were shot and killed by police in the U.S. in 2015, 25 percent had displayed signs of mental illness.

So instead of a medic in a white coat taking his blood pressure, one could argue, today's mentally unstable Black man is as likely to encounter a guy in a blue uniform spilling his blood.

What to do? Epperson has a list:

1. Train police to respond to mental health emergencies;
2. Integrate mental health services with law enforcement;
3. Create crisis teams to determine the best approach to police calls;
4. Establish triage centers with respite beds to provide temporary shelter and expert referral.

Epperson says, "Health service cutbacks have turned cops into gun-carrying therapists." But even if his ideas were put in place, Black people on the street or released from prison with mental illness will remain plundered and blundered. Oh, and Quintonio LeGrier still will be dead … another case of Black Injury.

The Drinking Water of Flint Michigan

But don't think for a minute Blacks have to be out on the street, acting crazy, to be so mistreated. Now we have the innocent children of Flint, Michigan, to tell us otherwise.

In 2014 state and local bureaucrats decided that Flint should obtain its drinking water from the Flint River while a replacement pipeline was being laid to Lake Huron. The river water was known to be more polluted than lake water, but for over 18 months it was pumped through the city's decaying lead pipes, despite complaints from the city's majority Black population that it was coming out reddish brown and bad-tasting.

Turns out the river water was also causing dangerously high levels of lead to build up in the bloodstreams of Flint's children. Lead is considered the No. 1 health threat to children and the effects of lead poison can last a lifetime. Not only does lead stunt a child's growth, it damages the nervous system and leads to learning disabilities. It's also linked to crime and anti-social behavior, ala Freddy Brown in Baltimore. Anybody spot the vicious circle here?

After much public outcry and media coverage, Michigan's governor has vowed to do better by Flint. But even if the federal government provides bottled and/or purified water indefinitely, and even if non-corroding water pipes are installed, that won't help the thousands of Black children already poisoned with lead. More Black Injury.

This concept of enduring damage and the need for adequate recompense is especially pertinent right now in our hometown of Chicago. The police here have shown a consistent inability to deal with Blacks with mental illness, even as hundreds more are about to be released from our state prisons and county jail. Relations between the Black community and the CPD are at a tipping point. And need I mention it's an election year?

The Political Litmus Test

For my part, all candidates seeking votes and/or financial support from minority businesses need to pass a litmus test – What will they do to remediate Black Injury? I further challenge all ministers who are asked that their pulpits be used, all media hosts, all fraternities and sororities and all community activists and college groups to invoke this test with any and all candidates seeking their forums for campaign purposes . Ask them:

1. Do you understand fully, as outlined above and elsewhere, the reality of Black Injury

2. What steps would you take to prevent Black Injury? (Hint: placing body cameras on, much less issuing Tasers to, all police is not enough.)

3. What is appropriate compensation for specific and proven cases of Black Injury? (Awarding the standard $5 million to families of those unjustly slain is insufficient. The University of Cincinnati, for instance, in compensation to the family of a Black man slain by campus police, recently awarded not just a multi-million dollar payment but also full four-year scholarships for the deceased's 12 children.)

Yet Black Injury cannot be compensated by a check alone. It must be accompanied by a continual contractually committed period of not less than 5 years of emotional, environmental, educational, employment-enhancing, mental and medical assistance – all of which should be part of any settlement.

These are the conditions I insist of anyone seeking my support. I urge you to do the same. It's not all that much to ask compared to the enormity of Black Injury.

FUND A LEARNING CENTER FOR CHICAGO'S MINORITY CONTRACTORS

Despite robust building programs, Chicago is without a locally based African-American general contractor capable of routinely bidding, bonding and building $60 million-plus projects.

This is especially curious since Chicago has a federal court approved minority contracting program stemming from past discriminatory practices.

One reason Black contractors have not developed here is due to the longtime and ongoing abuse of minority preference or set-aside programs by some large, white- owned construction firms. Phony "fronts," "pass-throughs" and letterhead-only "joint ventures" are too often used to meet minority contracting goals.

Recently, James McHugh Construction Co. agreed to pay $12 million to settle a whistleblower lawsuit for allegedly participating in a subcontractor scam in connection with major public works projects.

Reportedly, $40 million of the $150 million in work was to be subcontracted with minority- and female-owned firms. This did not happen. Instead the work was done in- house by McHugh or through a questionable arrangement.

A Tribune news story from May 2 said that McHugh admitted no wrongdoing and will not be barred from winning future government contracts. The company agreed to implement a compliance program and have an independent monitor oversee its subcontracting process for three years.

To some, $12 million may seem satisfactory as full penance. I think not.

The real damage is that the $40 million could have helped with the growth and development of female- and minority-owned firms.

So, how about this for a fix? Majority-owned firms engaging in the use of fronts or other abuses of minority set-aside programs should be barred from doing business with public agencies for several years.

And $2 million of the $12 million settlement paid by McHugh to the City of Chicago ought to be used to fund a technical assistance center for minority construction firms. An advisory team of construction estimators, fiscal managers, project managers and marketing experts would go a long way to assist underfunded and understaffed minority firms in growing their businesses. This center should reside within a highly reputable educational institution, such as the Illinois Institute of Technology or the St. Clair Drake Center of African and African American Studies at Roosevelt University.

Instead of serial slaps on the wrist for alleged wrongdoings, let's end the scams once and for all by developing a capable community of Black and other minority contractors benefiting from a great and fair-minded city.

OP-ED: TECHNO BRAINS

Vexed, amazed and bewildered by the stranglehold technology seems to have over the younger generation -- including young African-Americans -- I recently conducted my own investigation.

Scene 1: Three young ladies having lunch at a restaurant, each with their cell phones on the table and using them between bites. Why did they choose to meet and eat if they weren't going to engage one another?

Scene 2: At the Lyric Opera, during the performance – not the intermission – a woman has her "smart" phone out, reading it. Why pay $150-plus for a seat and not focus on the artists displaying their talent?

Scene 3: At a Catholic funeral service, during the actual mass – not the "peace be with you" greeting interlude – a woman was using the "smart" device in her lap. If she thought enough of the deceased to come to the service, why thumb her digital nose at the departed and all the surrounding mourners by showing such disrespect?

There must be answers. So I hit the books to find out.

In "Alone Together" author Sherry Turkle posits that we now expect much more from technology and far less from each other. Young "digital natives," Turkle argues, live in a constant state of waiting for connection.

"When my cell rings I have to answer," one youngster explains of this compulsion.

"When a text comes I have to see who it is and what they want."

Turkle points out that, for many, technology soothes and satisfies human vulnerabilities and needs in a way only direct human contact once did. We interact with technical devices in full knowledge of their limitations, including the inevitability of love unrequited.

Our smart phones, pads and computers provide the illusion of relief from loneliness, from our craving for attention, from our unmet desire for spontaneity.

What to do? Turkle suggests a return to simple good manners. Talk to colleagues down the hall; no cell phones at dinner, on the playground, in the car or in company.

But she advises us pre-digital critics to not be as judgmental as we feel. Turkle recommends compassion for those who are so dependent on devices that they cannot sit still for a funeral service or a lecture or a play. Gentle persuasion is called for, not scorn.

But don't get the idea, she cautions, that our differences are just a generational thing or that the kids are alright. They're actually in danger. And so are we.

Take texting while driving. Author Matt Richtel examines this issue in "A Deadly Wandering" He writes of a Utah lad who, while texting and driving, causes the deaths of two accomplished scientists.

"What is technology doing to us?" Richtel asks. "Can our minds keep up with the pace of change? How can we find balance?"

Richtel dips into the fascinating field of attention science, which has shown that purposive activity is invariably disrupted by extraneous stimuli ... and that the intended activity – be it reading or listening or car driving – is always diminished. In other words, texting while driving is a lethal mix.

More often it's just boorish. Back to the field:

Scene 4: At a downtown health club, a lady guest goes up a narrow flight of stairs, ever so slowly with eyes glued to her phone. Behind her were an elderly couple, one with a cane, looking confused about why their ascent was taking so long. But the texter never looked up, much less over her shoulder. If she slipped or tripped and injured the elderly, who would be liable? The digital zombie or the club?

Scene 5: I'm driving south on Columbus Drive and an urban ambler walks out in the middle of the block between cars intent on her phone. I make an abrupt stop to avoid hitting her. A cyclist falls off his bike while trying to pass me on the right. Car behind comes to a screeching halt to avoid a collision. All the while our preoccupied pedestrian crosses the street and never looks up.

So how do we as society address this walking and driving under the influence? And where is the Black thread in the technology Tapestry?

Full Disclosure: None of the females referred to above were Black women. But that doesn't mean we don't have issues.

Consider the Digital Divide, which can be defined as the actual or perceived inequalities between individuals within a boundary (as in ghetto) in their access to information and communication technology; as well as the knowledge and skills needed to effectively use this information for connecting.

We're told Blacks lag behind whites 20% in Internet use and in household connection to the Internet, and that the disparity increases with age.

Technology advocates say Blacks are 'on the wrong side" of the of this Divide and that our goal should be "to get everyone connected equally."

But who are these advocates and what are their motivations for seeking to wire us to the Big I, as if it were as simple as extending long distance telephone service.

One answer comes from Astra Taylor, author of The Peoples Platform – taking back power and culture in the digital age. She argues that Google, Facebook, Apple, Amazon, iTunes, AT&T and others want to get all Black People "connected" to further their own business imperatives. They want to accelerate media consumption and market forces that encourage compulsive on-line engagement. It's a process of consolidation, centralization and commercialism.

Consider the track record of these advocates. In 2001, California lobbyists for Cingular, Sprint and AT&T argued against safety bills that prohibited "being connected while driving". Claiming that " mobile phones posed no different distraction than eating," lobbyists for Sprint argued that a law banning hand-held phones could be used to discriminate against minority motorists. The carriers broadly argued that general education was sufficient to remind motorists about the risks of getting distracted by their devices. Yet by 2001 the California Highway Department cited cell phone use as a leading cause of accidents.

Today's aggressive marketing of mobile communications to minorities is reminiscent of tobacco companies inundating Black media and neighborhoods with ads, while knowing full-well the hazards of smoking.

So surrendered have we become to digitized "progress" that many readers no doubt consider all this curmudgeon-speak or the ranting of a conspiracy theorist.

And in fact, no informed person would question the enormous value of technology in matters small and large. Who can challenge the value of SIRI in helping an autistic child to better overcome their language limitations? Or the thousands of dollars saved by small businesses in office and administration costs by using electronic calendars and other applications? Or the millions saved by corporations in using Webinars in place of costly hotel and air travel?

Yet I urge educators, jurists, community activists and others concerned about where all this is heading to to consider the following points made by Matt Richtel in his Deadly Wandering:

1. Cell phone use while driving will result in jail time, revocation of Driver's license and civil lawsuits in cases of property damage;
2. Efficient multitasking is a myth, despite what AT&T ads say to the contrary;
3. The power of social connectivity, the need to stay in touch, is, for many both irresistible and addictive;
4. What's happening today with technology is not unlike the 1970's with drugs in terms of the pace of adoption and cultural acceptance … only its legal.
5. Net surfing is like a slot machine- you don't know what quality the information is- so you look at everything until something valuable comes along;

Suggestion: make "rules of the techno road" part of the curriculum in public schools, charters and community colleges? Teach the kids some attention science. And how about linking the right to use technology with its responsible use, the way we do with motorized vehicles or firearms?

Meanwhile, beware the wandering and distracted walker under the influence. The life you save may be your own.

Printed in the United States
by Baker & Taylor Publisher Services